Groundwork of
Philosophy of Religion

Groundwork of Philosophy of Religion

David A. Pailin

D. D. (Cantab)

EPWORTH PRESS

0 7162 0418 5

*First published 1986
by Epworth Press
20 Ivatt Way
Peterborough PE3 7PG*

Fourth impression 2001

British Library Cataloguing in Publication Data

Pailin, David A.
Groundwork of philosophy of religion.
1. Religion—Philosophy
I. Title
200´.1   BL51

ISBN 0–7162–0418–5

*Photoset at The Spartan Press Ltd
Lymington, Hants
and printed in Great Britain by
Biddles Ltd
www.biddles.co.uk*

IVCVNDAE
LAETAE
CARISSIMAE

Contents

Foreword

A book with a 'Preface' needs only a brief 'Foreword'. It would be wrong, however, to send this book out without acknowledging my debts to certain people. In the first place, the Rev. John Stacey deserves my thanks for asking me to write this work and thereby, unwittingly, giving me a summer's fun in doing it. I only hope that he doesn't come to regret his request. Secondly my thanks are due to my students over many years at Manchester University who have patiently endured my struggles with the problems discussed in this book, have offered corrections to my ideas and have shared in the excitement of intellectual discovery. Thirdly I must express my thanks to Miss Margaret Hogg who, with all her other duties, has found time to put my manuscript into elegant typescript. Above all, though, I am deeply grateful to two friends and colleagues, Dr Jacqueline L. Berry and Dr Vaughan Lowe who, in the middle of hectic lives in non-theological academic fields, found time to read through the manuscript as it appeared, made many extremely valuable comments on it and generally supported me throughout. They are not to be blamed for what now appears. Without them it would have been much worse. I am sorry that I could not take up all their suggestions about developing the points. The difficulty was that I had been asked to write a book and not a series.

14 July 1985   David A. Pailin

Preface

In relation to religious belief and practice the role of a philosopher of religion may be compared to those of a surveyor, a civil engineer and an architect. First of all it involves examining what is there. Philosophers of religion survey the religious scene in order to discover what is believed, what is meant by 'believing' it, why it is believed, and how belief is expressed in practice. In the course of this investigation they need to take into account what historians, sociologists, anthropologists, psychologists and philosophers have discovered about such matters, as well as what believers and theologians say about them. As philosophers of religion, however, they differ from these others in two respects. On the one hand, they seek a comprehensive understanding of religion which incorporates the findings of all valid insights into it. On the other, they are concerned about the justification of holding the beliefs and following the practices of particular religious faiths. They are not content with simply identifying what a faith is held to contain and why; they also want to assess the justifiability of entertaining that faith. In the course of their survey-work, therefore, philosophers of religion pay particular attention to the soundness of the foundations and construction of the 'buildings' of religious belief in order to determine to what extent they may be judged to be 'true' and how such judgments are to be warranted. In this respect philosophy of religion not only involves considering the traditional problems of the arguments for the existence of God, the reconciliation of belief in God's benevolence with the presence of evil in the world, the reality of miracles, and the likelihood of immortality, it also includes discovering how doctrines are influenced by the cultures in which they are formulated, why doctrines develop, how sacred texts are used and the manner in which it is considered appropriate to talk about God. Their survey, furthermore, seeks to discover where there are inconsistencies in the beliefs of a faith – as, for example, might be held to obtain between beliefs in divine foreknowledge and human freedom, or between divine omnipotence and human creativity.

Philosophy of religion, however, is not just a matter of producing a survey of what happens to be there in a religious faith. Since no system of belief and practice that has yet appeared seems to be without problems once it is subjected to critical attention, the philosopher of religion finds that there is more to be done than analytical description. Just as civil engineers investigate what types of structures can be built upon the kind of soil at a particular site and with the materials available, so, secondly, philosophers of religion consider what the relevant evidence for religious belief will bear and how the different components may be linked together in a credible manner. Granted, for example, the nature of our ways of apprehension, the character of the natural world, the records of history, and the qualities of human self-awareness, they consider what may justifiably be inferred from them. Granted the perfection of God, they seek to perceive whether – and, if so, how – it is possible to regard God both as eternal and as related to a temporally-ordered creation, or as unchanging and as caring intimately for individual human beings. Again, granted the existence of canonical texts – sacred scriptures – and credal confessions, they investigate what may and what may not be properly derived from them as authoritative sources for a contemporary understanding of faith.

The third major role for philosophers of religion is to present outline schemes of a credible faith. In this 'architectural' role they do not produce the final drawings and superintend the construction of a building from them. Instead, bearing in mind what the 'surveyors' and 'civil engineers' have discovered, they offer sketch plans of what might be possible, together with evaluations of the strengths and weaknesses of each case. In this role they may suggest why an existing structure should be retained or, if they so judge, how it might be modified to produce a more satisfactory one. Although it may seem to be always possible in principle for a philosopher of religion to present plans for a totally new form of religious faith, in practice it is extremely unlikely that any credible one would attempt to do this. A religious faith does not suddenly appear out of nothing: it emerges through a continuous process of alterations, adaptations and augmentations to some previous faith. The philosopher of religion contributes to these processes by suggesting how particular changes may improve the self-understanding of faith by eradicating incoherences between beliefs, by overcoming discrepancies between what faith holds to be the case and what experience tells us to be so, and by producing a story of the fundamental character of reality that makes sense to people today.

In this last, 'architectural', role the philosopher of religion comes close to and, in the case of philosophical or systematic theology, deliberately overlaps the role of the theologian. The difference between the roles is probably not very important and is in any case largely a matter of definition. However, so far as it is useful to distinguish them, some theologians hold that as such they are committed to accepting the basic truth of a specific faith and seeking, on that basis, to develop its doctrinal and practical implications. The philosopher of religion, in comparison, seeks to avoid presupposing the truth of a particular faith, but rather to consider how a true understanding might be developed, using some existing faith or faiths as the point of departure. The distinction is far from clear-cut. What is important, though, is that those who engage in considering problems of faith should be conscious of what they take for granted as the unquestioned foundation of their thought and what they leave open to be established or rejected.

Why should anyone want to engage in philosophy of religion? To many people it seems to be a pointless exercise whose only value is to provide some people with intellectual pleasure and even fewer people with a living by teaching it and meagre pocket-money from writing about it! To convinced believers, philosophy of religion often appears as an undesirable threat since examining the foundations and structures of their faith is likely to disturb even more what is already hard enough to believe. To non-believers it seems to be a waste of time because they are not convinced that there is anything to study beyond fond illusions. As for would-be believers, the practice of philosophy of religion, whatever its constructive intentions, seems only to make faith difficult by highlighting its problems. From all sides, then, philosophers of religion are regarded with suspicion. If they are not idiots who spend their life hunting for the crock of gold at the rainbow's end, they are trouble-makers who take a perverse delight in making a difficult situation even worse.

, To those who feel a sneaking sympathy for these criticisms, the philosopher of religion must respond that faith is too important a matter to be left unexamined. Faith concerns our judgment as to what is fundamental in reality and ultimate in value. Hence it concerns what makes sense of everything and so what gives meaning and direction to our lives as individuals and as social groups. Faith, furthermore, is not simply a matter of abstract, intellectual assent to a story about reality. Our values, our judgments and our conduct are, in the end, determined by our actual faith. Sometimes this determination is immediate: our thought and conduct in certain matters may be direct manifestations of our faith. We may love, for example, because we believe that God loves us. In other cases the influence on thought and conduct is mediated through 'intermediate principles' which themselves are formed in response to the basic commitments of faith but which are regarded as more open to question and revision as to whether or not they appropriately express our faith. In either case, however, the differences between the goals which people pursue and the ways in which they accordingly treat their environment and each other are linked to differences in their real (as opposed to alleged) faiths. Since, therefore, faith is a matter of our recognition of what we take to be ultimately true and of what controls the conduct of our lives, it is irresponsible to regard it as something which may be treated with indifference. As for the view that its object is an illusion, it may be replied that even if this be so, it is an inescapable illusion.

Each person has something which constitutes the final point of reference for life, which makes that individual 'tick' and constitutes the basic character of that person's life. This ultimate sticking point is their 'faith'. Ideally it is a coherent position determined by a single, self-consistent principle; in practice in many cases it is composed of a 'rag-bag' of presuppositions and principles which do not hang together in any obvious manner. The collection may even contain mutually contradictory elements which lead to internal tensions for individuals as they try to live by their faith. Faith of some kind is nevertheless a necessary component – and indeed the foundation – of human being. Where individuals finally differ is not over whether they do or do not have some faith, but over what particular realities or ideas constitute the object of their faith. It is therefore crucial, if people are to live in a responsibly self-aware manner, that they know what is the object of their faith and, if they wish their basic commitments in life to be justified, that they have reasonable grounds for assenting to that object as properly ultimate.

Since, furthermore, faith is an assent to what is held to be fundamentally the case, it involves questions about what is true. It is a serious distortion of the character of faith to consider that it can be content to see itself as merely the expression of arbitrary tastes, upbringing, prejudice, or blind choice. Philosophy of religion has consequently an important role for believers in so far as it examines, both in principle and practice, how the assents of faith may be rationally justified. Its concerns with truth-testing are not an optional extra, of interest only to cerebrally-directed would-be believers. Its concerns are of central significance to all those who wish to be fully human by self-consciously taking responsibility for the course of their lives. While faith is not simply a matter of reaching a conclusion on the basis of evidence and reasoning, it is nevertheless a state of commitment or captivation for which it is appropriate to seek rational justification.

The aim of the analyses and revisions produced by philosophy of religion is the establishment of what may be called 'honest belief'. Negatively this involves raising questions about the truth, significance and effectiveness of inherited systems of belief. It thus includes examining whether people today ought to be committed to the beliefs which they profess to hold and whether those beliefs adequately express the faith which they actually live by. In a famous story about a madman, Friedrich Nietzsche described churches as 'the tombs and sepulchres of God'. What he was pointing to in part was the gulf between the theistic faith which supposed believers affirm in church and the actual faith by which they conduct their lives once they have left its doors (and often when they discuss issues within its doors!). The philosopher of religion is interested in identifying both the purported faith and the actual faith, in comparing them, and in assessing their respective justification. Positively what the philosopher of religion seeks to establish is a system of beliefs which may be entertained as justified and significant by self-aware people living in the contemporary world. It is a quest whose attitude was well described by John Oman when he wrote that 'a true honesty is ever haunted by the fear of missing the highest and failing in the best, and it is guided by a humble search and patient aspiration which has little concern with mere argument'.[1] What is important in philosophy of religion is not cleverness but insight, not slick arguments but openness to the truth, not the protection of our prejudices but the readiness to open everything to the scrutiny of critical reason.

From what has been said, it must be apparent that the study of philosophy of religion raises an enormous number of questions. It must also be said – as a warning, perhaps – that it is far better at raising questions than at answering them. And when answers are offered, they are often far from wholly convincing. This situation, however, should not deter believers from engaging in the study. If their faith is to present itself as a plausible way of understanding reality and conducting their lives, it is no help to its credibility to attempt to ignore the problems posed by its critics. Nor is it any aid to faith to try to fob off those critics with unsatisfactory replies to their questions. Rather than be rebuffed with the comment 'You have found the answer because you have not appreciated the problem', believers engaging in philosophy of religion need to show that they understand the problems even better than the critics – for they are intimately aware of faith by their personal commitment to it. In the end such a probing, questioning, never finally satisfied approach to faith is an authentic response to the ultimate. For the theist, for example, God is that reality which is the final truth about all things. The search for truth, therefore, is not a drifting away from God but a demand which faith in God makes on believers. If God is truth, the quest for truth can never be alien to faith in God. Those who, in the name of faith, denounce the rational inquiries of philosophy of religion show, for all their zeal, that they do not have authentic faith in God. The faith which they are trying to defend is some pitiful illusion of their human creation. Genuine faith in God perceives that God, as the ultimate and holy, is for ever beyond our grasp and that faith must therefore be a continuous destruction of inadequate images in order to reach more (though never finally) satisfying approximations to the divine. The iconoclastic consequences of engaging in philosophy of religion is the expression of faith in God as its object.

To conclude this preface, four remarks about this introduction to philosophy of religion need to be made. First, this 'groundwork' is an 'introduction'. It does not pretend to be definitive (as if that were possible) in identifying the problems, let alone in answering them. Indeed, some readers may judge that it answers hardly any to their satisfaction. What it is intended to do is to outline some of the basic problems that arise in philosophy of religion and some of the more interesting responses that are made to those problems. It is to be hoped that these discussions will excite readers to pursue the matters further. What is provided here is an incitement to intellectual and spiritual adventures. Those who want a quiet life – and a dull (perhaps dead) faith – had better not read further.

Secondly, the problems that are to be discussed are those that arise particularly in the case of theistic faith and, even more particularly, in the case of Christian faith. While it is arguable that ideally a philosophy of religion should consider all forms of religious belief – from Buddhism to Islam, from Shinto to Mithraism, from Judaism to Hinduism – in practice it is presupposed that by far the greater number of readers of this study will be approaching the subject because of an interest in the Christian religion. Consequently what follows may be relevant to the understanding of other faiths but the issues are discussed primarily because they are significant for understanding Christian faith and they are discussed in terms of the beliefs and practices of Christianity. Those, therefore, who want an introduction to the philosophy of religion in terms of religion generally (if that be possible) or of some non-Christian faith in particular should look elsewhere.

Thirdly, there is the problem of using non-offensive language. Throughout this work I have tried to use 'all-inclusive' language. If at times I have slipped, I apologize and I regret the sexist overtones in some of the pieces from which I quote. In the penultimate chapter we will consider the character of religious language. From the beginning, however, there is the problem of what pronoun it is appropriate to use of 'God'. While the impersonal 'it' may help to stress the otherness of God, its use tends powerfully to deny the personal characteristics which are widely considered to be central to Christian belief since, according to this view, God is to be understood as one who knows, remembers, wills, acts, responds and loves. On the other hand to use the personal pronoun 'he' of God is to fall into the danger of attributing a sex-preference to God which is totally illegitimate. As recent feminist discussions have properly argued, the result is to reinforce the sexism of our culture in a way that is detrimental to half of humanity. To speak of God as 'she' or 's/he', however, is not only to be gimmicky. More reprehensibly it is likely to reinforce the sexism by drawing attention to it. In what follows, therefore, I have tried to avoid sexist implications by using 'the divine', 'the sacred' and 'the holy' as equivalent to a pronoun for God. While such usage may be criticized on the grounds that it uses abstract notions for the concrete reality of God, it may be defended on the ground that this substitution for a personal pronoun emphasizes the proper otherness of God. The divine is not another person to be treated as we treat the Katharines and Roberts of our human society. God is the holy one, and perhaps struggling with the basic language we use for God will help bring the point home to us.

Fourthly, many of the ideas discussed in the philosophy of religion are unfamiliar. I can remember that when I first began to delve into books on the subject, I found much of the material baffling. When I go back to the same books now, I wonder why I found them so difficult. Familiarity does not breed contempt but greater understanding. Those who find on a first reading that some of the ideas presented here are difficult to grasp may discover on re-reading that what once was hard to apprehend has become, with the benefit of the earlier struggles with it, comparatively clear. This is especially likely to occur with the issues considered in the first two chapters. Where this does not happen, it may be my fault for not being clear in my own understanding or for not expressing it clearly. I apologize.

Now, however, it is time to leave the comfortable base-camp of the preface and to move on to the cliffs and ridges of the study itself. The first face to be tackled is that of the relationship between faith and philosophy.

Chapter 1

Faith, Religion and Philosophy

'What has Athens to do with Jerusalem?' This question is often asked rhetorically by those who wish to protect religious faith from the unsettling investigations and demands of critical reason. Behind their assumed answer 'Nothing' lies a conviction that the realm of philosophy and the realm of religious faith in God are not only distinct but are to be kept thoroughly separate if each – and particularly religion – is not to be polluted by alien matter.

Such attempted isolationism, however, is bound to fail. So far as philosophy is concerned, religious claims about the ultimate structure of reality, about the human sense of the significance and value of life, and about the content of certain modes of experience are matters which not only are to be investigated but also identify possible components of the being which philosophy desires to understand. Furthermore, so far as religious faith affirms the final meaningfulness of all things, it is not a commitment which is alien to philosophy. It expresses, rather, one form of the basic presuppositions which underlie any philosophical enquiry. As for religion, philosophical investigations of its beliefs and practices are seen to be appropriate once it is recognized that faith intrinsically requires of believers that they should seek to understand their faith and be responsible for their assent to it. Philosophy in that case is neither a hostile alternative to faith nor a corrupting intrusion into it. It provides, rather, a valuable tool for developing our awareness of its contents and deepening our commitment to its truth.

Nevertheless, even if the rational enquiry of philosophy is not alien to religious faith, some believers may still feel that only believers can properly engage in such enquiry. Faith is thus protected by maintaining that it is essential to have faith in order to enquire into its content and truth. The judgments of outsiders have no significance. Hence, if their conclusions are to be taken seriously, philosophers of religion must be believers.

There is a degree of insight underlying this position which must not be ignored. Not long after the Norman conquest of England, Anselm affirmed at the start of his highly rational study of the doctrine of God, the *Proslogion*, that 'I believe in order to understand. For this also I believe, that unless I believed, I should not understand.'[1] Although it is arguable that in Anselm's own case this assertion was more designed to deceive potential critics of his rational approach in theology than to describe his actual method (a deception which has been successful in the case of most commentators on Anselm to this day), it is an assertion which makes an important point. Those who criticize a given position are not going to be taken seriously if it is felt that they do not know what they are making judgments about. The evaluations of a music critic who turns out to be tone-deaf, or of a colour-blind art critic, are of very limited significance. Similarly a devoted parachutist may claim that I will never be able to be aware of the peculiar thrill of that sport until I have stood at the door of an aeroplane, looked down and jumped. All I can reply is that I hope that I never will be aware of it!

By analogy, however, believers may argue that religious faith can only be properly understood by those who are committed to it. Looking on from outside fails to provide insight into the distinctive essence of it. When, therefore, unbelieving critics such as, say, Russell or Ayer or Flew, evaluate religious beliefs, their philosophy of religion misses the point of what they describe. As with tone-deaf or colour-blind critics of music and art, they must politely but firmly be told that they do not know what they are talking about and advised to turn their attention to what is within their competence. Such an argument, though, goes too far when it demands commitment as a precondition of significant evaluation. What is required by philosophers of religion is not assent to the truth of what they examine but an empathetic awareness of what religious faith means for those who have it. It is not commitment but understanding which is needed. Some perceptive critics of religion such as Feuerbach, Nietzsche, Freud and Hepburn have not been believers, but they have displayed a sympathetic appreciation of what they reject which makes their judgments important. As for professed believers, the depth and extent of their faith varies enormously and there is no litmus-test which can show if they believe enough in order to be able to criticize significantly. Indeed there is a good case for arguing that a totally unquestioning devotion is as poor a basis for understanding religious faith as is a total lack of sympathetic appreciation of it.

What, therefore, philosophers of religion must have is not faith but an adequate understanding of what they are investigating. They can only expose and evaluate the presuppositions, contents and significance of faith in God when they can imaginatively apprehend the thoughts and feelings of theistic believers. What they require is appreciation, not commitment. Unless the believers' position is to be totally mysterious to those who do not share it (and so any decision to believe quite inexplicable), we should not presume that a non-believer is never able, granted imaginative empathy, to understand faith adequately enough to be able to make a significant critical evaluation of it. To return to the example of the experience of parachuting: although I have never jumped from an aeroplane, I have looked out from aeroplane windows, stood on the edges of high buildings, committed myself to a rope in abseiling, and had experiences which create terror and thrill at the same time. While, therefore, it is true that I have never experienced for myself what it is to parachute, I do consider that I can claim to be able, by an imaginative combination of experiences which I have had, to attain a reasonable appreciation of what parachutists find in what they do. Similarly, in the case of religion, the requirement for those who study it is a sufficient degree of awareness of it, either by direct or by indirect experiences, to be able to comment intelligently on it. The question, therefore, to be asked of philosophers of religion is not 'Do they believe?' but 'Do they understand what it is to believe?'. This is not an easy question to answer. On the one hand it requires open-minded sensitivity to what they say about religion, on the other it presupposes a proper appreciation of what religion is. Only on the basis of both these perceptions can we presume to judge the adequacy of their understanding. It is, nevertheless, the kind of judgment which we frequently have to make as we decide how far someone has understood what they tell us about. It is a judgment whose possibility lies in our ability to understand each other – a possibility whose problematic nature we shall have to consider further in chapter 4 when we discuss faith and hermeneutics.

What is religion?

What, though, is religion? The word has already been used frequently. It is time we considered what it refers to.

Many attempts have been made to define what is meant by 'religion'. A few examples will indicate their variety. Paul Tillich spoke of faith as 'the state of being ultimately concerned'[2] and Paul

Wiebe has recently developed a similar view in which he equates religion with what is of 'profound interest':[3] 'Religion is that central human reality in which individuals and groups try to master what they judge to be the one profound ill of life on earth by confronting this ill with a good equally profound.'[4] This is a very formal, philosophical definition. An anthropological one presented by Melford Spiro is that religion is 'an institution consisting of culturally patterned interaction with culturally postulated superhuman beings.'[5] Ninian Smart, starting from the phenomena of religion, describes a religion as a tradition involving institutional organization, rituals, types of experience, doctrinal beliefs, mythic beliefs, and an ethical dimension, all interconnected into an organic whole.[6] What may be regarded as a religious view of 'religion' is given by Harvey Cox when he writes of it as 'that cluster of memories and myths, hopes and images, rites and customs that pulls together the life of a person or group into a meaningful whole' as it 'lends coherence to life, furnishes a fund of meanings, gives unity to human events and guides people in making decisions'.[7]

It would be easy to extend this list of definitions and defining descriptions for religion. Probably every one of them has some justification and identifies, from a particular point of view, distinctive characteristics of religion. In the end, however, the extension of the list would only provide further warrant for William James' conclusion that 'the word "religion" cannot stand for any single principle or essence, but is rather a collective name'. Thus 'we may very likely find no one essence, but many characters which may alternately be equally important to religion'.[8] Instead of trying to formulate a neat definition of the essence of religion, therefore, let us accept James' view of the matter (which in effect is implied in Smart's response to the problem) and try to specify some of the central characteristics of religion. Although not every one of these may necessarily have to be present for a religion to be recognizable as such, any identifiable religion will involve most of them and Christianity can be held to involve them all.

First, then, religion may be held to be characterized by its concern with what is ultimate in being, value and rationality. This is clearly the case with theistic religions for, as Anselm pointed out, God is to be thought of as 'that than which nothing greater can be conceived'.[9] More recently Charles Hartshorne has developed this notion to elucidate what is meant by speaking of God as essentially the perfect or the sole adequate object of worship.[10] It is also a distinctive quality of religion which lies behind Tillich's view of faith as 'ultimate concern' and his judgment that, since an ultimate concern must be unconditional, total, and infinite,[11] any 'philosophy of religion which does not begin with something unconditional never reaches God'.[12] The reason for the 'never' is that premises which refer wholly to what is conditional can never lead to an unconditional in a conclusion.

The ultimacy which typifies religious faith is, however, both objective and subjective. It is a duality which is reflected in the ambiguity of Tillich's phrase 'ultimate concern'. On the one hand this is a concern which is directed towards that which is taken to be intrinsically ultimate in itself. On the other hand it is a concern which possesses believers as that which finally directs their thought and action. The former of these qualities leads Tillich into all kinds of difficulties in finding an adequate way to speak about God. He is convinced, however, that 'every religious thought concerning God' must be founded upon the recognition that 'God is being-itself or the absolute'.[13] The object of religious faith, in other words, is that from which all else is derived, by which all else is to be valued, and in terms of which all else finds its significance. In itself, in contrast, it is necessarily underived, intrinsically good, and essentially meaningful. As such it is not surprising that it leads human thought to the limits of what it can apprehend and hints at mysteries beyond its competence. As for the latter of these qualities, the 'subjective reference' of ultimate concern, it is classically expressed in the commandment to love God 'with all your heart, with all your soul, with all your strength, and with all your mind'.[14] Søren Kierkegaard expresses it philosophically when he writes of religious faith as 'an objective uncertainty held fast in an appropriation-process of the most passionate inwardness' and as 'the infinite passion of the individual's inwardness' in contrast to the uncertainty of its object.[15] In less forbidding language, it is what finally 'makes a person tick': faith refers to the final commitments which determine who and what people are. When, therefore, we think of religion as a matter of faith we consider what people regard as normative for their lives.

A second way of characterizing religion stresses that it is concerned with what is 'holy' or 'sacred'. Nathan Söderblom, for example, wrote that 'holiness is the great word in religion; it is even more essential than the notion of God'.[16] It is a view of religion which was classically developed by Rudolf Otto in a work entitled (in English translation) *The Idea of the Holy*. Here Otto describes 'holiness' as 'a category of interpretation and valuation peculiar to the sphere of religion'. It is experienced as 'a unique original feeling-response' which is quite unlike anything else, an 'absolutely primary and elementary datum' which cannot be defined except in terms of itself.[17] A sense of what it is, however, may be awakened in us by directing attention to other experiences which resemble aspects of the sense of the holy. Such experiences are those of creature-feeling – 'the emotion of a creature, submerged and overwhelmed by its own nothingness in contrast to that which is supreme', mystery, awe, dread, horror, overpoweringness, urgency, otherness, and fascinating attractiveness. The sense of the 'holy' that is distinctive to religion is not any one of these feelings but that which combines qualities similar to all of them in one mode of experience. This understanding of religion emphasizes that religion is to do with that which is intrinsically and unconditionally to be worshipped. It is not primarily a matter of understanding nor one of moral behaviour. It is the awareness of the sacred, of that which is to be adored with utter respect. According to biblical stories, it was the presumption of touching the Ark, the object identifying God's presence, that produced Uzzah's death; it was the sense of the being of God that evoked in Isaiah a sense of deep profanity and in Job of the error of seeking to question God.[18] According to the vision of the Revelation of John, the heavenly beings unceasingly proclaim the divine holiness and give glory to God,[19] while Gerhard Tersteegen suggests the solemn silence of adoring awe as the proper response to the presence of the divine:

> God is in His temple:
> All within keep silence,
> Prostrate lie with deepest reverence.

It is a sense of God which needs to be remembered in the days of hearty services of worship and feverish social activism. Without it religion may become a hollow shell – a lifeless caricature of itself.

Among the experiences by which Otto attempts to evoke an awareness of what is meant by 'holiness' is that of 'creature-feeling'. His discussion of it pays critical attention to Friedrich Schleiermacher's attempt to locate the heart of religion in a feeling of absolute dependence. This, indeed, may be regarded as a third, distinct, way of characterizing religion. At the end of the eighteenth century Schleiermacher criticized the 'enlightened' critics of religion who regarded it primarily in terms of rational conclusions and moral principles and then dismissed it as presenting, at worst, 'senseless fables' and 'rude superstition' and, at best, 'the ill-put together fragments of metaphysics and ethics'. Whatever the form, the critics find it to be 'without rhyme or reason'.[20] In his *Speeches on Religion* addressed to these 'cultured despisers', Schleiermacher argues that they have crucially failed to perceive the authentic nature of religion. Religion is primarily 'the immediate consciousness of the universal existence of all finite things, in and through the Infinite, and of all temporal things in and through the Eternal'. In phrases reflecting the Romantic movement, Schleiermacher says that religion is 'to have life and to know life in immediate feeling, only as such an existence in the Infinite and Eternal'. It is 'a life in the infinite nature of the Whole, in the One and in the All, in God, having and possessing all things in God, and God in all'.[21] Doctrines, abstract ideas, formal principles and moral practices are secondary products of this mode of awareness. Later, in a more systematic treatment of the issues, *The Christian Faith*, Schleiermacher made a fundamental distinction between feeling, knowing, and doing as modes of self-consciousness. Religion is primarily a matter of 'feeling' – of 'a feeling of absolute dependence' – which accompanies all our being when we are fully self-aware. God is thus held to be 'the *Whence* of our receptive and active existence, as implied in this self-consciousness'.[22] It is important to note that Schleiermacher regards the 'feeling' which is at the heart of religion as an authentic mode of awareness. Whereas when we speak of ourselves as 'feeling' hope or dismay, for example, we are only reporting our subjective states, the 'feeling of absolute dependence' is understood to provide us with a reliable perception of the ultimate nature of reality. What, then, Schleiermacher's work draws attention to is the way in which religion is connected with the human sense of fundamental creatureliness. Human being, according to this view of religion, finds its worth and meaning in that which is other than itself and intrinsically transcends all creaturely reality. Whatever the significance of human autonomy and responsibility, its final satisfaction is only to be found in God. Religion is the awareness of this.

Recognition of the 'otherness' of God leads to a fourth view of what characterizes genuine religion. This is the view that whereas there are many inauthentic faiths which human beings have invented and false gods which they have imagined, authentic religion is a matter of divine self-revelation. Human thought based upon human experiences of the world in which humanity finds itself can never, according to this position, discover anything besides the human and imaginative projections of human being. If, then, we are to have a genuine knowledge of the divine as that which is essentially other than the human, it must be given to us by the divine. It is an argument which John Ellis developed in *The Knowledge of Divine Things* in the middle of the eighteenth century. He concludes that 'groveling silly' human beings could never 'rise up' by their own rational powers 'to a clear comprehension of an infinite and uncreated nature'.[23] The only way to a knowledge of God must be 'by its own Manifestations' and this is what 'Grace and Mercy have supplied. Nothing (without a Miracle) can ascend to Heaven, but what first came down from thence.'[24] For much of the twentieth century a similar view of the sole source of true knowledge of God has been powerfully advocated by Karl Barth and his followers. According to Barth both the transcendence of God and the limits of human reason (limits which have been made more severe because of the effects of the Fall) prevent humanity discovering truth about God by its own efforts. Human attempts to attain such knowledge are 'criminal arrogance'; theology is properly to see itself as a 'ministerium verbi divini' – a ministry of the divine word which is given to humanity.[25] In *Dogmatics in Outline*, Barth sums up his position thus: 'God is thought and known when in His own freedom God makes Himself apprehensible . . . God is always the One who has made Himself known to man in His own revelation, and not the one man thinks out for himself and describes as God.'[26] Although this view is open to basic criticisms – how, for example, could something be recognized as a revelation of God if there was no prior awareness of a God who could be self-revealing? – it is a strongly held understanding of authentic theistic faith and must not be ignored in any attempt to identify what is seen as the characteristic nature of religion. Many believers who do not accept that religious belief must be wholly a matter of revelation do maintain that revealed elements are a vital part of their faith.

A fifth view of religion stresses the moral aspects of faith and practice. It sees religion largely as a matter of behaviour and its thought as expressions of the principles of right conduct. When, for example, Lord Herbert of Cherbury early in the seventeenth century attempted to outline the components of true religion, he began with a belief in the existence of a deity who is to be worshipped but he went on to hold that 'the connection of virtue with piety' is 'the most important part of religious practice'. His further points reinforce this view for they concern the human sense of sin and the expiation of crimes, and a postmortem state in which human beings receive rewards or punishments for their conduct in this life.[27] A fundamentally moral understanding of religion is shared by a number of modern interpreters. Immanuel Kant, for example, held that a rational religion 'must consist not in dogmas and rites but in the heart's disposition to fulfil all human duties as divine commands'.[28] Matthew Arnold asserts that 'the true meaning of religion is . . . *morality touched by emotion*'.[29] According to his analysis of religion 'the antithesis between *ethical* and *religious* is . . . quite a false one' for both are essentially concerned with practice and conduct.[30] In a famous paper Richard Braithwaite argues that religious assertions are used to 'announce allegiance to a set of moral principles';[31] thus 'God is love' is a way of reporting an intention to live in a loving manner. As we shall consider in chapter 10, the link between religious beliefs and morality is not without its problems. Nevertheless, the inclusion of a moral element in any adequate appreciation of the character of religious faith seems indisputable. As the first letter of John puts it, 'if a man says "I love God", while hating his brother, he is a liar'.[32] Belief in God and moral conduct seem to be inextricably bound together.

As well as being concerned with moral conduct, both private and social, religion is, sixthly, often held to be distinguishable by the ways in which it involves its adherents in communal cultic activities. Rituals, of course, are not peculiar to religion. Brownie packs and regimental messes have their special ways of doing things! Group adherence, furthermore, is common to many aspects of human life, for human beings are social animals who feel a need to belong. Nevertheless, as Spiro's definition of religion indicates, a religion is probably to be understood as a 'cultural institution' whose members participate in the joint activities of some form of worship. Indeed, it may be that it is the presence of what is regarded as an essential element of communal activity which provides the basis for distinguishing between a *religious* faith and assent to a metaphysical understanding of the ultimate nature of reality and to the proper principles of morality. The forms of the cultus differ enormously – from the stillness of a Buddhist meditation garden or a Quaker meeting to the intricacies of a Parsee ritual or an Orthodox liturgy – but no religion seems to be without some forms of worship which are regarded as essential to it. The basis of membership also varies considerably. In some parts of the world, for example in Thailand, the notion of 'religion' is hard to apply since adherence to a faith is not readily distinguishable from being a member of society in those areas. For other faiths membership involves distinctive confessions and practices which separate its adherents from fellow members of their secular society. Whatever the faith, however, it is normally held to involve a sense of bonding to fellow-believers in a community. To be a Christian, for example, is not just a matter of accepting a certain creed and ethic; it is also widely regarded as a matter of seeing oneself as a part of 'the body of Christ', of sharing in worship with the other 'members' of that body, and of allowing one's understanding to be moulded by the teaching given in the community.

While religion may have essential social and cultic aspects, it may also be held to have a peculiarly personal and private character. Even those who stress the importance of group-activity in the practice of a faith often emphasize that in the end faith is a matter of an individual's personal response to reality. Thus authentic religious faith may, seventhly, be characterized as a highly personal and individual matter. According to Søren Kierkegaard faith is a matter of 'the individual's inwardness' as an existing person. The truth of faith is something which each individual must grasp 'existentially and in existence'.[33] It is also something which may be secret and private to the individual: the believer as such lives in the world, according to Kierkegaard, 'incognito' because 'there is absolutely nothing that marks him off from others, absolutely nothing that could serve as a hint of his secret inwardness'.[34] Faith is one's own business: 'there is no disciple at second hand'.[35] A less existentialist version of this view of religion is given by Alfred North Whitehead in *Religion in the Making*. Here he describes religion as 'the art and the theory of the internal life of man, so far as it depends on the man himself and on what is permanent in the nature of things . . . Religion is what the individual does with his own solitariness . . . Accordingly, what should emerge from religion is individual worth of character.'[36] Later in his Gifford Lectures, *Process and Reality*, he interprets religion as 'the translation of general ideas into particular thoughts, particular emotions, and particular purposes . . . Religion is an ultimate craving to infuse into the insistent particularity of emotion that non-temporal generality which primarily belongs to conceptual thought alone.'[37] Religious faith, that is to say, is the way in which individuals make truths their own and allow them to fashion their lives. Here the difference between metaphysical insights and religious faith is not a distinction between the individual assents of philosophical understanding and the corporate involvement of religious adherence but one between the general principles identified by philosophy and the personal commitment of a believer. 'But who do you' – you as individual, solitary, alone – 'say that I am?' is a basic religious question. Faith is not a matter of hiding behind authorities: it involves the frightening exposure to individual being.

Why, then, do people concern themselves with religion? In some cases believers might answer that they have a disinterested concern about what is so. In most cases they are likely to answer along the lines that religion provides the means to a fuller life, that it enhances their being, that it offers 'salvation'. In these replies we are pointed to an eighth characteristic of religion, namely that it is seen as offering salvation in some way or other. At a popular level it is on this basis that evengelists 'sell' their gospels: by sharing their faith others will find life in place of existing death, satisfaction in place of frustration, purpose in place of aimlessness, forgiveness in place of death, wholeness in place of disintegration. At a more sophisticated level, Paul Tillich's theological 'method of correlation' argues that the meaning of the Christian gospel is to be perceived by seeing how it corresponds to and meets the fundamental existential needs of human being.[28] It is the salvific element which James Henry Leuba sees as the decisive characteristic of religion: 'Not God, but life, more life, a larger, richer, more satisfying life, is, in the last analysis, the end of religion. The love of life . . . is the religious impulse.'[39] A similar conclusion is reached by Gerardus van der Leeuw in *Religion in Essence and Manifestation*. After a wide-ranging study of the phenomena of religion he asserts that the goal of all religion is – and always has been – salvation: 'It may be the enhancing of life, improvement, beautifying, widening, deepening; but by "salvation" there may also be meant completely new life . . . received "from elsewhere". But in any case, religion is always directed towards salvation, never towards life itself as it is given.'[40] Although the underlying metaphors may now have only very limited appeal, Charles Wesley was, according to this view of religion, reflecting its heart when he wrote:

> To save what was lost, from heaven He came:
> Come, sinners, and trust in Jesus's name;
> He offers you pardon, He bids you be free:
> If sin be your burden, O come unto Me!

The claim that religion is salvific, however, brings from some critics the riposte that religion is like a placebo: it is only effective in the case of those who believe in it. The object of its faith, 'God', is really a product of the believer's imagination. This brings us to the ninth – and last – way of characterizing religion which we shall mention: this is the view that religious beliefs express projections of our ideals, reifications of our values (i.e. presenting abstract values as if they were concrete objects or actual persons). Some present this analysis of religious beliefs in order to destroy their credibility. Ludwig Feuerbach, for example, argues in *The Essence of Christianity* that 'Consciousness of God is self-consciousness, knowledge of God is self-knowledge. By his God thou knowest the man, and by the man his God; the two are identical. Whatever is God to a man, that is his heart and soul.'[41] When, therefore, people list the attributes of God, they are listing the values which they regard as supreme and ascribing to them a reality over against themselves. When they feel guilt at failing to live up to those values, they may describe the situation as one of having offended 'God' but in reality they are confessing to being alienated from their ideals. A similar interpretation of religion in terms of our psychical constitution is given by Sigmund Freud. In *The Future of an Illusion* he describes religious ideas as 'illusions, fulfilments of the oldest, strongest and most urgent wishes of mankind'. Belief in 'the benevolent rule of a divine Providence', for example, is the way we find a comforting replacement for our childish confidence in the protective powers of our fathers when experiences have taught us their weaknesses.[42] It is arguable, though, that the projective character of religious beliefs is not necessarily to their discredit. Gordon D. Kaufman, for example, in his *Essay on Theological Method* and *Theological Imagination* has convincingly developed the view that theological understanding is a constructive activity.[43] The structure of human understanding may be such that it is only through such projective or imaginative activity that we can apprehend the nature of the ultimate and divine. Indeed it is plausible to argue in the case of belief about a divine incarnation that in such an occurrence God provides us with a story or a model by which we may grasp the divine nature in the most appropriate way that it is possible for us. Whether such a view of the revelatory purpose of a divine incarnation be tenable or not, it does not undermine religious faith to hold that its beliefs concretize and amplify our perception of the nature of God by using reifying projections of humanly perceived ideals. It may well be that the resulting stories are the most adequate way in which human beings can apprehend the character and will of that ultimate and holy being which we name 'God'. Imagination is not to be avoided by theologians and believers. It may turn out to be one of the ways, if not the way, to discover the reality of God.

What, then, is religion? Our discussion of some of its major characterizations suggests that it is a complex entity for which there is no simple definition, nor has it any single essence which identifies it. The term 'religion' refers to an undefined number of actual faiths whose dominant characteristics form in each case a complicated network that overlap and criss-cross similar or identical features in other faiths to a significant extent. Consequently 'religion' may be said to be a term whose boundaries are 'fuzzy'. It denotes a reality whose identity is a matter of what Ludwig Wittgenstein speaks of as 'family resemblances'.[44] By this phrase he points to the way in which the various features of the members of a family which bring them to be recognizable as belonging together as a family, form various series of resemblances which overlap and criss-cross in complicated ways. The characteristic features of different religions similarly overlap and criss-cross.

What has philosophy to do with religion?

Having, then, considered some of the ways in which religion may be understood, it is time to return to the question with which this chapter began, 'What has Athens to do with Jerusalem?'. Granted the nature of religion which we have indicated, what has philosophy to do with its understanding? How, in other words, does philosophy of religion engage in philosophical activities in its surveying, engineering and architectural roles in relation to religion? In one way the rest of this study provides a material answer to this question as it investigates various aspects of religious understanding. As a preliminary and more formal answer, however, it is important to recognize that the label 'philosophy' covers a number of distinct intellectual activities, and to reflect on how various of these activities have been and are used in the tasks of formulating, grounding, developing and understanding religious faith.

Among the intellectual activities that can be called 'philosophy' and which are particularly pertinent to religious faith are metaphysics, logic, epistemology and analysis. We will briefly note what is involved in each of them before outlining the different ways in which philosophical enquiries have been applied to the matter of religion.

'Metaphysics' is what many people immediately think of when they meet the word 'philosophy'. The term originated as a name for the works of Aristotle which came 'after' ('meta') his works on nature ('phusika'). It has, however, come to refer to attempts to perceive that which is universal and ultimate, which is the necessary ground of all things, and which transcends or underlies the empirical, contingent world of immediate, empirical observation. In 'metaphysics' philosophers try to identify the fundamental reality, being itself, and to discern how its nature determines the constitution, purpose and meaning of all things in a significant way. Tillich speaks of it as the discovery of 'the principles, the structures, and the nature of being as it is embodied in everything that is'.[45] Whitehead describes it as the attempt to grasp the 'first principles' which can never fail to be exemplified in all that is and in all that could ever be and which, therefore, provide 'a coherent, logical, necessary system of general ideas in terms of which every element of our experience can be interpreted'.[46] He also points out that it is very difficult to perceive these universal principles: because they are exemplified in everything, they cannot be distinguished, unlike the way in which our knowledge is generally obtained, by comparing cases where they apply with those where they do not apply. For much of the twentieth century metaphysics has been in disfavour in Anglo-Saxon philosophical circles because philosophers have doubted the possibility of achieving coherent understanding of such matters. Their objections are not to be ignored, based as they are on important insights into our meaningful use of language, but neither are they necessarily overwhelming. The questions which metaphysics seeks to answer are ones which are unavoidable for self-conscious beings who seek to determine whether there is any point in being or whether it is an absurd accident in a meaningless cosmos and, assuming that there is a 'point', what it is.

A rapidly expanding field in philosophy over recent decades is the study of logic. Here philosophers attempt to identify the procedures, application and significance of valid reasoning processes. These range from analyses of the simpler forms of syllogistic reasoning to the complex refinements of modern symbolic logic and modal logic. The study of logic, however, is not confined to the identification of conclusive patterns of demonstration (and, by contrast, fallacious ones) so that we can know why it is valid to conclude from 'All human beings are mortal' and 'David is a human being' that 'David is mortal' – and why it is invalid to conclude that because 'David teaches philosophy of religion' and 'David is bald' that 'Teachers of philosophy of religion are bald'. Such discoveries may have their uses in detecting fallacies but often they only formalize what is already obvious to careful thought. More interesting, especially for the student of religious understanding, is the way in which the study of logic may include the examination of the informal, complex procedures by which we arrive at reliable conclusions by estimating the cumulative force of different pieces of evidence and the converging significance of various factors. This is the kind of reasoning by which we reach judgments, for example, about the guilt of the accused at the end of a trial, or about the reasons why things happened as they did in some historical event, or about the proper diagnosis and treatment of a patient.

A third form of philosophy is 'epistemology' – the study of what we can warrantably regard as knowable and the determination of what lies beyond our proper competence, and the study of how we know what we can claim to be able to know. Although Plato's concern with how we come to a knowledge of the 'Forms' which empirical objects seek to imitate reminds us that this aspect of philosophy is probably as old as philosophy itself, it has particularly characterized the fundamental concern of modern philosophers from Descartes and Locke to the present time. Descartes began by trying to determine what could not possibly be doubted and what followed from it, Locke by seeking to identify the nature of human understanding and hence what may be held to lie within its scope. The work of Hume and Kant examined the issues further and suggested that the range of knowledge was much more restricted than Descartes and Locke, and their followers, had considered. Kant, in particular, maintained that the examination of the competence of human reason showed that the nature of things as they are in themselves, and hence of any trans-empirical reality, is beyond our knowledge. All we can legitimately claim to *know* are our structures of experience and of thought and the objects of which we are aware in terms of those structures. His 'critical' appraisal of thought has had great influence in philosophical thought during the past two centuries. In particular it has led metaphysicians and philosophers of religion to consider carefully what is meant by 'belief' in relation to religious faith, its relationship to 'knowledge', and its justification.

Finally, for our purposes here, there is the analytical form of philosophy. Philosophers who follow this approach do not seek to discern new truths about the final nature of reality. They try to clarify what people mean when they make certain statements and how those statements are regarded as justified by those who make them. In this way philosophers attempt to sort out confusions and avoid the misapprehensions which occur when people are not clear about what they and others are 'really' saying. A classical statement of this understanding of philosophical activity is given by Ludwig Wittgenstein in *Philosophical Investigations*: 'A philosophical problem has the form: "I don't know my way about". Philosophy may in no way interfere with the actual use of language; it can in the end only describe it. For it cannot give it any foundation either. It leaves everything as it is.'[47] Although the claim that this is the only legitimate form of philosophy is to be resisted, for ultimate questions do not disappear by holding that philosophers have other, more mundane tasks to see to, the development of this form of philosophical activity, especially in Anglo-Saxon circles, during the present century has brought much-needed light and rigour to understanding. While, for example, it has not made it any easier to justify the truth of claims about the reality of God, it has made it clearer what those claims express and what is involved in justifying them.

Having, therefore, indicated the metaphysical, logical, epistemological and analytical roles of philosophy, we may try to outline a rather formal answer to the question 'What has Athens to do with Jerusalem?'. In other words, what emerges when one or more of these different forms of philosophical thought are applied to religious understanding? Here again there are several basic positions which reflect different views of the relationship between philosophy and religion. M. J. Charlesworth has discussed four of them in *Philosophy of Religion: The Historic Approaches* – 'philosophy as religion', 'philosophy as the handmaid of religion', 'philosophy as making room for faith' and 'philosophy and the analysis of religious language'.[48] His study provides interesting examples of each of them from major religious writers. In the remainder of this chapter I simply want to indicate the basic content of each of these positions and to add a fifth, 'philosophy as the study of the reasoning used in religious thought'.

'Philosophy as religion' is found in those cases where metaphysical understanding of the nature of ultimate reality is seen as providing both an object to be worshipped (or an ideal to be contemplated) and a value-system to direct the conduct of life. In such cases the content of the religion is determined by human thought. This does not mean that what is adored and its intrinsic value-system are human inventions which have no ontological status apart from the human mind which has conceived of them. The rational thought of metaphysical understanding involved here is held to be a perception of what actually is the case ultimately. Thus although a few atheistic optimists like Feuerbach and Don

Cupitt may urge us to worship the admitted inventions of our minds (which, I confess, I do not find an inspiring prospect), philosophy as religion normally occurs where rational reflection on the highest principles and on the nature of things is considered to give true insight into what is ultimately so, whether we recognize it or not. As such it is held to provide a totally sufficient basis for faith and practice. What this position excludes, or at least excludes as being essential, is any additional element of understanding and direction which is claimed to have come to humanity through acts of revelation by the ultimate and divine.

Classical examples of philosophy as religion can be found in the adoption of Plato's understanding and, even more, in the later development of neo-Platonism by Plotinus and Porphyry. In *The Republic*, Plato writes of the Good as that which 'gives the objects of knowledge their truth and the mind the power of knowing'. It is that on which all else depends for its reality, but is itself beyond what we can comprehend. It is unsurpassable in dignity and power.[49] This 'Good' is the proper goal of all activity and its existence is 'divined' by everyone even though it is 'difficult to say just what it is'.[50] In recent years Iris Murdoch's *The Sovereignty of Good* indicates how a contemporary Platonic 'philosophy as religion' might be developed. She affirms the importance of retaining 'the idea of Good as a central point of reflection' and of recognizing that 'Good, not will, is transcendent',[51] and then suggests that 'faith' is to be understood as the quest for increasing perception of the character of the Good. In Plotinus philosophy as religion emerges as a form of energizing mystical contemplation. The intellect is to be used to pass beyond itself in order to adore the One which is the origin of all being and value. In the vision of the One we 'obtain the end of our wishes'. We 'are no longer discordant, but form a truly divine dance about it'. In this situation we find total felicity for we behold 'the fountain of life, the fountain of intellect, the principle of being, the cause of good, and the root of soul' and are animated by it.[52] Hard to understand as Plotinus may be, his work suggests that some forms of philosophical reflection may have profoundly disturbing effects as they offer a totally absorbing vision of the true end of all being.

A contemporary philosopher whose work and life provide an interesting example of a theistic philosophy as religion is Charles Hartshorne. In *The Logic of Perfection* he tells us that 'about the age of seventeen, after reading Emerson's *Essays*, I made up my mind (doubtless with a somewhat hazy notion of what I was doing) to trust reason to the end. In pursuit of this ideal, I have tried to make my thinking about metaphysical and religious questions good thinking, good by the proper criteria of thinking, rather than of persuading, edifying, or expressing emotion.' Although he goes on to confess that this ideal is easier 'to proclaim than to adhere to',[53] comparison of his intellectual work with his personal attitude to life reveals a remarkable consistency between them. He believes and acts according to what he rationally concludes. Basically his faith may be summed up in the proposition 'God is love'. He concludes, without any appeal to revelation, that it is possible to show the rational necessity of affirming the reality of God as an essentially perfect and utterly worshipful being who is conscious of and responsive to all that occurs in the world, and from this he infers that such a being can only be coherently conceived as loving. Although more or less (usually less) significant objections may be raised against his arguments, Hartshorne maintains with some justification that 'there is something irrational in choosing not to believe in God. There seems no other way than the theistic to conceive the objective correlate of personal integrity.'[54] His work offers a 'philosophy as religion' which is rich, effective and fundamentally in accordance with Christian faith about God.

A different view of the relationship between philosophy and religion does not deny the actual achievements of rational reflection in providing some knowledge of God and of human destiny but it holds that any such achievements can never be adequate for a living and saving religious faith. It may be possible, for example, to show the rational justification of holding that God exists, is eternal, all powerful, just, to be obeyed, and so on. It may even be possible to show that human beings are morally responsible to God and immortal. Nevertheless, so this point of view maintains, any such conclusions need to be augmented by divine revelation if people are to arrive at the faith which God requires of them for salvation. The result may be described as a two-tier model of religious understanding. The lower tier consists of truths which may be discerned by human reason; the upper tier consists of further information about the divine nature and will which is revealed to humanity by God in order to make necessary additions to what it can grasp by its own powers. Reason does, however, have an important role in relation to these revealed truths: it judges whether they bear the marks of authentic revelation and so are to be accepted as coming from God.

The classical exponent of this view of religious understanding is usually held to be Thomas Aquinas. In two great works, the *Summa contra Gentiles* and the *Summa Theologiae*, Aquinas explores in detail what may be discovered about the existence and nature of God – such as the simplicity, the perfection, the infinity, the immutability, and the unity of the divine – before proceeding to discuss the 'divine truth' which 'surpasses every effort of reason' and which God makes known 'out of a superabundant goodness'.[55] Included in the latter are the doctrines of the Trinity, of the Incarnation, and of 'the ultimate end of man such as the resurrection and glorification of bodies, the everlasting beatitude of souls, and matters related to these'.[56] It should be noted, though, that Aquinas has doubts about human reason's ability in practice to reach the truths which are in principle attainable by it. He suggests, therefore, that God 'fittingly' provides a revelation of these truths also so that they may be acquired quickly and accurately.[57] In the end we may be confident about our rational conclusions because and so far as they agree with what God declares in revelation.

Since the time of John Locke, however, the characteristic view in modern thought has been that the standard of truth lies in what reason establishes: supposed revealed knowledge is acceptable so far as it does not contradict what reason declares and it is confirmed by rationally acceptable tests as being from God. It is a position which Locke develops in some of the later chapters of Book Four of his *Essay Concerning Human Understanding*.[58] It is a pattern which is well illustrated in the form and contents of Samuel Clarke's Boyle Lectures for 1704 and 1705. He first attempts to demonstrate the being and attributes of God from the casual structure of the world and concludes that 'nothing is so certain and undeniable as the Necessary Existence of God, and the consequent Deduction of all his Attributes'.[59] Having, then, 'endeavour'd to lay firmly the first Foundations of Religion' in this way, he proceeds to the task of 'proving and establishing the Truth and Excellency of the whole Superstructure of our most Holy Religion' by showing 'the unalterable Obligations of Natural Religion, and the certainty of Divine Revelation'. In this task he sees himself as opposing 'certain vitious and profane Men' who seek 'to excuse their Vices and Debaucheries' by denying these latter truths. The conclusion of his investigations is that God provides as 'many and certain Proofs'[60] of these matters as is possible in such cases. Consequently there is 'all the reason in the World to oblige' us 'to believe' what reason shows and what revelation declares about God and humanity.[61]

A very different view of the relationship between philosophy and religion holds that the philosophers' role is to show the inadequacy of human reason in reaching and judging any understanding of the being, nature and will of God and, thereby, to establish the essentially revelatory basis of all genuine knowledge of God. Those who adopt this position do not only deny that rational reflection can adequately produce a religion; some of them also deny that reason can discover anything significant about God by using its own powers. According to the extreme version of this position, all valid knowledge of God must come from the divine and be accepted in faith. The value of philosophy is that its metaphysical, epistimological and logical investigations, if correctly carried out, will make clear the incompetence of human reason in matters concerning the divine. In this way it will check the pretensions of human thought and thereby, as Kant put it in describing the significance of his *Critique of Pure Reason*, limit reason in order to make room for faith.[62]

Our earlier discussion of the view that authentic religion must be based upon acts of divine self-manifestation indicates how the works of John Ellis and Karl Barth provide theological examples of this position. An earlier example is to be found in William of Ockham's treatise upon God's knowledge of the future. In this work he points out that the philosopher, using human reason, judges that God cannot know, in cases where there is a range of future possibilities, which one will actually occur. On the other hand, 'the authorities of the Bible and the Saints' are held to prove that God does have such foreknowledge.[63] Faced with this apparent contradiction Ockham attempts by various kinds of subtle reasoning to reconcile the two positions. Where, however, he is unable to find a way of harmonizing them, he maintains that it is the dictate of faith which must be correct, however odd it may appear to natural reason. Although Ockham's appeal to authorities may not be acceptable, the way in which he deliberately subordinates what reason judges to what faith declares, when the two disagree, is an example of how some theologians who have some confidence in rational reflection may nevertheless consider that it is incompetent to judge basic issues about belief in God and the importance of revelation.

In the middle of the nineteenth century Henry L. Mansel produced Bampton Lectures on *The Limits of Religious Thought* in which he maintains that reflection on basic attributes of God shows that we are here attempting to deal with matters beyond our mental capacity. He considers in particular the three conceptions of 'the Cause, the Absolute' and 'the Infinite' and argues that while they are 'all equally indispensable' to a proper view of the divine, analysis of their implications shows that they cannot be attributed together to 'one and the same Being' without 'contradiction'.[64] From this he draws two conclusions. The first is that the self-contradictions into which reason inevitably falls when it attempts to speculate about God are divinely given 'beacons . . . in the mind of man, to warn us that we are deviating from the track that He designs us to pursue'.[65] The other is that God has revealed 'in a manner accommodated to the finite capacities of the human thinker' how 'He wills that we should think of Him' in order to be correctly related to the divine.[66] The self-manifestation will not satisfy our intellect but it will be a sufficient guide for our proper conduct in relation to God. In contemporary theological debates the priority and exclusiveness of revelation for a genuine knowledge of God has been strongly maintained by Thomas F. Torrance. In *Theological Science*, for example, he states that we attain true knowledge as we 'respond faithfully and truly to all that He declares and discloses to us of Himself'. God has 'absolute primacy' in our knowledge of the divine. 'In our knowledge of Him, He remains the Lord, He comes first and remains first, and maintains His ascendancy over all our knowing of Him . . . Knowledge of this God cannot be moulded according to our plastic ideas or controlling archetypes; that would be idolatry. Rather must our knowing of God be brought into conformity with what He reveals of Himself, and under the control of what He gives us of Himself.'[67] The role of philosophical investigation, then, is to show, on the one hand, that this is the necessary condition of authentic knowledge in such matters and, on the other, to demonstrate the incapacity of human beings to reach such knowledge through non-revelatory reasoning.

A fourth view of the relationship between philosophy and religion takes up the view of philosophy as analysis which has dominated Anglo-Saxon philosophy for much of this century. It maintains that the role of the philosopher in terms of religion is to analyse religious statements in order to clarify their proper meaning, logical status, and implications. Such philosophy of religion does not attempt to prove the truth or development of the content of religious understanding but, rather, seeks to discover what religious people are expressing when they speak about their faith, what are the kinds of grounds which they consider appropriate for justifying their claims, how their religious statements are connected to each other, and what functions these claims perform in relation to their understanding and conduct generally. In pursuing these investigations, however, philosophers of religion are not always acting in a wholly descriptive manner. Their analyses, by identifying what seem to be misunderstandings and confusions in religious claims, may have a radically revisionary affect on faith.

Although the pursuit of this form of philosophy of religion is usually regarded as a characteristically twentieth-century concern, its basic approach can be seen in earlier works. When, for example, Xenophanes stated that 'the gods of the Ethiopians are black with snub noses, while those of the Thracians are blond, with blue eyes and red hair',[69] he was drawing attention to the way in which descriptions of the divine apotheosize the characteristics of those who produce them. It is an interpretation of the content of talk about God which was radicalized and also applied to the reference of that talk by Feuerbach and Freud, as we noted earlier, in their projection theories of religion. Again, when David Hume, in his criticisms of the arguments for natural religion and for revelation, concludes that these things must be a matter of 'faith' rather than of 'knowledge', he is in effect identifying – though probably in his case ironically – the logical status of such claims. Kierkegaard's studies of the nature of faith are similarly understandable as an attempt to identify its proper logical status.

Among contemporary philosophers this view of philosophy of religion has been strongly urged by Dewi Z. Phillips. In an early work, *The Concept of Prayer*, he states that 'it is not the task of the philosopher to decide whether there is a God or not, but to ask what it means to affirm or deny the existence of God'.[70] What is being sought is 'conceptual elucidation; that is, the philosopher wants to know what is meant by "real" ("exists") in the statement "God is real (exists)"'.[71] In terms of belief in God, this means examining the contexts in which people make such a statement, the reasons they offer for making it, the consequences which they consider follow from holding it, and so on. In terms of prayer, it means examining what people do when they pray – for 'the ultimate appeal is to actual usage itself, that is, to the activity of praying'.[72] The purpose in seeking to understand the activity, though, has a destructive as well as a constructive aspect, for Phillips wants 'to stop ways of talking about prayer which lead to confusion' as well as trying 'to say what people *are* doing when they pray'.[73] Such analyses, of course, are always liable to the objection from those who do what is supposedly being analysed 'But that is not what I am doing!'. Nevertheless, as we shall see, particularly in chapter 11 when we discuss religious language, the result of such studies has been an illuminating awareness of the multi-faceted and complex structure of such talk.

The final form of philosophy of religion which is to be outlined in this chapter is that which is concerned with the reasoning used in religious thought. In some ways it may be seen as a component of the analytical view of the relationship between philosophy and religion. It does, however, have sufficient importance and characteristics as a study in its own right to deserve to be mentioned separately. The conviction underlying this philosophical approach to religion is that believers are human beings and hence both the human structure of their thought and the particular cultures in which they find themselves condition what they believe. Basically, then, the philosopher of religion here is interested in identifying the factors which influence faith and the ways in which these factors affect the expressions of faith, both in doctrines and in practices. Several of the following chapters deal with different aspects of this study and refer to classical and modern treatments. There is, for example, the investigation of the effects of culture upon faith. In a work which is now nearly a century old but whose findings are still important, *The Influence of Greek Ideas and Usages upon the Christian Church*, Edwin Hatch considered how the early formulations of the Christian faith were influenced by their Hellenistic context.[74] More recent studies by Maurice Wiles and John Hick, in which the former has raised questions about the contemporary value of Greek thought-forms in expressing Christian doctrine today,[75] and the latter has speculated on what might have emerged as a doctrine of Christ if Christianity had initially moved eastwards into India rather than westwards into Europe,[76] have aroused a certain amount of concern about orthodoxy in some self-consciously Christian circles. The hostile character of some of this concern shows the present need for theological education about the findings of this form of philosophy of religion. Among other controversial matters which it investigates are the ways in which doctrines develop, the use of reports of historical events in coming to judgments about the divine, the manner in which texts (especially those of sacred scriptures) are interpreted by believers, and the relationships between scientific discoveries about the natural world and theological thought. Above all there are questions concerning the ways in which the perception of the nature of God is humanly and culturally relative. Since these, however, are issues to be considered in later chapters, it is unnecessary to say more about this form of philosophy of religion here. It is time to move on to other questions. Having, then, discussed how the 'Athens' of philosophy may in principle be considered to have dealings with the 'Jerusalem' of religious faith, we must now consider what these dealings suggest in practice about religious understanding and, in particular, about theology and reason.

Chapter 2

Faith, Theology and Reason

In the previous chapter we considered what may be understood by the notions of religion and philosophy and the relationships between them. Two other basic notions involved in religious understanding are those of theology and reason. It is now time to turn our attention to them and to their relationships.

Theology may be defined as the self-consciously rational attempt to produce a systematic account of the beliefs contained in a religious faith. According to the common interpretation of this definition, faith is the primary datum; beliefs express what this faith holds to be the case in reality; theology is the result of reflection upon those beliefs. Theology is thus dependent upon beliefs, and beliefs upon faith. We shall note later that this view fails to appreciate the ways in which rational considerations may contribute to theological understanding and then, in turn, influence belief and faith. For the moment, however, we need to consider what is meant by 'faith' and 'belief' in order to perceive what is involved in theology.

Faith

'Faith' in this context refers to a person's fundamental existential commitment. It signifies what ultimately determines the kind of person an individual is, so far as this is a matter of personal concerns and not simply the resultant of natural and environmental factors such as those which genetically decide that individual's physical and mental characteristics. Faith itself is a complex phenomenon which is constituted by and expressed in a range of attitudes, dispositions, values and practices. Theistic faith, for example, may be held to involve a person in attitudes of hope and confidence, in dispositions of concern and respect, in entertaining certain values as categorical imperatives, and in practices of worship and benevolence. Bound up with all these, however, and combining them into a coherent position, are certain claims about what is ultimately the case in reality. For theistic faith, for example, these are claims about the reality and will of God. It is these claims which justify the attitudes, dispositions, values and practices which are involved in the faith. Furthermore, the nature of God is such that claims about the divine are only properly grasped when they are seen to require appropriate attitudes, dispositions, values and practices. They may thus be described as 'self-involving' claims in that their authentic accept-ance is held to 'involve' those who accept them in adopting appropriate responses. They cannot be held to be true in the unconcerned way in which we may accept that Queen Anne died in 1714.

The way in which the acceptance of certain claims about what is the case is self-involving – and the way in which the involvement shows that the significance of such a claim has been grasped – is easily illustrated. Suppose you rush into a room where I am sitting doodling with a crossword and shout 'Your daughter has just been awarded a starred first in her finals'. If I abstractedly reply 'Oh, really!', you would have good reason to infer that my response shows either that I am not listening or that I have not understood what is meant by 'starred first in finals' or that I do not appreciate what it is to be a father. 'Understanding' what is being said would be expected to involve me in a very different kind of response. So it is even more in the case of most reports about God. If we accept them as valid, we show that we have failed to grasp their intrinsic significance if we dismiss them with an uninterested 'Oh, really!' – as if we were Lancastrians who were being told that the Yorkshire cricket team had just managed to draw with a retired parsons' team! To be told about God is to be told about that which is ultimate in being and value, about that in terms of which everything else finally makes sense, and about that which is intrinsically and unsurpassably worthwhile. It is to be told about that which we cannot but respond to in the awe and wonder and self-giving of true adoration and, so far as it is proper, in seeking to embody the qualities of that divine being in our lives.

Belief

Beliefs express the components of faith which make claims about what is the case. Many people, though, are largely unaware of the content of their faith. They live by their faith rather than are explicitly conscious of it. Often it is only when it is challenged – by crises which cast doubt on their convictions or by sceptics who question the way they live – that they begin to discover what it is that they are finally committed to. What they then declare to be the truths upon which their lives ultimately depend are what they take to be their beliefs. It must be recognized, however, that these explicit statements of belief do not necessarily represent the actual components of their faith in a satisfactory way. For one thing, they may have failed to discern significant elements in their faith and so present only a distorted picture of it. It is not easy to become fully conscious of the general truths, such as truths about God, which we consider to apply necessarily to all that is real and all that is possible. Discernment is much easier where there is observable contrast between cases where the truth does apply and cases where it does not – for example, it is much easier to identify what is signified by the presence of John, because we can contrast it with experiences of the absence of John, than to discern what is signified by the presence of God because, whatever may be the state of our sense of awareness of that presence, the nature of God's reality means that there is no actual or possible situation in which God is or conceivably could be absent. For another thing, in stating what they hold to be their beliefs, people may in fact be misled by traditional expressions or inadequate reflection into making claims which do not accurately reflect the faith which they live by. Many theists, for instance, say that they believe that God is outside time – it seems a proper way to speak about the eternity of the divine – and yet consideration of their faith shows that they are convinced that God is aware of and responsive to them as individuals whose personal being is temporally ordered. It is arguable, though, that such a faith only makes sense if the divine being is held to have a temporal aspect. Again, although they may say that they believe God to be impassible and unchanging, it is clear that they live on the basis that God loves and creates. What is usually happening in such cases is that people are adopting traditional modes of expression to express their faith, failing to notice that a careful analysis of some of those expressions of belief reveals that they contradict their basic commitments. Without raising questions of integrity, therefore, it seems on two counts that the statements of belief which people provide may to some extent be misleading expressions of the actual faith by which they live. They may be misleading because those who give them have not adequately grasped what constitutes their faith and they may be misleading because they have adopted inaccurate modes of expression for it.

Theology

In considering beliefs, therefore, it is always important to compare what are said to be the beliefs of a faith with what people living by that faith indicate to be its actual beliefs. This comparison is one of the tasks of theological reflection. An interesting example of it is found in Schubert Ogden's paper 'The Strange Witness of Unbelief', printed in his *Reality of God*. Here the faith and professed beliefs which are being examined are not those of a theist but of the atheistic Jean-Paul Sartre as expressed in his lecture 'Existentialism is a Humanism'. Sartre's claim is that the existentialist assertion of the radical freedom and responsibility of human beings, which is expressed in the slogan 'existence precedes essence', is only possible if there are no rules, prior to human existence, which determine what human being is and what human beings must do. Belief in the reality of God, however, is held to entail the reality of such rules. Sartre thus takes up Dostoyevsky's remark that 'If God did not exist, everything would be permitted' and asserts that it is because God does not exist that everything is permitted and human being is radically free. Each individual is responsible for the values and conduct of his or her own life. We choose for ourselves what we shall be and what we shall value. Sartre puts it thus: 'when I confront a real situation . . . I am obliged to choose my attitude to it.'[1] I cannot avoid choosing nor can I avoid bearing responsibility for the choice. Since God is excluded, we must be seen to be those who 'invent values'. To assert this means 'that there is no sense in life *a priori* . . . but it is yours to make sense of, and the value of it is nothing else but the sense that you choose'.[2]

Ogden responds to ·this thesis by arguing, first, that it is inconsistent and so must be abandoned and, secondly, that its major insight into human being only makes sense in terms of correctly understood theistic belief. To establish the first point Ogden argues that when Sartre asserts that human beings are free, he is in fact ascribing to them a nature that precedes their choices – namely, the nature of being a free being. Furthermore, Sartre holds that human beings are not free not to choose: they are under a demand to choose and are responsible for their choices. Ogden points out that in making this case Sartre not only uses language containing strong moral overtones but also maintains that each individual must recognize that the choice which she or he makes is for all humanity. This last claim is, though, further to impose *a priori* moral conditions on human being. Sartre is thus inconsistent. According to his presentation human beings are not simply what they choose to be: their existence is defined by *a priori* limitations.

In spite of this basic inconsistency, Ogden does not dismiss Sartre's position out of hand. He shares the latter's 'unqualified affirmation of the fact and value of man's freedom' and his 'rejection of any thoroughgoing moral skepticism'.[3] He points out, however, that these judgments imply that human choices have ultimate significance. It is impossible, though, to justify such a claim if they are considered only in terms of human existence. We perish. While the effects and memories of some of our attainments may survive us for a time, in the end they will share our oblivion. Human beings can give only very limited significance to human being. Ogden also maintains that the ultimate significance of human choices cannot be justified by reference to God's awareness of them if the classical view of God is correct. This is because that view regards the divine as 'a reality wholly necessary and absolute, and so without real internal relations to the contingent beings of which he is the ground'.[4] What Ogden points to in this summary of the defining characteristic of the classical view of God is the way in which it interprets the divine ultimacy and perfection as implying that God must be thought of as unchanging in all respects. From this it follows that God cannot be regarded as being affected by and so as being genuinely aware of such events as human choices and human actions. Consequently there can be no way of justifying claims about their significance by reference to God's recognition of them. Ogden, however, is not deterred by the fact that the classical view of God does not warrant claims about the ultimate significance of human being since he considers that it is to be rejected as a fundamentally unsatisfactory understanding of the God of theistic faith. In its place, using the insights of Charles Hartshorne, he advocates a neo-classical view of God according to which God is to be understood as one who is bound to the world 'by genuine ties of real internal relationship'.[5] In other words, God is to be held to be thoroughly aware of and affected by all that occurs. Nothing happens without God noticing it and its happening being embraced in the divine reality. According to this view, furthermore, our actions must be seen to be 'ultimately meaningful or worth while'[6] because they are experienced, valued and everlastingly preserved in the divine consciousness.

When, in chapter 7, we discuss the attributes of God, we will consider further the significance of claims about the inadequacy of the classical view of the divine and the need for a revised understanding of it. What Ogden's argument illustrates for our purposes in this chapter is how the rational reflection of theological understanding, in exploring the relationship between faith and belief, may show that what is professed to be believed does not in reality correspond to what is actually involved in the commitment of faith. This, however, is not the only role of theological thought. As well as seeking to identify the actual beliefs involved in faith, theology employs rational reflection in order to produce clearer formulations of belief, to discern the relationships between beliefs, and to develop the implications of beliefs for both thought and practice.

So far the discussion of faith, belief and theology has largely been conducted in a way that coheres with the assumption, mentioned earlier, that theology is to be seen as dependent on belief, and belief on faith. The result is a parasitic view of theology which regards it as essentially confessional in character. Theologians are accordingly held to be expositors of the faith of a community whose work is to be validated by its accuracy in expressing that faith. Although the attempt to express the faith in a rationally coherent and systematic manner may result in formulations which sound strange to the ordinary members of the community, this is only because they are unfamiliar with the technical terminology that is being employed – just as grandparents may be baffled when their grandchildren tell them that they have been 'partitioning the sets' at school today since they do not know that this is the language of the new mathematics for 'division'. Basically, though, what the theologians are supposed to be doing is to express the faith of the members of the community in a precise manner. John Macquarrie thus defines theology as 'the study which, through participation in and reflection upon a religious faith, seeks to express the content of this faith in the clearest and most coherent language available'. He goes on to emphasize that theology is to be understood as speaking 'from the standpoint of faith' and that this means that 'it is some specific faith that expresses itself in theology, not just faith in general but the faith of an historic community'. Theologians are accordingly to see themselves as 'spokesmen for their community, charged with a special responsibility within it'. They are not, as *theologians*, to express 'a private faith'.[7]

This view of theology is very common. It justifies those members of communities of faith who become indignant when, in their judgment, theologians of their community present distorted expositions of its faith in attempts, for example, to render it intelligible or believable to people generally. It is, however, a view of theology which is to be fundamentally questioned. For one thing it apparently makes the identification of the authentic nature of faith a non-theological matter. This odd conclusion comes about because if theologians are simply to expound the faith of a community, they must start with that 'faith' as given. If, then, disputes arise within the community about what does and what does not have a place in its faith, theologians cannot even try to help find a solution. All they can do is to say, if you hold that the faith is constituted in *this* way, then *this* theology will express it; and if you hold it is constituted in *that* way, then *that* theology will express it. Many people, though, will regard such a limitation on the scope of theology as absurd. While believers may suspect that many of the disputes within their community are caused by theological arguments, it seems reasonable to consider that those who rationally reflect on faith should also have some influence in judging the proper nature of that faith.

A second objection to the wholly confessional view of theology is that it fails to recognize how rational reflection has in practice contributed to theological understanding and, as a consequence, has influenced belief and faith. Doctrines of the unchangeableness, timelessness, impassibility and simplicity of God are, for good or ill, largely the result of rational reflection on the significance of the ultimacy and perfection of the divine as a totally adequate object of worship. They do not emerge from considering the believer's experience in faith of the personal graciousness, receptivity and responsiveness of the divine. Later we shall consider how these doctrines show the need for careful analyses of the qualities to be properly attributed to the divine. For the moment it is enough to note that whether they distort or illuminate our understanding of God, such understanding is partly the product of our reason's conclusions about how it is appropriate to conceive of the divine being. To hold that theology is wholly dependent on the givenness of faith is, therefore, to ignore how some of its doctrines emerge.

Thirdly, theologians should, I suggest, be as concerned about truth as about the contents of the faith of a given community. To the extent that they are committed to a particular faith, it is presumably because they regard it as containing the truth about God, the world and human being. If, however, their investigations into the contents of faith show that it is making false claims, it would be odd to hold that they must see their role as one of trying to hide the truth and bolster the error. Not only would such a view of their role undermine the general credibility of their work. It would, more importantly, be a denial of the primary object of faith and of their understanding, God. As was suggested in the preface, God is that which is ultimately so. Hence no understanding of the truth can ever be contrary to a valid perception of the divine. If the recognition of truth requires a revision of faith's position, then the theologian must accept the responsibility of urging such a change. Theological work, that is, must be appreciated as being revisionary as well as descriptive in relation to a community of faith.

So far, then, as theology is held to be essentially related to a given faith, it is important to recognize that its proper criteria are, as Schubert Ogden puts it, the twin ones of 'appropriateness' and 'credibility'. The former requires the theologian to produce an interpretation of faith which is appropriate to the meaning of its normative expression – for Ogden this is to be located, in the case of Christianity, in the apostolic witness of faith. The latter requires the theologian to develop an interpretation that is 'credible to human existence as judged by common experience and reason'[8] – in other words, an understanding which may justifiably be regarded as true. An alternative view of theology is to ignore its background in communities of faith (except so far as they provide the social context in which theological thought has developed in the past and have influenced that development) and to see it as concerned with perceiving the ultimate nature of things. According to this view of its character, theology differs from metaphysics in that while they have the same goal, theology is committed to the attempt to grasp ultimate reality in terms of being which is worshipful, perfect and personal or agential (i.e., as one who acts as an agent that influences what happens), whereas metaphysics generally is not so limited. The faith and experience of communities of religious believers provide possible sources of insight for such theological understanding but its sole criterion is that of credibility.

In the end it is probably not very important which of these views of theology is preferred so long as those who engage in it are clear about the one that they are following. Those who feel loyalty to some community of faith and consider that it has basically apprehended the truth are likely to adopt the former position while those who prefer to feel themselves unfettered in their freedom of thought will incline to the latter. I will leave it to readers to judge which one I am attracted to. The reason why, in any case, the choice between them is not very important is that in the long run they effectively amount to the same thing. As the later discussions of hermeneutics, tradition and the development of doctrine will indicate, whatever formal authority may be ascribed in a community to certain canonical or normative expressions of its faith, in practice those expressions are interpreted and expounded in such a way that they affirm what is currently regarded as the truth. Although, therefore, those expressions are supposed to provide the standard for theological understanding, it is the criterion of credibility which is finally the determinative one in deciding the contents of that understanding.

Theological understanding, however, is a matter of rational reflection, whether the rational reflection is upon the faith of a community, or upon the nature of ultimate reality, or is a study which combines the two by using the former as one way of gaining insight into the latter. Having, therefore, considered what may be understood by 'theology', it is time to turn attention to 'reason'. Four questions need to be considered: What status has reason in theological understanding? Is reason reliable? What is meant by reason? And in what ways is reason employed in theological understanding?

Reason

The place of reason in theology needs to be considered because there is a suspicion in some quarters that it is an evil virus which seeks to infiltrate into the healthy body of faith in order to destroy it. Ordinands, on leaving for theological seminary, are sometimes advised by well-meaning, if benighted, believers 'Don't let them spoil you!'. Behind this word of caution lies the fear that once a person's faith is opened to rational scrutiny (as if many seminaries did this anyway), it will be subverted. It must be preserved by being protected from all such threats. Such concern is, of course, a recipe for perpetual childishness. People grow as they face challenges and discover either how to solve their problems or to live with them. Faith grows as it is subjected to doubts and challenges and finds how to respond to them.

While, however, the need to grow in faith may be admitted, timid believers may still urge that the use of reason is basically alien to faith. When people use their reason, they are deciding for themselves. They are thus exercising their autonomy and this, according to the objectors, is the antithesis of the obedience to God which authentic theistic faith requires. The use of reason, that is, is held to express the fallen nature of humanity and, furthermore, that fallen nature is also held to have corrupted reason so that its conclusions are distorted.

If this view were accepted (and it can arguably be dismissed as self-contradictory in that it apparently uses reason to argue against reason), it would follow that human beings could in no way be held responsible for their faith – and for their unbelief. Those who accept the doctrine of divine determinism may be happy with this position but its implications are horrific, both in terms of God and in terms of human being. For 'God' it means that the divine is immediately responsible for everything that occurs: such a God would hardly be a credible object of adoration. For human being it means that what we consider to be our decisions and morally responsible actions are in fact only illusions of such. All is controlled from elsewhere. If, though, the determinist position is rejected, the importance of reason in human being becomes evident. If reason were banned we would have no way, except the very problematic (because uncheckable) ones of private and corporate illumination, to discriminate between true and false, between sense and nonsense, between right and wrong, between valid belief and wanton credulity, between the proper implications of belief and improper ones. Faith of whatever sort would become either something into which we are coerced like puppets or a matter of arbitrary choice. Those who wish to blame God for everything, even our faith and unfaith, may be prepared to entertain such a view but it neither does honour to God (for it implies that the divine is unable or unwilling to allow others to share in the divine creativity) nor allows human being to have any significance. And those who do hold such a view cannot expect others to regard it as true because they have rejected the only way in which such a judgment could be made.

Admittedly human reasoning sometimes succumbs to temptations to try to determine matters beyond its competence. The basic concern of many philosophers, as we shall consider shortly, has been to try to prevent this by determining the bounds of justified understanding. It is also true that later reflection sometimes shows that conclusions which reason reached earlier were mistaken, or distorted by current prejudices. The role of critical reason is therefore to review apparently sound positions to establish if they can still claim to be valid. Nevertheless, in spite of its defects, reason is the only tool which we have for arriving at responsible decisions. It may not be a perfect tool, at least not in the hands of those like ourselves, but we have no other instrument by which we may reach warrantable judgments.

Rather than repudiate reason in theological matters, we should note what John Baillie says about its role. In his *Invitation to Pilgrimage* he cites with approval a remark of L. P. Jacks that 'God is pleased when the publications of the Rationalist Press are really rational, and angry when they are not'. Baillie then comments, 'What is wrong with the world is not that it thinks but that it refuses to think'. Reason is not something that believers should abhor for it is 'the description of how God meant us to think, and hence is the reflected image of His own thought'. Consequently 'faith and reason must not then be enemies but the best of friends'.[9] Whether, therefore, we accept Baillie's theological justification of reason or merely accept that reason is the only way we have for making responsible decisions, it seems that its use in theological thought is unavoidable if that thought is to be deemed a significant form of understanding.

But is reason reliable? This is our second question. Towards the end of the seventeenth century John Locke classically expressed the canon of reason which has become the hallmark of modern thought when he stated that 'he governs his Assent right, and places it as he should, who in any Case of Matter whatsoever, believes or disbelieves, according as Reason directs him'. To act thus is to do one's 'Duty as a rational Creature' by using 'the Light and Faculties' which God has given us for this purpose.[10] Locke's *Essay concerning Human Understanding* was accordingly an attempt to determine the nature and define the proper bounds of rational understanding. A similar quest had earlier been initiated on the Continent with René Descartes' *Discourse on the Method* and his *Meditations on First Philosophy* in which he sought to determine what is to be held to be known, first by establishing what cannot possibly be doubted and then by seeing what necessarily follows from these indubitable propositions. The views of Descartes and Locke, however, had a paradoxical effect. While establishing the canon of reason as the criterion for understanding, they also initiated a still unfinished investigation into the nature and limits of reason. This investigation has resulted in increasing suspicion about its powers and extent.

In the eighteenth century the works of David Hume and Immanuel Kant concluded that we can legitimately claim to know much less than had been previously supposed. Hume's attempts to be rigorously empirical in his thinking[11] made him aware of 'the wretched

condition, weakness, and disorder' of human thought.[12] The search
for understanding seems fated to be unsatisfied for 'when we trace
up the human understanding to its first principles, we find it to lead
us into such sentiments, as seem to turn into ridicule all our past
pains and industry, and to discourage us from future enquiries'.[13]
Kant was provoked by Hume into a critical examination of reason.
The result was the claim that the universal truths of philosophy
describe how we cannot avoid thinking about things. What we think
we discern about the world – and even more about ultimate reality –
is determined by these inbuilt structures of perception and principles of thought. We can never, therefore, justifiably claim to know
what reality is 'in itself'.

The critical review of reason's powers continued in the
nineteenth century. In Britain Sir William Hamilton explored the
constitution of knowledge and claimed that it was 'relative' to and
conditioned by our 'faculties'. We are able to know 'nothing
absolutely and in itself'.[14] Consequently 'we philosophise to escape
ignorance, and the consummation of our philosophy is ignorance;
we start from the one, we repose in the other; they are the goals
from which, and to which, we tend; and the course of knowledge is
but a course between two ignorances . . . The highest reach of
human science is the scientific recognition of human ignorance.'[15]
Although Hamilton's views were trenchantly criticized by John
Stuart Mill, the latter recognized that, when correctly interpreted,
references to 'the relativity of human knowledge' express a notion
that is 'true, fundamental, and full of important consequences for
philosophy'.[16] In Denmark, Søren Kierkegaard emphasized that
'truth' must be defined in terms of 'the existing individual' who lives
by it: 'the truth is precisely the venture which chooses an objective
uncertainty with the passion of the infinite.'[17]

There were, of course, other points of view being expressed.
Hegelian thought, in particular, gave fundamental status to mind.
In spite of its obscurities and difficulties, it enjoyed considerable
prestige. The work of scientists and technologists was also often
held to show what 'reason' could achieve. Nevertheless, the study of
reason in the previous century and, even more, in the present one
has led to something of a crisis of confidence. On the one hand we
are now well aware, through the work of psycho-analysts, of the
way in which we use reason to prove by sophisticated arguments
what we wish to believe. In practical affairs the current state of
international relations, of economic activities, of social structures
and of political affairs make it seem ludicrous to suggest that human

being is to be distinguished by its rationality. Whereas in one way reason has been amazingly effective in producing scientific and technological advances, those advances have also highlighted humanity's gross inability to use reason to control its productions for its own general welfare. As for metaphysical, theological and ethical thought, not only has there been no achieved agreement about fundamental principles but recent work has stressed the relativity of thought to such an extent that the goal of such agreement has appeared to some to be ludicrous while others have eschewed all pretensions at transcendental understanding. As a result what Alfred Ewing said in 1941, in a paper on 'Reason and Intuition', is all the more pertinent today: 'the conclusion strongly suggested to very many minds is that, while we may use reason as a reliable instrument to argue from given ultimate premises to conclusions based on them, these premises are themselves merely instinctive beliefs with no possible rational justification, the mere product of evolution or of feeling'.[18]

What must not be overlooked, though, is that these criticisms are presented as rational criticisms of reason. It is only because they are held to be the result of rational reflection that they are presented as being justified. Consequently, as Ewing points out, the so-called 'revolt against reason' is not logically coherent if it is regarded as a rational revolt against reason as such and not merely as 'a suspicion as to whether people who pretend to be reasonable or think themselves reasonable are so in fact'.[19] We discover whether they are reasonable by subjecting their views to rational examination. The justification of the reliability of reason, therefore, does not depend on some claim that in certain identifiable circumstances its findings will always be true. It depends upon the self-critical role of reason which continuously subjects its methods and its conclusions to critical examination and accordingly is always conscious of their possible unreliability. Reason, in other words, is trustworthy because it seeks to discover its own limitations and its own failings. It is also, as has already been suggested, our only instrument for reaching responsible judgments. Consequently, in spite of the qualifications which have emerged since the time of Locke from the study and use of reason, it is still the case, as Whitehead puts it, that 'ultimately nothing rests on authority; the final court of appeal is intrinsic reasonableness.'[20]

What, though, is reason? It is much easier to use the term than to specify its content. As long ago as 1729 a certain Dr Hildrop complained that current controversies about the reasonableness of belief suffered from 'Misunderstanding, Perplexity, and Obscurity' because people did not define their terms and, in particular, did not clarify what is to be meant by 'that much perverted and abused Word Reason'.[21] It is a complaint which has been heard many times since then. The problem is aggravated because, as G. J. Warnock, points out, there is 'no universally agreed or uniquely correct sense of "reason"'.[22] In the end it is probably preferable not to try to define 'reason' beyond giving a very simple and formal one such as John Baillie's 'Reason may be defined as the ability to recognize truth when it is presented to us'.[23] Instead we should concentrate attention on what is involved in such recognition and thereby, in effect, provide a descriptive answer to the question of reason's nature.

Reason involves two components which we may call 'reasoning' and 'intuition'. The first of these concerns the ways in which we may convincingly move from premises, or evidence, to conclusions. Logic is the study of these reasoning processes and in the forms of syllogistic reasoning, identified first by Aristotle, philosophers have classically attempted to define its valid types. Locke, however, pointed out that our reasoning powers are not so limited in practice: 'God has not been so sparing to Men as to make them barely two-legged Creatures, and left it to *Aristotle* to make them Rational, *i.e.* those few of them that he could get . . . to examine the Grounds of Syllogisms' but 'He has given them a Mind which can reason without being instructed in the Methods of Syllogizing'. Unfortunately Locke himself went on to qualify this insight by suggesting that nevertheless all 'right reasoning may be reduced' to syllogistic forms.[24]. Others have recognized that this is not so and have explored the various ways in which reasoning is properly conducted. John Henry Newman, for example, did this in the discussions of 'informal inference', 'natural inference' and 'the illative sense' in *The Grammar of Assent*. Here he investigates the powers which we have 'of judging and concluding' without any need to resort to a 'technical apparatus of words and propositions'.[25] More recently Stephen Toulmin has investigated 'the nature of the rational process' in *The Uses of Argument*, using jurisprudence as a model for discovering how we argue cases and settle claims.[26] As he puts it in his later *Human Understanding*, people 'demonstrate their rationality, not by ordering their concepts and beliefs in tidy formal structures, but by their preparedness to respond to novel situations with open minds – acknowledging the shortcomings of their former procedures and moving beyond them'.[27]

Although Toulmin's warning against attempts to codify all reasoning into 'tidy formal structures' is a proper reminder of the subtle and complex processes that constitute most acts of reasoning in practice, it is possible to identify some of the forms which are in principle used in such acts. There are, of course, the syllogistic forms from which certain conclusions indubitably follow once suitable premises have been established. For example, if 'All As are B' and no 'C is B', then it must follow that 'no C is A', whatever we substitute for A, B and C. The problem with this kind of reasoning, though, is that it is difficult to establish the necessary premises and, when they have been found, to reach conclusions which were not already obvious when the premises were being determined. It is a rigid form of argumentation which often cannot cope with the elusive complications of practical affairs.

Another form of reasoning which has received a great deal of attention is the inductive form of reasoning which reaches general conclusions on the basis of the consideration of individual instances. For example, having observed that swans on the Thames are white and swans on the Avon are white and swans on the Rhine are white . . . , it might be held reasonable to conclude that 'all swans are white'. This form of reasoning traditionally was regarded as the basis of scientific discovery and, in proportional forms, is the basis of the use of samples to discover general states and statistical probabilities (whether of the quality of a product or the views of a population). The illustration, however, also reminds us that the conclusions of inductive processes are always open to falsification as the range of observation is increased. 'All swans are white' ceased to be a satisfactory conclusion once black swans had been found in Western Australia.

Two other types of reasoning which, in some forms at least, may be classified as inductive but which deserve separate mention are arguments by cumulative reasoning and arguments by converging probability. In the former, various disparate pieces of evidence are brought forward, none of which by itself offers any strong support for the case being advanced. Taken together, however, they may add up to a convincing argument, provided that each piece of evidence carries some weight towards the conclusion. Argument by converging probability substitutes in effect a geometrical model of the point where different bearings meet for the simple arithmetical model of a cumulative argument. Here it is suggested that the different pieces of evidence, while they may be very varied in character and significance, all point to one particular conclusion.

There is, finally for our purposes, reasoning by finding a 'story' which makes sense of the evidence. Very often this form of reasoning is combined with the previous ones. A conclusion is held to be 'proved', more or less convincingly, to the extent that the different pieces of evidence 'add up' to it, point towards it and are made sense of by it, and to the extent that, in a similar way, apparently contrary pieces of evidence can be convincingly explained away as mistaken or as actually irrelevant to the case at issue. It is this complex kind of reasoning that is found in practical matters, whether we think of the formal procedures of a court of law, or the academic defence of the interpretation of the reasons for some historical event, or the day-to-day decisions we make in deciding which house to buy.

Earlier we suggested that reason has two components. We have outlined 'reasoning'; we must now consider 'intuition'. The view that intuition is a respectable part of reason may be surprising to some people, bearing in mind the way in which phrases like 'that's an intuition' are used as polite ways of saying 'that's a guess for which no justification is (currently) available'. In his paper on 'Reason and Intuition', however, Alfred Ewing points out that what he calls 'intuition' is an essential component of all rational reflection and argument. It is that 'immediate insight' which is employed in all reasoning processes. It is by intuition that first we recognize what are valid premises and significant evidences, that secondly we perceive the validity of the connections between the different stages in an argument, and that thirdly we judge the strength of the conclusion reached by an argument. For example, in the case of the syllogism 'All As are B, No C is B, *therefore* no C is A', we do not use reasoning to 'see' that the conclusion follows ineluctably from the premises; we directly recognize it to be so. If we were to try to show by reasoning that the connection is correct, then there would be steps in the argument which we used which would likewise have to be shown to be correct, and so on unceasingly. The only way that we could stop the process and argue the case is by immediately recognizing that some connections are valid. This recognition is a matter of intuition. Similarly if we turn our attention from the reasoning processes which establish the stages of an argument to the premises from which the argument starts, either some premises must be accepted as self-evidently valid (i.e. recognized by intuition to be correct) or the argument can never start. If we have to justify the premises, then it can only be done by means of arguments which start from other premises which are intuitively accepted as valid.

Thirdly, intuition is involved where the premises or evidences do not conclusively demonstrate a conclusion. In such cases – and these are by far the majority of our actual reasoning processes – we have to judge the 'weight' of the case, the 'balance' of probabilities, the 'significance' of the evidence. In the end, therefore, when we have laid out the argument as clearly as we can and compared it with other arguments to different conclusions about the matter at issue, we have to rely on an estimate of the strength of the argument which cannot be justified by other reasoning processes.[28] This estimate must either be intuitive or derived from estimates which are intuitive. All reasoning processes thus use intuition in recognizing the truth of their premises, the significance of their evidence, the validity of their logical steps, and the strength of their conclusions. As Ewing puts it, reason includes '"intuition" or the seeing something to be true, not because it is inferred from other propositions or established by observation, but because of its own intrinsic nature it must be, or at least is, true'.[29]

A common objection to intuitions is that by their very nature they precede argument, are therefore unjustified by argument and, in practice, provide a way in which erroneous ideas are foisted on to others. Ewing recognizes that the notion of intuition is 'liable to gross abuses' because people may persuade themselves that their 'prejudices represent real intuitions' or use 'the appeal to intuition' as a way of avoiding the need for 'a careful examination' of what is to be accepted on this basis.[30] It is also unfortunately evident that with the best will in the world people have sincerely disagreed about intuitions or have come to realize that what was once generally accepted as an intuition of the truth is mistaken.[31] Ewing responds to these difficulties by holding that intuitions both need to be and can be carefully checked to see if they are justified. This 'testing and care' will never completely eliminate the risk of error but it will significantly lessen it.[32] Among the tests that are applicable to an intuition are the extensiveness (ideally the universality) of its recognition, the experience of the persons having it in the kind of material concerned,[33] the clarity of the apprehension of what is intuited, the consequences of holding it, its coherence with other things which we claim to know, and the degree of unprejudiced care with which the situation has been considered.[34] Admittedly the result of these tests will itself be finally a judgment of our intuition but by using them we may hope to avoid being dupes of false intuitions. Here again, therefore, we find that it is the reflective, self-critical activity of reason that justifies its use.

Having outlined the status, reliability and nature of reason, we come to the final question for this chapter. In what ways is reason employed in theological understanding? Seven roles are readily identifiable. Since much of what is to be found in the following chapters exemplifies these roles, it will only be necessary to outline them briefly here.

The roles of reason

The first role is that of drawing out the implications of religious beliefs. In this way reason provides a means of discovering what is involved in entertaining a particular faith. Consider, for example, a fundamental tenet of theistic faith – the belief that there is a God who is the proper object of worship. Rational reflection may consider what follows from regarding some-one (or something) as a proper object of worship. It may thus be argued that such a being must not only be unsurpassable in value but also be everlastingly and necessarily so. As such the divine is not to be judged or evaluated but is that by reference to which all else is to be judged or evaluated. The conclusion that the divine must necessarily be unsurpassable in value (for otherwise we would be forced to judge at any time whether this being is still properly worshipful) may be held to imply further that the divine must be essentially unchanging. The reasoning here is that since the divine perfection is unsurpassable in value, it cannot be conceived to be able (logically able) to improve itself – i.e. to change for the better. Neither, though, can it be conceived as able to change for the worse since it is always essentially unsurpassable. If, though, it cannot change, either for the better or for the worse, the conclusion is drawn that God must be simply unchanging. From this it may be held to follow that the divine is impassible – unaffected by all that happens – for passibility would imply a capacity for change in God. Although, as we shall argue shortly, this reasoning is probably mistaken, it has exerted considerable influence on traditional theistic thought.

A second, and parallel, role of reason does not start from religious beliefs but from rational insights into the ultimate as the object of religious faith and similarly seeks to draw out their implications. An example of this use of reason in theological understanding is provided by the kind of argument which starts from the perfection of God and ends up by maintaining that everything that happens is brought about by God. The initial insight is that God is perfect – by definition God, as Anselm put it, is 'that than which a greater cannot be conceived'. Because of this it is held that all power must be ascribed to God (i.e. God must be held to be 'omnipotent'), for if what we thought was God only had a great deal of power but lacked some bit of power, a greater being than what we thought of as 'God' could be envisaged – namely a being that had the power we ascribed to 'God' and the other bit as well. Only a being that has all power, therefore, adequately fits the rational insight into what is meant by God. But if a being has all power, then everything that occurs must be an expression of that power since there can be no other sources of power to bring things about. If that is so, then our belief that we have a certain autonomy to choose and to effect things is an illusion. What we do is really an activity of God's power and, therefore, God is responsible for all that occurs. Although, as we shall suggest shortly, careful reflection suggests that this argument is fundamentally faulty, it too has influenced traditional theological understanding and illustrates another role of reason in such understanding.

The third role of reason is to investigate the compatibility (and hence to expose incompatibilities) between what is presupposed by faith and what is maintained by theological understanding. Ogden's argument against Sartre, which was outlined earlier, illustrates this by comparing Sartre's existential faith and his atheistic philosophy. A glaring case in Christian thought occurs when believers pray to God, manifestly presupposing that the divine hears, is compassionate and is responsive, while asserting that they believe that God is impassible and so must be untouched and unaffected by all that occurs – including, presumably, by people's prayers. Reason's role in such cases is twofold. First it points out the contradiction between what is assumed by faith and what is implied by the beliefs which supposedly express it. Secondly it seeks to suggest how the problem may be overcome – for example, by arguing that the practice of petitionary prayer is inappropriate to a mature recognition of the perfection of God (a position which many would regard as destroying faith), or by holding that the doctrine of divine impassibility, so far as it is held to imply the non-awareness and non-responsiveness of God, is the product of a gross misunderstanding of what is meant by the perfection of the divine. We will consider this issue further when we discuss the attributes of God in chapter 7.

A fourth role of reason, which has been hinted at in the previous paragraph, is to revise and correct what are regarded as the implications of belief and of rational insights into the ultimate. The arguments which were used earlier to illustrate how reason draws out such implications may now be used to provide examples of the correcting role of rational reflection. In the case of the argument from the essential worshipfulness of God to the divine impassibility, further consideration may be held to show that the inference is unsatisfactory. It errs because it mistakenly regards logical inability to change in one respect (i.e. inability to be other than perfect) as implying inability to change in all respects. The implication is false. The point is most clearly made by looking at a concrete case. For a being to be perfectly and unceasingly loving (whether we think of God or of a counsellor or of a friend as that being) means, on the one hand, that in each situation that being will respond in a way that is the perfect expression of love in that situation. On the other hand, though, such appropriate responsiveness means changing the concrete actuality of the response according to what is truly loving activity in that situation. If, for example, John is disappointed at losing a business deal, Mary's love will involve her in being supportive and understanding; if he is excitedly sharing the joys of an electric train with their son, it will involve her in enjoying that happiness; if he is struggling with an intricate engineering problem or with producing a Chinese meal, it may well involve not offering to help but keeping the children amused elsewhere. Similarly in the case of the divine, for God to be unceasingly loving, when love is an active response, God must act in different (and so changing) ways according to what will best enhance the interests of the beloved.

As for the argument from divine perfection to omnipotence, this too is arguably faulty because it makes the nonsensical assumption that all power can be coherently ascribed to one being. In fact power is a relational concept. One being may have power over another but the notion implies that the latter has some power which the former is able to overcome. A being which had all power, rather than supreme power, would in effect be powerless, because there could be nothing over against that being in relation to which the 'power' could be exercised. Since, therefore, the notion of omnipotence as an absolute monopoly of power is self-contradictory, implications which supposedly follow from it are invalid.

Reason's fifth role in theological understanding is that of trying to reconcile and harmonize theological doctrines which are really or apparently incompatible with each other. It is an exercise of reason which was much in vogue in medieval theology. The numerous commentaries on the *Sentences* of Peter Lombard involved subtle attempts to show the mutual consistency of the various texts which the *Sentences* cite from patristic authorities. Anselm's *Proslogion* provides another good example of this use of reason. By careful distinctions, which are sometimes more subtle than convincing, its author attempts to find ways of affirming both the compassion and the passionlessness of God, and both the justice (in terms of distributive justice which punishes the wicked) and the mercifulness (in terms of forgiveness) of God. Throughout Christian theology this use of reason has probably been most tested by attempts to find ways of expressing the doctrine of the incarnation in a rationally coherent manner which is also theologically orthodox as it affirms of Jesus Christ that he was fully God and fully human and one person. The doctrine of the Trinity has probably been less subjected to such treatment because it seems less amenable to it.

The sixth role of reason is that of rendering theological understanding plausible to current thought by showing that it is compatible with and, even better, incorporates and makes sense of what other forms of understanding indicate to be the character of different aspects of reality. Believers, for instance, sometimes affirm that God is 'the Lord of history'. As Charles Wesley puts it,

> God ruleth on high,
> Almighty to save

while the Psalmist declares that God is 'a safe retreat' and 'refuge' which ensures that 'no disaster shall befall you, no calamity shall come upon your home'.[35] Theologians turn to rational reflection to find ways of making such faith in God credible in view of the savageries and injustices of historical existence — or of showing that such faith is not a proper understanding of the faithfulness and worshipfulness of the divine. Another huge problem arises from the need to reconcile belief in God with what we find to be the character of the natural world. It seems that belief in the reality of God must entail that God is the ground and origin of all things. Accordingly theologians today face the task of overcoming the credibility gap between current biological and cosmological discoveries and beliefs about God's creative activity which often seem determined to speak as if the discoveries of the past century had never occurred. Belief in God will only be plausible when reason finds ways for theology to understand divine creativity which are compatible with and make intentionally significant what other rational investigations discover to be the character of natural processes.

A seventh role of reason in thought about religion is to establish ways of justifying faith's claim to provide the true understanding of the ultimate nature of reality. This activity of reason is sometimes called 'apologetics'. As a preliminary it may be considered necessary to give grounds for holding that it is legitimate to seek verification of faith's contents, both by showing that faith involves claims about what is the case and by overcoming philosophical, theological and religious objections to the propriety of seeking truth-tests for such ultimate matters. Having made clear the legitimacy of the task, theologians then have to find ways of fulfilling it. John Henry Newman's *Grammar of Assent* is one example of many examinations of what is required. He suggests that assent in faith, as in other matters, requires us to apprehend what it is that we are asked to assent to, to have reasons for regarding it as likely to be true, and to be persuaded in our conscience that we must make a decision and that the decision for faith is the correct one. Others suggest that the verification appropriate to religious faith is more clearly understood when it is seen to resemble the truth-tests appropriate to a metaphysical position – namely, that the understanding is internally coherent, consistent with what is found to be the case in reality, universalizable in that it applies to all reality, and fruitful in that it leads to further insights. Perhaps the best model for theological verification is that of a story which fits the available evidence and makes sense of it (at least makes sense of it in a way that is more convincing than is the case with other available stories). What reason here seeks to do, in one way or another, is to show that a faith, as expressed in a theological understanding, provides the most convincing story by which we are able to make sense of reality, both as we find it in our experience and as we consider its ultimate nature. Hence it is reasonable and responsible to hold that faith.

Having, then, looked in the first two chapters at the formal and preliminary matters of the relationships of faith to religion, philosophy, theology and reason, it is now time to consider some particular aspects of the understanding of religious faith – both of faith as it is understood and of faith as itself providing understanding. Among the fundamental ones are those that arise from faith's interpretative aspects as it is, on the one hand, affected by its cultural context and, on the other, involved in discovering significant interpretations of texts, historical events and natural processes. In the following four chapters we shall consider each of these issues in turn.

Chapter 3

Faith, Culture and Doctrine

The faith by which we live and which is expressed in theological understanding is an attempt to make sense of the world in which we find ourselves. As such it is influenced by what we take to be that world and what we consider, in view of our beliefs about the ultimate character of reality, to be the appropriate way of responding to it. The world, however, is not simply 'given' to human beings. While some parts of our reality just are, other parts are the products of human activity and alterable by other human activity. The former parts are what we usually call 'nature'. The fact that masses attract each other according to the laws of gravity, that e = mc^2, and that we need vitamin D$_3$ in order to survive are three of the human abstractions by which we attempt to grasp the horde of 'givens' that constitute the natural side of our world. We cannot change them and it is not profitable to complain about them. That is the way things are. We can, though, use our knowledge of these givens to alter our situation to our advantage. A doctor, for example, can show us how to treat certain medical conditions by providing remedial doses of a form of vitamin D$_3$ that those suffering from the conditions fail to produce for themselves.

There are, however, other parts of the reality in which we find ourselves which are the result of human creativity acting on the basis of the given structures of the natural world. This is what we may call the world of 'culture'. In this usage the term does not apply only or even primarily to the realm of aesthetic activity – to music, literature and art. It applies to all that human beings have produced. In his illuminating study, *Christ and Culture*, H. Richard Niebuhr describes culture as 'the "artificial, secondary environment" which man superimposes on the natural. It comprises language, habits, ideas, beliefs, customs, social organization, inherited artifacts, technical processes and values.'[1] It is the product of human effort and is only assimilated by effort. Infants are not born with an inbuilt culture as they are born with a digestive system; they have to struggle (in most cases) to become civilized by learning the values and procedures of cultured life in society.

In numerous cases the cultural products of human activity are not what was envisaged by those who undertook that activity. Intentions and results have a disturbing habit of not coinciding. The current social, political and economic situation provides good examples of this. Advances in technology were intended to ease human life but they threaten to destroy the fabric of society by depriving large numbers of people of the significance of work. Political movements, both of the right and of the left, which were to produce individual liberty, have often resulted in most individuals being tyrannized by power-structures, either of the masters of free enterprise or of the bureaucrats of planned societies. Schemes for economic advance have led to an even greater divide between rich and poor; the development of industries in the Third World has led to massive destruction of industrial activity in the older industrial nations. Nevertheless, whether as intended or not, by far the larger part of the reality in which we find ourselves is the result of human activity. Although there are still vast tracts of this planet which are basically still as nature has evolved them, the environments of most human beings are largely the result of moulding by human activities. This is not only true of urban areas but also of the countryside. The rural scene is the consequence of centuries of activity. The plants we grow have been developed by human ingenuity. Furthermore, the social scene in which we develop and which heavily influences our understanding of what it is to be 'human', to a great extent is the result of human movements. We cannot, for example, alter the fact that it is women who bear babies, that children need educating, that some old people become unable to look after themselves. Corporately, however, and largely unconsciously, the large groups of people we call societies come to decisions about how people within those societies will be expected to respond to such facts as these. There seems to be no 'natural necessity' which dictates whether society should be matriarchal, patriarchal or sexually egalitarian; whether we should combine in the smallest units of society in monogamous, polyandrous or polygamous ways; whether our social order should be authoritarian or libertarian; whether society should be divided into exclusive castes or classes or into a hierarchy of merit. Furthermore, and perhaps most disturbing of all for those who desire the security of a given reality, even our values are largely cultural products. While some very general principles may be held to transcend cultural determination, their actual implementation in practical goals is very much subject to cultural formation. How justice, freedom and human rights are actually understood, for example, differs interestingly from society to society and even within societies, although general consent may be happily given to them as values that are formally to be pursued. At less refined levels, what one culture hears as fine music is to another a cacophony; what one community sees as praiseworthy devotion to disinterested intellectual enquiry is to another a waste of resources which contributes nothing to the gross national product.

Granted, then, the world of culture which so largely determines the context of human being, four questions arise. How does faith relate itself to culture? How does culture influence the way in which believers understand their faith? How does faith express itself in ways appropriate to its cultural context? And how are valid developments in theological understanding to be identified? What is involved in these questions will become clearer as we discuss each of these problems in turn. It must be recognized, furthermore, that these discussions are not purely theoretical and speculative. Living faith involves concrete decisions about and responses to the world of culture. Only so does it become authentic and real.

The relation of faith and culture

First, then, how does faith relate to culture? Within the history of Christianity various answers have been presented to the question of the authentic relationship of the believer to the world of contemporary culture. One of the responses to be found in traditional Catholicism, for example, has been that the demands of Jesus are too demanding to be a practical option for ordinary people who have to take part in the life, work and social activities of the world. Thus, a bank manager would soon be in trouble if he always obeyed the command, 'Give when you are asked to give; and do not turn your back on a man who wants to borrow.'[2] There are too many evilly-disposed people in the world for such an ethic to be appropriate. Accordingly this particular 'Catholic' response suggests that most Christians should follow a demanding but yet generally practisable ethic derived from the Old Testament and Stoicism while a few, seeing themselves as called to a higher form of life, should separate themselves from the world and seek to live out the life of the gospel teaching in religious institutions.

Others, however, have refused to accept this solution. They argue that every Christian must follow radically the teaching of Jesus, whatever the individual and social consequences. Their response is the sectarian attitude to the world. Those who accept it refuse to take part in the institutions of society that use force or make judgments. Some even refuse to join any group to which those that they consider unbelievers may belong. Most Christians however have rejected this position. They consider that their faith calls them, among other things, to active participation in the world's politics, industry and legal systems. It is an illegitimate avoidance of the responsibility of Christian citizenship to be merely passive recipients of the benefits (and the disadvantages) of social living.

Two other responses, therefore, have tried to work out how Christians are both to accept the full force of the gospel and to live actively in the world. Luther's solution, when he had realized that the monastic response did not produce the perfect life, was to recognize that no one could fulfil all the demands of righteousness and so to trust in the justifying grace of God. Christians were thus to engage in the world's affairs as those who sought to fulfil the demands of God while acknowledging their failure to do so and relying on divine forgiveness. The other solution, typical of more recent periods, stresses the possibility of improvement in human life rather than its deficiences. It looks for the achievement of a more Christian society and presents the gospel as an inspiring vision of what may – and eventually will – come to be. Some who currently adopt one or other of these responses find Jesus to be a disturbing, revolutionary leader who draws Christians into the ambiguities of the struggles for justice and freedom in the world. It is, however, a position which is wider and older than its present expressions in the so-called 'liberation theologies'.

If, though, we step back from the confused scene of history and consider schematically how faith may in principle be related to culture, we find that there are five plausible ways. Each of them is discussed by H. Richard Niebuhr in *Christ and Culture*. He points out that while no Christian community may ever have adopted any of these options in an exclusive manner, one or other of them has at different times and places exercised a dominant influence on how Christian faith is understood and exercised.

The first option sees Christian faith and culture as fundamentally opposed to each other. Would-be believers are to be confronted by the demand to decide for Christ or for the world. They cannot belong to both for no one can authentically serve two masters. To hold to one is to renounce the other. Converts are to avoid wordly contamination by leaving the world. Christian existence is ideally perceived in terms of the membership of holiness groups which set themselves apart to live in Christ and under Christ. The only authentic authority is Christ: believers have no duty to the cultural world and its ways. From the standpoint of faith Christians see their true goal in other-wordly terms and may even look eagerly for the destruction of the current world-order. Some so stress the all-sufficiency and sole validity of the grace of God that they condemn all human effort to change the world as intrinsically sinful. Christian obedience is thus held to demand rejection of culture's values and institutions.

A second view of Christianity adopts almost the opposite approach. It affirms a fundamental agreement between Christian faith and culture. Jesus is here perceived as showing in his life and thought what human being can achieve. The proper goals of the development of culture find exemplification in him. He thus provides the image which all are to emulate. They do this, however, not by renouncing culture but by affirming all that is good in their cultural heritage and by seeking to foster it so that it comes to characterize all forms of human being. Jesus himself is seen as part of that cultural heritage and the memory of him, as the image of the Christ of faith, is the inspiration for future advances in it. Christ and culture are harmonized because the former is seen as the underlying spirit which has led to the genuine achievements of the latter from the beginning of civilization.

The third option emphasizes the discontinuity between Christ and culture. While Christ is presented as the culmination of humanity's proper aspirations, he is not seen (in contrast to the previous position) as a development which emerges from the cultural process. Rather he is one who breaks into history to reveal to human beings their true goals and the way to attain them. This is insight which humanity could never discover for itself: it had to be presented to it from 'beyond' or 'above'. The cultural quest for values, therefore, is not to be condemned but neither is it to be wholly approved until it recognizes that its proper end lies beyond what human beings by themselves could ever attain. The spirit of God revealed in Christ is the 'logos' of creativity which has always been stirring human existence but in Christ a radical transformation of the human situation has occurred by a divine intervention which highlights the evils present in culture and provides a divine remedy to them. Christian faith thus affirms a divinely produced synthesis of the human and divine both in the person of Jesus as the Christ and in the Christian understanding of the true course of cultural development.

A fourth option finds itself unable either to affirm such a synthesis or to deny that each side to it has some intrinsic validity. It consequently understands the relationship between faith and culture in dualistic or paradoxical terms. Believers have the uneasy task of seeking to obey two proper authorities whose demands may conflict. On the one hand, Christians must recognize that they are human beings and are under an obligation to be supportive members of the human community, accepting the impositions and using the opportunities provided by social life. On the other hand, and at the same time, they are as Christians to be totally loyal to Christ and utterly committed to doing his will. For such an understanding the life of faith, as Richard Niebuhr puts it, is lived 'precariously and sinfully' in the hope of a final justification beyond history but appreciating that in this life there is unescapable 'polarity and tension' between Christ and culture.[3]

Finally there is the view which sees the Christian as seeking the transformation of culture. While it recognizes that there is enormous opposition between the mind of Christ and the values and practices of society as we now find them, it also appreciates that culture, as a human product, is open to reformation. It accordingly holds that the Christian faith does not seek the destruction of culture's forms but their gradual conversion into harmony with the mind of Christ. This transformation happens in history. Salvation is not a transworldly event but the actualization of the kingdom of God on earth. Human culture, as we inherit it, is distorted by evil but it is corrigible and, according to the Christian hope, eventually will be perfected.

None of these views of the relationship between faith and culture, as we have mentioned, has ever been realized in a pure form. None of them, furthermore, can warrantably be presented as *the* Christian solution for every time and place. This is not just because a proper reticence stops us presuming to know the mind of God with such clarity and totality, even granted that God has a preferred solution to the problem. Nor is it just because we are largely the products of our culture and, therefore, are very limited in our capacity to assess its significance and to make judgments about what may be constructed out of it in the future. Above all we have to see that faith's judgment on culture must be relative because human perceptions of the nature of faith and the character of the culture which provides its context vary considerably from time to time. The correct relationship for one situation may be wrong for another. The nature of that correct relationship may also involve a more or less coherent combination of two or more of the five stances which we have identified. What believers cannot do, however, is to avoid making a decision. As beings who exist in culture, who are moulded by culture and who themselves form culture, they must decide responsibly how to react to it – and then live out that decision of faith while appreciating that it can only be provisional and relative. Without such a decision and its practice, their faith will remain as a series of theoretical assents without substance or significance.

The relationship between faith and culture, however, is not confined to the issue of faith's appraisal of its proper attitude towards culture. In many ways faith, at least as it is apprehended and theologically expressed, is to be seen to be moulded by culture. We must, therefore, now turn to our second question, How does culture influence the way in which believers understand their faith?

The influence of culture on faith

As a basis for answering this question, it is important to appreciate how our culture influences what we perceive and in what ways we understand it. We do not first experience something and then find concepts by which to describe it and make sense of it. What we experience, so far as it is something which we are aware of experiencing, is the product of basically three factors. There are our inbuilt structures of reception and assimilation which belong to us simply as human beings; there is the impact which the 'something' makes upon our organs of awareness (whether physical or mental or both); and there are the ways of 'sorting out' and 'making sense of' which we happen to possess. Consider, for instance, my current awareness of the slate roof of a building opposite. Such an experience is not just the result of the way in which certain physical processes involving light-waves interact with certain physical organs in my eyes, and the results of those interactions are transmitted to and sorted into orderly patterns by my brain. The experience is only possible because I also have learnt the concepts of 'roof' and of 'slate' and of 'building'. If any of those concepts were not available to me, my awareness of what I was experiencing would be different. Such cultural conditioning, though, is not limited to the learning of concepts. It also applies to their applications and the judgments which we make on the basis of them and which form part of what we take as our 'experience'. Compare, for example, my response to the question 'What's in that field?' with that of Tom who is a dairy farmer. I answer 'Cows': he says 'There are a group of young Holsteins who look as if they need feeding up, an old Jersey and an Angus bull.' What Tom 'sees', because of his interests and training, is interestingly different from what I 'see' although we are standing side by side.

It is, however, not just at the level of immediate awareness that we are conditioned by the concepts available to us. Such influence becomes even more pronounced when we consider how we reach what we regard as 'understanding'. How we may understand depends upon the possible ways of understanding with which we are acquainted. Significant advances in understanding occur much more because we find new ways of making sense of things of which we were, in some respects, already aware than because new objects have come into view. Indeed, the more profound advances in scientific thought usually seem to occur because those involved conceive of something as likely to be the case and then look to see if their expectations are confirmed or falsified, rather than because they have unexpectedly stumbled across something unanticipated. What we 'stumble across' is far more likely either to be ignored or to be interpreted in terms of other things of which we are already aware than, by itself, to produce new developments in thought.

When considering the influence of culture on the understanding of faith, therefore, it is important to appreciate that, to a great degree at least, our concepts and our structures of understanding are provided by our culture and thus are, to some extent, temporally and geographically relative. There may be some structures which are necessary to all human thought as such. Kant thought so and attempted to identify them as the *a priori* 'categories of understanding'. Whether or not this Kantian position is justified (and in any case while its categories are fundamental, they are few and formal), it still remains the case that how we observe things and what sense we make of them predominantly depends upon what we have learnt from our culture.

At a basic level this occurs with the language(s) which we learn to use. How we identify things and discriminate them from other things depends upon the terms we have at our disposal – compare, for example, my restriction to 'cows' and Tom's knowledge of different kinds of cow in the earlier illustration. Similarly, if I walk though a field, I see 'grass'; a botanist walks through it and observes an enormous range of distinct plants, some of which he may classify as different 'grasses'. Until the term 'agnostic' was coined in the second half of the nineteenth century, there was no straightforward way of distinguishing in the English language between those who positively assert that there is no divine being and those who are unsure whether there is or is not a deity. Accordingly in earlier usage 'atheist' referred to both positions and as a result the difference between them was obscured and tended to be over-looked.

The influence of language upon thought is not restricted to the range of conceptual distinctions which it makes available. How we understand is also subtly affected by the grammatical structure of the language in which we seek to apprehend and express our thought. To take a simple but far-reaching example, English (like most other languages) has a basic noun and verb structure. Nouns refer to objects; verbs describe what those objects do or have done to them. For most purposes such a structure of language is unproblematic. It does, however, carry with it the implication that an object is a self-identical entity which does not change, since the same label is applicable to it on different invasions. The Jackie I meet today is the same person as I met yesterday and was called Jackie. The desk I write on today is the same desk as I wrote on yesterday. For most practical purposes this is quite satisfactory and any major deviation from it would be liable to produce a non-communicative, absurd world where there was no way of identifying anything, and so of thinking at all, because there was no continuity. On the other hand, in certain ways neither the person whom I call Jackie nor the desk is the same as yesterday. Experiences as well as physiological changes have happened to Jackie in the interim that have necessarily changed who she is to some extent. The desk, similarly, is not a static object but is composed of an enormous number of 'particles' or 'forces' which are continuously interacting between themselves and with other 'particles' and 'forces' impinging upon them. The difficulty with the noun-verb structure of language is that it obscures the fundament-ally processive nature of reality and makes it hard to grasp intellectually.

It is not only by means of language that culture influences our understanding. Among other factors, the experiences which it gives rise to, the values which it entertains, the relationships which it finds significant and the artefacts which it produces all affect the ways in which we think. Talk of humanity sharing 'one world' is going to be apprehended differently today when we can see on television what happened a little while ago in Korea or Ethiopia, when we can get relief to stricken areas in a matter of hours, when we are aware of how actions by one group of people may have devastating effects for all, than it was in the sixteenth century when people in England were ignorant of large parts of the world and had no way of significantly influencing events in them. In the case of values, how we understand the proper goals of human being will be directed, to some extent, by whether we have been educated in a culture that stresses individualism or corporateness, freedom or obedience, satisfaction or duty, creativity or conformity, personal rights or communal good. The notion of 'evolution' is one which illustrates how our grasp of relationships in one area of understanding may be taken up and influence thought in others. What began as a biological concept to make sense of how the present structures of living beings have come about is now applied to such disparate structures as the development of societies and the production of the latest model of a car. Much of our thought and expression, furthermore, involves metaphors taken from the productions of our culture. We talk of 'fine-tuning' in economic matters, 'pump-priming' in giving aid, and 're-charging the batteries' in holidaying. These are metaphors taken from engineering and would be impossible in cultures where the respective pieces of engineering had not been invented. Sometimes the use of metaphors or models or analogies from artefacts in the culture is not simply an attractive way of expressing our understanding. It provides a means of insight into what is unfamiliar or puzzling. For example, the model of rotting vegetation out of sight at the bottom of a well but producing gases which erupt on the surface has proved for some psycho-analytic theories a useful model for investigating what is happening when a person's conscious life is unexpectedly disturbed.

Faith as we perceive it and theological understanding are, of course, not exempt from these conditioning factors. Both the ways in which they are expressed and the thought which they contain are culturally influenced. Consider, for example, the ways in which Christian theologians have attempted to express the special character of the person of Jesus. The language – and hence the ideas – which were employed in the formative period of the church were taken from Jewish and Greek sources. Jesus was described as the Messiah or Christ, the Son of David, the Son of God, the High Priest, the Word ('logos') of God, the Lord, and so on. Even though the meanings of these terms may have suffered modification in their application to the case of Jesus, their original contents could not be totally excluded if they were to preserve their significance. As a result the manner in which Jesus came to be understood in classical Christian orthodoxy was to a considerable extent controlled by the concepts available in the Jewish and Greek cultures where the Christian church initially developed. As John Hick has suggested, it is interesting to reflect on what might have happened if initially the dominant expansion of Christianity had been eastwards. If it had developed in the setting of Indian cultures, it is likely that the theological discussions and credal definitions would have been in terms of modifications of the Hindu notion of 'Avatara' (which signifies the 'descent' of the deity to the world in a physical form in order to ward off some peril) or of the Mahayana Buddhist doctrine of a 'Bodhisattva' (which refers to one who has come to a perfect relationship with the ultimate but who continues to live a human life in compassion for others in order to show them the way to perfection).[4] Such development would not have basically occurred because the Eastern concepts were better than those used in the West. It would have occurred because these were the concepts that were available to people in those areas as they thought about Jesus.

It is important to appreciate, though, that the influence of culture in this respect is not just on the expression of faith and of theological understanding. The concepts available affect what is grasped as being the content of what is expressed. At times we may have a sense that our words do not adequately express what we want to say but we cannot find any more adequate modes of expression. In such a case we cannot specify even for ourselves how our words fail us – for the problem is with words. We cannot compare what we want to say with what we do say because we have not got the words to say what we want. On the other hand, once we start to think about things, we are inescapably moulded by the ideas contained in the language available to us, even though we may try to indicate that we are using some terms in a modified manner. References to the 'resurrection' of Jesus provide an example of what may happen. It is probable that what originally took place in the experience of the earliest Christians was a unique occurrence for which they had no directly appropriate terminology. They therefore took over the notion of resurrection, which was generally then used to refer to apocalyptic expectations concerning the destiny of the dead at the end of this age, and used it as best they could to signify the Easter experience. In some ways, therefore, 'resurrection' became a metaphor for the notion of transformation into a new mode of life. The adoption of the language of 'resurrection' left two problems.

One was that the implications of the notions of 'resurrection' began to influence how Christians understood what had originally occurred. In other words, having used 'resurrection' terminology to describe the event, 'resurrection' ideas influenced what was later taken to have been that event. Secondly, we have now no convincing way of comparing the satisfactoriness of the 'resurrection' language with the original event because it is now difficult to get behind the Christian appropriation of that language to perceive what it originally meant and, even more importantly, because we cannot get 'behind' the language, as it were, to discern what event it was seeking to express – if, that is, it was an historical event and, even more, an historical event unlike any other. Current debates about these matters, therefore, should always be tentative because we cannot be sure how far the original language adopted by the church distorted what it was used to apprehend and to convey.

The values of a culture are another potent influence upon faith and theology. Granted that the Christian faith proclaims a God whose love is displayed in the crucifixion of Jesus and whose relationship to human beings is one of such caring awareness that even the fall of a sparrow is noticed,[5] it is surprising to find acknowledged Christian thinkers affirming that God is 'not compassionate' because the divine does 'not experience the feeling' and is 'affected by no sympathy for wretchedness' (Anselm),[6] that 'it is impossible for God to be in any way changeable' and accordingly that 'in God there is no real relation to creatures' (Aquinas),[7] and that God 'is not entangled in our predicament' but enjoys 'unruffled beatitude' (E. L. Mascall).[8] What has happened is that Christian understanding has, in these respects, been captivated by the values enshrined in and expounded by classical culture. Instead of allowing the conviction that God is normatively revealed in Jesus to dominate its thought, the church was overwhelmed by the combined forces of the culture out of which it had emerged and the culture whose members it was seeking to convert. As a result it produced a composite understanding of God constructed from Roman, Hebrew and Greek sources. As Whitehead puts it, it largely forgot 'the brief Galilean vision' which points to 'the tender elements in the world, which slowly and in quietness operate by love' and found images of God in 'the ruling Caesar, . . . the ruthless moralist', and 'the unmoved mover' of 'an ultimate philosophical principle'.[9] The problem for theologians today is to be sensitive enough to current value-preferences to avoid, as much as possible, being similarly trapped by contemporary culture.

How does faith express itself?

Another aspect of the relationship between faith and culture emerges, however, when we consider our third question, How does faith express itself in ways appropriate to its cultural context? From what has been said in answer to the previous question, it might be concluded that faith is an unwilling victim of cultural influences and that it should seek to free itself from such moulding. While that conclusion might be defended on the grounds that it calls for a properly self-critical attitude in theological understanding, what it asks for is neither possible nor desirable. It is not possible because, as we have indicated, believers and theologians must use their culturally-given ideas when they try to understand. They have no other resources. It is undesirable because if faith and theology are to be taken seriously, they must be seen to make sense of the world in which people currently find themselves and in terms which people currently regard as significant.

The works of Edwin Hatch, Adolf Harnack and Rudolf Bultmann indicate what this may mean in terms of theological understanding. Hatch begins the Hibbert Lectures for 1888, *The Influence of Greek Ideas and Usages upon the Christian Church*, by pointing to the 'difference of both form and content between the Sermon on the Mount and the Nicene Creed'. The former offers a law of conduct, assumes beliefs, is predominantly ethical, and 'belongs to a world of Syrian peasants'. The latter is partly historical and partly dogmatic, uses metaphysical terms, has no ethical content, and belongs 'to a world of Greek philosophers'. Why did this change in the presentation of Christianity come about? Hatch's reply is that 'the change in the centre of gravity from conduct to belief is coincident with the transference of Christianity from a Semitic to a Greek soil'. In the lectures, therefore, he traces how Greek thought and practices influenced the formation of Christianity in its first centuries. What is interesting for our purposes, though, is Hatch's claim that 'the religion of a given race at a given time is relative to the whole mental attitude of that time'. Religious phenomena are part of 'the whole complex life of the time, and they cannot be understood except in relation to that life'.[10] Furthermore, at the end of the lectures, he suggests that one argument for the divinity (and, we may add, an explanation of the durability) of Christianity may be that it has proved itself able to grow in the soils of different human societies 'by assimilating to itself whatever elements it found there'. Such growth is 'integral and essential' to the life of

Christianity for only so does it present a message that is appropriate to each situation where it finds itself.[11] A similar conclusion is reached by Harnack. In *The Expansion of Christianity* he points out that the study of Christian history shows it to have developed by using contemporary ideas for its self-expression and self-under-standing. Its syncretism, though, is that appropriate to 'a universal religion' for 'every force, every relationship in its environment, was mastered by it and made to serve its own ends'.[12] Elsewhere Harnack puts it that Christianity is to be understood as a spirit which has 'permanent validity' but which has to adopt appropriately different forms in actualizing itself in different cultural settings.[13] In more recent times, Bultmann's concern about the presentation of the gospel, which we shall consider further in the next chapter, has reflected a similar insight. While he criticizes the older liberal theologians like Harnack for treating Christianity as essentially a matter of 'eternal, timeless truths' (and arguably does less than full justice to Harnack's view that it is a 'spirit' which is permanent), his own aim is to find a way of expressing the gospel which brings home to contemporary people its challenge and offer. The core of the problem is that the New Testament presents the gospel in what Bultmann describes as a 'mythological conceptuality' basically derived from Jewish apocalypticism and Gnostic redemption myths.[14] This conceptuality may have been a suitable vehicle for communicating it in the first century but today it produces serious misunderstanding both of what the gospel is about and of the genuine affront which it presents to human thought. In order to preach the gospel adequately its New Testament expressions must be 'demythologized' – interpreted, that is, in ways which make the Christian proclamation of God's saving act clear to contemporary people. Bultmann's own solution to the problem of how to do this is by employing categories developed in Heidegger's existentialist philosophy. This solution may be criticized in various ways. What is less open to dispute is the validity of the problem. In each age the gospel has to be presented in a form that is appropriate to its cultural setting. Only so will it be communicated.

Thus far we have considered the question of the expression of faith as if it were primarily a matter of discerning its meaning as something which fundamentally remains the same and then having to find suitable ways of expressing it in current ways of thought. Part of understanding, however, is application: we grasp something as we perceive how it can be used.[15] This insight implies that an adequate understanding of a faith must not only take into account its previous expressions but also identify its contribution to meeting current needs.

Paul Tillich adopts such an approach in his *Systematic Theology*. He argues that theology must seek to unite 'message and situation' by means of what he calls 'the method of correlation'. What this means is that the theologian 'tries to correlate the questions implied in the situation with the answers implied in the message' by means of a process of reciprocal adaptation. What Tillich wants to avoid, on the one hand, is a theology which expounds its perception of the gospel's offer of salvation without taking into account how people understand their basic needs and, on the other hand, a theology which allows people's understanding of their needs to determine what the gospel must be. Taken to extremes the first view is liable to invent unreal needs in people (just as, for example, a quack doctor may invent bogus ailments to persuade us to buy a remedy from them) while the latter is liable to invent a gospel to offer them an illusion of salvation. Accepting that the gospel is the divine response to the basic problems of the human situation, Tillich therefore aims to make 'questions and answers, situation and message, human existence and divine manifestation' interpret each other.[16] What this means is that the theologian must investigate both previous presentations of the faith and current analyses of the human predicament. In order to satisfy the latter requirement, the theologian (and the preacher) needs to be sensitive to the illumination which art, literature, music and drama throw on the current problems of life, as well as to the ways in which psycho-analysis and popular movements reveal people's anxieties.

Although the demand that the gospel be expressed in practically relevant ways is not new – compare the Christian Socialists in mid-nineteenth century Britain and the later Social Gospel movement in the United States – it is an emphasis which has received much attention in recent decades. The radical theologies of the 1960s, whether or not they adopted the slogan 'The Death of God' (a slogan which had a wide range of distinct interpretations), were generally united by their concern to address their message to 'modern humanity' – a partly mythical entity which seems to have been largely composed in reality of well-educated, economically comfortable, rather traditionless members of Western society, especially in California and the north-eastern quarter of the USA. What was significant about these theologies was their serious interest in contemporary human experience and their desire to interpret faith so that it spoke to that situation. The danger in their approach was that they were liable to accept the culture of 'modern humanity' too uncritically and, as a result, to try to make the gospel conform to it. Paul van Buren, for example, maintained that since people 'no longer believe in a transcendent realm where their longings will be fulfilled', it is necessary to present to them a 'secular', non-supernatural (and hence non-theistic) interpretation of the Christian faith.[17] Others may warrantably retort that to do this would be to present an essentially non-Christian faith and that one function of the Christian gospel today is to expose the inadequacy of such a secular world-view. Either way, though, the interpretation of the faith is related to how people understand their reality and hence is shaped by, even if its content is not simply provided by, contemporary culture.

The radical theologies had a basically intellectual application to the contemporary world. They were largely about theoretical understanding. The liberation theologies which superseded them at the front of theological fashion regard the practical applications and material expressions of faith as of fundamental importance. It is argued that the crucial test for theological understanding is not to be found in theoretical criteria but in the actions which the understanding gives rise to. According to José Míguez Bonino, a 'theological interpretation' must be judged by the 'kind of praxis it supports, reflects, or legitimizes'.[18] The Johannine phrase about '*doing* the truth' is used to support the view that there is no valid distinction between 'a theoretical knowledge of truth and a practical application of it. Correct knowledge is . . . disclosed in the doing.' There is no such thing as 'neutral knowledge' for 'we think always out of a definite context of relations and action'.[19] The 'theologians' who are to be listened to, according to such an analysis, are those who speak from the context of involvement in Christian action in the struggle to bring social, economic, political, racial and sexual liberation to those who are oppressed.

Although some who seek to develop liberation theologies are not wholly convinced by the view of truth produced by Marxist sociology of knowledge, they do generally accept that cultural background – and, in terms of this theology, particularly the social situation – prejudices thought and that the most important aspect of faith is its implementation in social action. Such implementation, however, demands an analysis of the structures of oppression in order to be able to perceive what the gospel of liberation must involve. At the end of *The Crucified God*, Jürgen Moltmann speaks of the presence of God as an explosive and liberating spirit which seeks to set all things free and to fill them with meaning. 'Brotherhood with Christ' thus means 'suffering and active participation'[20] in liberating activity which has five dimensions – economic, political, cultural, industrial and ontological as it seeks to end economic need, political oppression, cultural alienation, the ecological crisis, and the feeling of the senselessness of life.[21] Others have concentrated attention on particular issues. Gustavo Gutierrez, for example, is concerned in *A Theology of Liberation* to summon the church to realize that following Christ means being 'on the side of the oppressed classes and dominated peoples' in Latin America in the active struggle to liberate them from all dehumanizing forces.[22] For James Cone there is 'a desperate need for a *black theology*, a theology whose sole purpose is to apply the freeing power of the gospel to black people under white oppression'.[23] The liberating work of Christ is thus specifically applied to the conditions of black people, and black protest movements are interpreted as manifestations of the current activity of God.[24] In *God of the Oppressed* he puts it that Christ is '*truly* black' because he '*really* enters into our world where the poor, the despised, and the black are, disclosing that he is with them, enduring their humiliation and pain and transforming oppressed slaves into liberated servants'.[25] Other theologians direct the message of liberation to the case of the half of humanity that suffers oppression in most societies and races. They properly challenge ridiculous prejudices which see the divine as male and find permanent theological significance in Jesus' having been a man and which, consciously or not, are used to justify male domination. As Rosemary Radford Ruether urges in *To Change the World*, the role of Jesus as 'liberator does not reside in his maleness, but, on the contrary, in the fact that he has renounced this system of domination and seeks to embody in his person the new humanity of service and mutual empowerment'.[26]

Investigations into the ways that Jewish and Greek thought conditioned the formative period of Christian understanding and consideration of current attempts to perceive the significance of that understanding for contemporary life provide two examples of the ways in which faith expresses itself in a manner appropriate to its cultural context. The fact that faith is so moulded is not surprising. If faith is to be a significant grasp of the ultimate nature of reality by which believers can make sense of and orientate their lives, it must clearly apply to the reality in which they find themselves. Otherwise it will offer only pointless speculations about theoretical postulates. On the other hand, the effects of culture on the understanding and practice of faith reminds us that all perceptions of faith are culturally relative to some extent. Furthermore, because our cultural presuppositions provide the basis of our judgments, it is difficult to become aware of how they direct our understanding. Even if it is not impossible, it is at least difficult to become conscious of the possible relativity of the structures by which we think. This recognition of the inescapable relativity of thought brings us to the final question for this chapter. How are valid developments in theological understanding to be identified?

The question of valid developments

The claim that Christian doctrine has developed and continues to develop is an uncomfortable one for many believers. Desiring to find in their faith security, they want it to remain the same, a divinely fixed point. Consequently they are happiest when they are told that their belief is that which was 'once and for all time delivered to the saints of old'. They are happy with the name 'The Apostles' Creed' for the summary of their faith: it asserts a link with the first disciples. Essentially Peter's confession of faith, the rock upon which the church is founded, is their faith. It is all very reassuring. It is also quite illusory and, so far as authentic faith is concerned, betrays a fundamental refusal to have relationships with the living God. So far as Christian theological understanding is to express Christian faith, we need to appreciate what Harnack said in *What is Christianity?*: 'it is not a question of a "doctrine" being handed down by uniform repetition or arbitrarily distorted; it is a question of a *life*, again and again kindled afresh, and now burning with a flame of its own.'[27]

In the fifth century Vincent of Lérins laid down a threefold test for orthodox Christian faith. True doctrine is what has been believed everywhere, always, and by all ('quod ubique, quod semper, quod ab omnibus creditum est'). Unfortunately any attempt to apply this test would either beg the question (by its selection of which believing communities were to be considered) or would have to conclude that Christian doctrine has possibly never existed – for the New Testament records of the church show that believers from the earliest days were not wholly agreed. Historical investigations, furthermore, have shown how Christianity, like other religions, is a 'cumulative tradition' which develops and alters its perception of itself. Development occurs, in doctrine and in practice. The crucial question is how we are to distinguish valid changes from distorting deviations.

In his *Essay on the Development of Christian Doctrine* John Henry Newman suggested that there are seven 'notes' or characteristics which distinguish a genuine advance from a perversion. Granting that they are 'of varying cogency, independence and applicability', he sees these 'notes' as enabling us 'to discriminate healthy developments of an idea from its state of corruption and decay'.[28] Genuine developments are marked by (1) preservation of type – in spite of its enlargements and applications, the doctrine remains at heart the same, (2) continuity of principles, (3) power of assimilation – the ability to incorporate external materials into itself, (4) logical sequence – the later developments follow in a reasonable sequence from the original teaching, (5) anticipation of the future – earlier forms contain clear indications of the later developments, (6) conservative action upon the past – not destroying what has gone before but tending to preserve its achievements, and (7) 'chronic vigour' – showing the power to assimilate, to revive after decline and to persist as a living force. These 'notes' were an advance on earlier views of doctrinal developments which saw them either as a matter of stating explicitly what had always been held in the tradition of the church or as cases of logical inferences from the premises of already acknowledged doctrines. They also allowed Newman to become a Roman Catholic by showing, in his judgment, that the contemporary Roman Catholic church was a genuine development of the one church of the fathers.

In the judgment of many others, however, these 'notes' failed to solve the problem of identifying authentic developments in Christian doctrine. They are very general and various mutually conflicting understandings of Christianity could be held to satisfy them. Newman's own use of them shows how their application in practice is liable to beg the question. What to him are desirable developments seem to others to be rank corruptions of the genuine, original form of Christianity. Since Newman's time various other criteria for identifying valid developments have been put forward. Some have suggested that appeal needs to be made to the 'consensus' among believers. This is unsatisfactory in principle because the need for criteria of authentic development arises when no consensus is available and in practice because it would always be likely to be prejudiced in favour of the religious desire for security and opposed to the disturbing freedom of God. Another suggestion is that the touchstone of true doctrine is to be found in the 'essence' of

Christianity. Unfortunately, even if the idea of identifying such an 'essence' is acceptable (and many dispute its validity), this criterion fails because it is disagreement about the character of that 'essence' which leads to the search for such a criterion. Others have maintained that it is wrong for us to try to determine what is true by formulating and applying what seem to us to be reasonable criteria. Faith is God-given and the genuine believer must simply be responsive to the self-authenticating 'Word of God'. Here, too, the criterion fails in practice for, notoriously, sincere believers sometimes fundamentally disagree about what the 'Word of God' is obviously declaring. To by-standers their disputes are likely to indicate that it is not easy to distinguish between subjective arbitrariness and divine 'Word' when appeal is made to inner conviction. Finally there are the criteria which Maurice Wiles suggests as the proper aims for theology in his illuminating *The Remaking of Christian Doctrine*. These are 'coherence' and 'economy'. The former is a matter of checking whether different doctrinal affirmations are mutually consistent. The latter requires the theologian to distinguish between what the evidence of faith requires us to hold and what is the result of imaginative expansiveness.[29] While, however, these principles should undoubtedly control the development of theological understanding, their actual application seems to leave open too wide a range of possibilities for them alone to be satisfactory criteria of true development.

In the end the solution to the problem of authentic development may be seen to emerge from a consideration of why theological understanding does develop. Where they are not the product of a theologian's unbridled imaginings, changes occur in order to overcome problems with the present form of understanding. Seven forms of these problems are readily identifiable. Five of them are theologically valid but two of them are suspect. First, doctrines may be altered to make them mutually consistent. No faith can be acceptable which maintains incompatible beliefs. Secondly, a doctrine may be modified to make it agree with reality as we find it. No belief is going to be plausible which contradicts our unquestionable experience. Thirdly, the way in which a belief is expressed may be changed in order to communicate its content more clearly and accurately. Fourthly, a doctrine may require amendment to show that it is an appropriate way of understanding the proper universality of God who is the ground and goal of all reality. The intrinsic demand for comprehensiveness in perceptions of the divine may thus lead to developments in thought. The fifth and sixth reasons for doctrinal developments are much less theologically respectable but nevertheless have affected Christian thought. The fifth is the desire for doctrines which suit the convenience of some individual or, more likely, some group. Popes, not surprisingly, have been interested to advance developments which enhance their status while, as we have seen, the representatives of the oppressed are now keen to bring about doctrinal changes which support their causes. Sixthly, developments in Christian thought may be brought about by the character of those who are involved in formulating it. Ernst Troeltsch, for example, suggested that differences between early Lutheranism and Calvinism can be ascribed in part to differences in the character and disposition of Luther and Calvin. Seventhly and supremely, though, developments in theological understanding occur because people wish their faith to be seen to correspond to what they are convinced is the truth. Doctrines, therefore, are developed because believers wish to find in them a true understanding of the ultimate nature and meaning of reality. The other reasons for development are in effect subsidiary aspects of this over-riding concern to establish and express what is true.[30] In the end, therefore, the proper tests for authentic development are not found internally in Christian tradition by looking to earlier and perhaps original forms of the self-understanding of Christian faith. They emerge as we take seriously that the truth is in God – indeed, is intrinsic to the divine being – and that nothing that is true understanding can be a false doctrine, however much it may radically alter received ideas. The tests of true development are the tests of truth generally.

Chapter 4

Faith, Hermeneutics
and the Bible

According to a leader in *The Guardian* in September 1977, Chairman Hua had recently advanced a novel interpretation of Karl Marx's 'From each according to his abilities, to each according to his needs'. The Chinese understanding of this socialist principle is that it means 'From each according to his ability, to each according to his work' – those who work harder are to receive more and all else is 'idealism run wild and metaphysics rampant'. By this remarkable exegesis the Chairman of the Chinese Communist Party was apparently using Marx to advocate policies which would be approved by Professor Milton Friedman! It is a form of activity which has long been suspected to occur in Christian thought. Although believers may generally subscribe to the normative authority of the Bible, in practice hardly any, if any, of the conflicting interpretations of Christian faith have seemed to face any embarrassment when asked for biblical justification. As John Locke once put it, when people are urged to study the Bible, the result is 'that the scripture serves but, like a nose of wax, to be turned and bent, just as may fit the contrary orthodoxies of different societies'.[1]

The problems of interpretation cannot be avoided by simply repeating biblical texts. Not only are most of those repetitions in a translation from the original Hebrew and Greek and hence affected by the interpretative conditioning of all translation of literary documents, the choice of which texts are to be cited in a specific case and the presupposed understanding of what they mean are acts of interpretation. When, therefore, people assert 'But the Bible says . . .' and quote a text, they are interpreting the Bible whether they acknowledge it or not. The study of the interpretation, exegesis and application of texts, which is what the term 'hermeneutics' refers to, is consequently fundamental for all Christian theology so far as it regards the Bible as a source for its understanding.

The study of hermeneutics is not confined to the problems of the warrantable apprehension and application of biblical texts. Its basic principles and findings apply to all kinds of literature. They need to be appreciated by philosophers wrestling with the works of their predecessors and contemporaries, by historians working on documents, by literary critics studying novels, poetry and plays, by lawyers referring to statutes, by biochemists analysing journal reports and laboratory records, by theologians considering works of doctrine, indeed by everyone of us as we read anything – including you as you read this. Different forms of literature, however, also have peculiar problems of their own. Since, therefore, this work is primarily concerned with Christian thought and practice, we shall focus on the hermeneutical problems which arise with the study and use of the Bible.

The nature of the Bible

Interpretations of the Bible which desire to be taken seriously as interpretations (in contrast to imaginative reflections which use biblical texts as a 'pretext' for independent thought – like the preacher I once heard who gave an excellent sermon on just pay but who used as his text Romans 6.23) should start from a recognition of the basic characteristics of the Bible as a literary document. In particular seven qualities need to be borne in mind. Some of them may seem too obvious to be worth mentioning but it is disturbing how frequently those who use the Bible in fact abuse it by forgetting their significance.

The Bible, first of all, is to be regarded in many ways not as one book but as several. Normally the interpretation of a book can and should start from the presupposition that it is a unity – a single work by one author expressing a consistent position throughout. As a result a difficult passage in one part of the book may be elucidated by what is more clearly expressed in another part. Some books, however, are collections. Between their covers are a selection of items which may express a range of opinions and even a variety of types of literature. The Bible is such a book. It not only contains different forms of literature (law, history, poetry, letters, gospels and so on); its materials express a range of opinions which do not always cohere. For example, the Deuteronomic historians sought to show how the justice of God is realized in history as the righteous prosper and the wicked are punished whereas the book of Job is a protest against any such optimism. What this means is that interpreters should be extremely cautious before they refer to 'the teaching of the Bible' or 'the biblical understanding' of some point of doctrine or practice. Before such claims are warranted it is necessary to show that the different documents do so agree. Furthermore, the diversity of the points of view contained in the biblical materials means that the old exegetical principle of allowing the Bible to be its own interpreter is unjustified. The fact that Matthew 2.15 interprets Hosea 11.1 as referring to the flight into Egypt is not a good reason for holding that this is the correct understanding of the Hosean verse (and even less a reason for holding that prophecy required Jesus ever to go to Egypt). Similarly, it must not be presumed that when different biblical works both use the same term, say 'salvation' or 'the holy spirit', they mean the same thing by it and so can be used to amplify each other's understanding of it. Consequently, while the Bible as a whole is held to be canonical, the diverse character of its contents means that its canonicity cannot be regarded as narrowly defining some particular position as the only Christian one.

Secondly, while some of the biblical documents, especially the legal works, seem to have been carefully drafted and may reasonably be subjected to fairly close exegetical elucidation, much of the material has not been so carefully prepared. Some at least of the prophetic books appear to be compilations from surviving fragments, and Paul's letters, with the possible exception of Romans, were occasional pieces directed to specific situations. When they were written (or dictated) it was never anticipated that many centuries later exegetes would submit them to minute analysis and find theological significance in their specific choice of words and grammatical forms. Rather than treat the materials as if they had been produced by lawyers who deliberated over each phrase before they used it in order to ensure as far as possible that it exactly said what was desired and could not be misinterpreted if accurately analysed, it is more plausible to see them as generally written by non-professionals to meet some immediate need and with some particular recipients in mind. When Paul, for instance, wrote in strong terms to the 'stupid' Galatians, his concern was to make that particular community aware of how he judged their behaviour. His language would have emerged as what was suitable to make his views clear to them. He was not thinking how the letter might also be used by Christians in a Cheshire village or a Japanese suburb nineteen centuries later to guide their faith and conduct in a world which he could never have envisaged. If he had had such posterity in mind, he would possibly have taken more care over his choice of language and certainly over his grammar in dictating it. To treat the Bible in the detailed way that many commentaries still do is only justified if the text is supposed to have been produced by a mind at least as acute as those of the commentators and with a clear grasp of all the implications that can be derived from the material. Since, however, the documents show too many human failings to be attributable to God, such treatment seems unsupportable.

The third characteristic of the biblical materials is that they are basically a collection of religious writings and to be interpreted accordingly. It is a mistake to treat the texts as if their authors were primarily concerned to make other sorts of claims. The stories in the first two chapters of Genesis are not cosmological accounts which are to be compared with what scientists hold about the origin of the universe. They make religious claims, such as that reality is fundamentally purposive and good and that humanity has a special status in the order of things. The so-called 'historical books' of the Old Testament are not unbiased accounts of what happened but expressions of religious concern about obeying the will of God in history, a concern which leads to a political success story like that of Omri being briefly dismissed while Josiah's politically disastrous reign is given extensive treatment. The Acts of the Apostles uses an historical format to express the universal significance of the Christian faith. The Gospels are not neutral biographies which seek to describe their subject in a balanced fashion. They are the products of and seek to evoke passionate commitment to Jesus as the Christ. They are not really interested in discovering how he seemed to those who originally followed him but became disillusioned and left. The story of Jesus is used instead to present 'good news' and the call to faith. While, therefore, biblical materials contain many references to nonreligious items, such as current views on the nature of society and about why things happen in the world, historical events, and agricultural practices, those materials are to be understood as incorporating these references, where they are not merely incidental background items, because they are understood to provide ways of communicating and justifying religious convictions.

It should also be realized, fourthly, that the biblical materials both are the products of believing communities and were (and still are so far as they are held to be canonical) authorized by one. The documents reflect stages in the development of an ongoing community of faith. It is not the case that the Bible (or parts of it) first appeared and then a community formed in response to its teachings. What was written emerged out of the needs and concerns of the community, was moulded by those interests, and was finally chosen to be in the canonical collection because it was considered to offer a valuable contribution to guiding of the community's life. Above all it must not be forgotten that what we now have as the canonical Bible contains a more or less deliberate choice by the Christian community from a range of materials that were available to it, some of which have survived. The selection was made, furthermore, on the basis of the community's existing faith and practice and thus shows us how Christians at that time understood their faith. To appeal from the community to the Bible today is therefore to appeal in effect from what the church is like today to what it was in the patristic period. It is not self-evident, though, that the earlier form or forms of a community's self-understanding of its constituent faith are to be regarded as necessarily the determinative standard for its current belief and practice. Later reflection on the faith may be expected to produce more perceptive insights into it.

A fifth characteristic of the biblical materials, which follows on from the previous remarks, is that they reflect a wide range of levels of theological development. Some of the Old Testament is the product of a long period of reflection on the relationship between the divine and the human in the light of the formative events and succeeding history of the Jewish people. In contrast, while some parts of the New Testament may show more profound insights than other parts, all of it comes from a period when the Christian community was still in the early stages of sorting out the significance of the event of Jesus. Although its faith was based on the conviction that Jesus was – and is – the Christ and that in his life the character of God has been disclosed, it was far from clear what this meant in terms of God, Jesus and humanity. It is a mistake, therefore, to look to the New Testament for sophisticated expressions of the Christian faith, and anachronistic to attempt to derive classical (or modern) christological and trinitarian doctrines from its statements. Such doctrines may be there *in embryo* but this does not mean that they are there in a developed and identifiable form, for when the materials were written there was no way of perceiving how the church's understanding would eventually develop. The so-called 'Protestant principle' of believing only what the Bible explicitly asserts thus led in the eighteenth century to Arian christologies and

Unitarian rejection of trinitarianism. When the New Testament authors spoke of Jesus in terms of 'Lord', 'Messiah', 'Word' and so on, they were not using these titles in the full knowledge of what they might be held to imply about Jesus but because they seemed appropriate at the time. As the community's awareness of its faith developed, so did its understanding and exposition of the significance of these titles. In the New Testament materials we are presented with a rudimentary stage in the development of Christian doctrine.

While, however, doctrinal aspects may need to be developed, it is important, sixthly, to recognize that the understanding which is expressed in some parts of the Bible is based upon a mature experience of life and accordingly presents a faith which only mature persons are likely to be able to appreciate properly. It is a point to which Christopher Evans drew attention in an essay in his stimulating collection, *Is 'Holy Scripture' Christian?*.[2] When, for example, Paul attacks the law, he may reasonably be held to be repudiating not just religion as law but also all rules of morality. Such rules may have an educative role in bringing people to perceive what sin is, but the authentic life of faith is by immediate response to the grace of God. It is a life which involves a sophisticated view of ethics – a view which Augustine expresses as 'Love carefully and then what you will, do'[3] (Dilige, et quod vis fac) and Harry Williams as the 'admittedly appalling' risk of taking 'generous self-giving love' as 'the ultimate moral value'.[4] It is not a policy of conduct which may safely be presented to immature people, for the demands of freedom and love will be liable to be too much for them. Initially they need a morality which provides clear rules and suggests that happiness comes from following them. Hence, as Evans suggests, school-teachers find it more comfortable to teach Acts' version of Paul's career than to present his own understanding of faith in his letters. Many churches, we may add, continue the same treatment, either unaware or afraid that their congregations might contain mature people who have grown beyond such treatment.

The seventh characteristic of the Bible is that it is not to be regarded as a sacred book. It is interesting, in this respect, to compare Muslim attitudes to the Qur'an with Christian ones to the Bible. According to Muslim teaching, what is contained in the Qur'an is the uncreated Word of God which existed before the creation of the world and which was transmitted in Arabic through the Prophet. Accordingly the text itself is to be treated with grave respect. An Islamic journal which I recently received contains this note: 'The sacred verses of the Holy Qur'an and the Traditions of the Prophet have been printed for the benefit of our readers. You are asked to ensure their sanctity. Therefore pages on which these are printed should be disposed of in the proper Islamic manner.' Such an attitude to the Bible would be fundamentally alien to the Christian faith as properly understood. For Chrsitians God alone is intrinsically holy. Sacred places, sacred functionaries, sacred objects are notions which belong to other faiths: where they emerge in supposedly Christian contexts they reveal the infiltration of superstition. Furthermore, not only is the Bible not a 'sacred book' nor a 'sacred oracle' for Christian faith: it is also not properly to be described as the 'Word of God'. This phrase properly describes the medium, namely Jesus as the Christ, through whom, according to Christian belief, the divine nature and will is directly expressed to humanity. The role of the Bible is to witness to that medium and to express how believers have apprehended its message. It is not that medium. In the end authentic Christian faith is a living response to God which uses the Bible as a means to perceiving the divine but which thoroughly repudiates any suggestion that that book is to be treated as something sacred.

Ways of interpreting the Bible

Having noted these seven preliminary – but basic – points about the Bible, we come to the question, How is the Bible to be interpreted? It may be claimed to be fundamental for Christian understanding but the history of that thought shows how diversely it has been interpreted. Leaving aside, then, the question of its authority and the problems that arise because of the apparent variety (and mutual incompatibility) of its ideas, is there any way of moving towards a 'correct' interpretation of its materials? Several attempts have been made to answer this question. We shall mention first what may be described as two theological responses to this hermeneutical problem and then consider how others have identified the heart of the problem in cross-cultural communication. Finally we shall note some insights that come from literary criticism.

One solution to the problem of how the Bible is to be understood maintains that God has inspired the production of this work and through the Spirit will make its meaning plain to all who will listen in obedient faith. The correct interpretation of the Bible, therefore, is not a result of scholarship or institutional direction. It occurs when

believers open themselves to confrontation by the 'Word' as it is
mediated to them through the Bible and as God chooses so to
confront them. It is thus a matter of faith and a work of divine grace
in believers rather than something which believers can achieve by
their own efforts. Karl Barth received his theological education
under some of the greatest biblical scholars in Germany at the start
of the twentieth century but when, in 1920, he addressed students
on 'Biblical Questions, Insights, and Vistas' he said this:

> The Bible is the literary monument of an ancient racial religion
> and of a Hellenistic cultus religion of the Near East. A human
> document like any other, it can lay no *a priori* dogmatic claim to
> special attention and consideration . . . For it is too clear that
> intelligent and fruitful discussion of the Bible begins when the
> judgment as to its human, its historical and psychological
> character has been made and *put behind* us.[5]

Biblical scholarship is not very important if, like Satan, it is to be
dismissed. For Barth such study presents an obstacle between the
reader and the Word mediated through the Bible. By our own
efforts we cannot even discern that the Word is so mediated: we
discover it as God chooses so to address us and to enable us to hear
that address.

This view of the Bible as self-interpreting (or, perhaps, as
divinely communicated) corresponds to an important characteristic
of all understanding, namely, that it cannot be forced. No matter
how sophisticated our grasp of hermeneutical methods, in the end
our grasp of the meaning and significance of a text is a type of direct,
immediate experience. It happens – suddenly we 'see' what it is
expressing whereas previously it seemed fuzzy and puzzling. There
seems no need, though, to attribute such a happening to the work of
the divine Spirit – unless all understanding is to be so attributed. It is
an experience that belongs to our study of all kinds of texts. The
major problem with this view of interpretation, however, is that it
leaves us with no way of deciding, beyond subjective inclination,
between conflicting exegeses of a passage, each of which sincerely
claims to be an authentic-apprehension of the current 'Word'. For
each person to be justified in asserting that what the Bible 'says' to
him or her is the true grasp of the self-interpreting 'Word' through
the Bible is to lead to a state of confusion. It is also to leave the Bible
open to the 'eisegesis' when people read into it their individual
prejudices and claim them to be biblically justified.

The other 'theological' solution to the problem of correct exegesis holds that it is the duty of the church to determine how the Bible is to be understood. On the one hand this claim can be held to be justified on historical grounds. The Bible is the product of the believing community and its contents were selected and authorized by that community. The community, therefore, should be recognized to have the responsibility of deciding today which interpretations accord with its faith. On the other hand it is argued that God gives to the church magisterial power in order to prevent the errors of private judgment. The Council of Trent asserted this position:

> Furthermore, in order to restrain petulant spirits, It decrees that no one, relying on his own skill, shall . . . presume to interpret the sacred Scripture contrary to that sense which holy mother Church, – whose it is to judge of the true sense and interpretation of the holy Scriptures, – hath held and doth hold . . .[6]

Three centuries later John Henry Newman took up the Ethiopian's question to Philip when asked if he understood what he was reading, 'How can I, unless some man shall guide me?' and argued that a revelation can only be held to have been given if an authority is also provided 'to decide what it is that is given'. This office is to be undertaken by the church.[7]

It may be thought that this view of biblical hermeneutics is not a Protestant one. Formally this may be so but in practice one frequently finds that Protestant groups have their own informal view of what is the correct interpretation of the Bible and find it hard to accept the possible legitimacy of significantly variant views. The problem with such an answer to the problems of interpretation is that it is not self-evident which body is to be the authorized interpreter and how it is to act. Various ecclesiastical institutions may claim the position but none are above suspicion. Popes, Bishops, Councils, Synods, Conferences and so on turn out on examination to have too many human traits to be credible candidates. At best their decisions seem to be guided by currently accepted theological views and at worst by selfish interest. The 'consensus of the faithful', on the other hand, is too vague and begs too many questions to be a practically effective principle for identifying correct exegesis. Those who advocate it see it as the endorsement of what the majority have agreed on but this leaves open a number of prior questions about which there is no agreement. Who, for instance, decides what the consensus comes to and that the majority is sufficient? What is the community in which the majority is sought? Is it that of the Christian community at large or some section of it – and, if so, which section and why is it determinative? The principle, in any case, offers a highly conservative approach and fails to meet the problem of whether a new interpretative insight is valid or not. So far as biblical exegesis is concerned, its implementation over the past centuries would probably have meant that Christians would still be required to believe that the natural world had been produced in six days, that Jonah had been swallowed, that Jesus had made over a hundred and twenty gallons of wine for a wedding feast which had already drunk up the provisions, and that there was a bodily ascension to heaven.

Most of those who consider that neither of the 'theological' solutions to the problem of biblical hermeneutics is satisfactory presume that the proper task of the interpreter is to grasp what the original authors (or compilers) had in mind when they produced this literature. Correct exegesis, in other words, is a matter of apprehending what the author was desiring to communicate. The hermeneutical question then largely becomes one of how this is to be achieved, especially in view of the fact that the biblical authors and interpreters today belong to widely differing cultures.

Early studies of hermeneutics were much concerned with formulating principles for correct exegesis. A chapter in Isaac Watts' *Improvement of the Mind* (1741) is one of numerous examples. Aware of the ambiguity of language and in order to guide the reader 'to hit upon the ideas which the writer or speaker had in his mind', Watts lists twelve rules. Among other things, readers should 'be well acquainted' with the original language of the passage, including its idioms and specialist uses. They should compare how an author uses words and phrases in different places and interpret individual passages in the light of the author's overall scope and design. What is said allusively or metaphorically should be explained by what the author elsewhere says more strictly and expansively on the subject. The meaning of an assertion can, further, be more clearly discerned by considering what the author considers to follow from it or what objections are brought against it. Above all readers are to take care that their own prejudices do not distort their interpretations: they are to treat every author as they would wish to be treated by others.[8] Such rules, of course, apply to all kinds of literature. Sometimes, though, the character of the Bible is held to require special treatment. Thus Samuel Davidson begins his extensive study of *Sacred Hermeneutics* (1843) by suggesting that the heavenly source of the Bible means that it 'should not be rashly approached'. It should be expounded by those who not only have the proper intellectual and literary skills but also have 'a singleness of desire to know the mind of God'.[9] The danger with the addition of such religious qualifications to the principle that the Bible is to be interpreted in a way appropriate to any text is that it is liable to be used to deflect critical analysis into channels comfortable to the faithful.

The character of proper hermeneutics was a problem which exercised Friedrich Daniel Ernst Schleiermacher during the first decades of the nineteenth century. In the manuscripts which he left he recognizes that more is needed for correct understanding than the observance of grammatical rules. Initially the aim of interpreters of a text is to grasp the inner coherence of what its author is expressing. This involves reconstructing 'the whole internal process of an author's way of combining thoughts' and of expressing them. To do this interpreters need to be conversant with the structures of the language which the text uses and aware of the ways in which that language may modify a thought as it is used to express it. They also have to know the intellectual background of the text, its context in the life of its author, and the situation of those to whom it is addressed. The possession of such information, however, is not sufficient to enable an interpreter to step into the frame of mind of the author. What is further required is a general understanding of how people think and, in particular, the exercise of empathy in respect of the particular author and text. The presupposition of this activity is that all human beings share certain basic characteristics which enable them to 'divine' what is happening in the mind of others. The result is that the interpreter perceives why the author wrote at all and used particular forms of expression. Interpretation may thus be regarded as an artistic achievement in which we seek to become 'sensitive to the particular way an author combines the thoughts, for had those thoughts been formulated differently, even in the same historical situation and the same kind of presentation, the result would have been different'.[10] In the end, however, the aim of the interpreter is to go beyond the author by grasping the subject-matter more clearly, accurately and comprehensively than the author had managed. Hermeneutics may thus be compared to that aspect of a 'meaningful conversation' where we try to 'lift out its main points' and 'grasp its internal coherence', and then 'pursue all its subtle intimations further'.[11] Its success in any particular case would be marked by the original author saying 'Yes! That is what I was trying to get at!' It is also an infinite process for a text is not seen as an end in itself. A text is a way to understanding. New interpretative perspectives and contexts may find through it previously unperceived insights.

Schleiermacher's major contribution to hermeneutics lies in his recognition of the role of empathetic divination (i.e. of the power to enter into the thoughts and feelings of the author) in hermeneutics and his assertion of a shared humanity which allows it to be possible.[12] We can, for example, expect to be able to understand what Jeremiah and Paul and Augustine and Hegel were getting at in their writings because they were human beings living in the same kind of natural and historical reality and having the same fundamental structure of existence as we have. We can therefore appreciate their problems and benefit from their insights. Others, however, wonder if such empathetic understanding is as possible as Schleiermacher believed or is available in the way that he suggested.

Adolf Harnack's studies of patristic thought made him aware of how the early expressions of the Christian gospel included dispensable materials derived from the prevalent ideas in contemporary culture. As we noted in the previous chapter, he regards these cultural influences on doctrine as unavoidable if Christianity were to present its message in a credible form. He also considers that Christianity has always had the capacity 'to strip off' any ideas which it has adopted from a culture and to 'unite itself to fresh coefficients' for understanding and expressing its faith.[13] This ability to use and to drop different thought-forms is the basis of his view of the correct method for biblical hermeneutics. According to Harnack the exegete should seek to determine the everlasting and unchanging truth – or, better, 'spirit' – which lies behind and is more or less adequately represented in the historically relative and culturally influenced forms of the New Testament. Exegesis is a kind of historical analysis which aims to discern the essence of Christianity from its various self-expressions. Rather misleadingly he presents his position in a famous passage in *What is Christianity?* (1900) in terms of a 'kernel and husk' model. Discussing how the 'faithful disciples' of Jesus responded positively to Paul's teaching which 'in important points seemed to depart from the original message', Harnack states that

What was kernel here, and what was husk, history has itself showed with unmistakeable plainness, and by the shortest process. Husk were the whole of the Jewish limitations attaching

to Jesus' message . . . In the strength of Christ's spirit the
disciples broke through these barriers . . . Without doing viol-
ence to the inner and essential features of the Gospel . . . Paul
transformed it into the universal religion . . .[14]

The model of kernel and husk is 'misleading' because, in the case of
a nut, stripping away the husk reveals the kernel. As Harnack
appreciated, though, this is not possible with statements of the
gospel. Even though he offers various summaries of the essential
character of the Christian faith, he also recognizes that all such
statements are culturally relative ways of communicating its fundamental spirit. What exegetes may do, however, it to identify
certain texts which, for all their temporal conditionedness, express
the truth of the gospel most clearly and then expound them in ways
that make its spirit plain to their contemporaries. Other texts may,
contrariwise, be left aside because their way of putting the gospel is
so alien to current thought that they are obstacles to its present
apprehension.

In the epoch-making essay, 'New Testament and Mythology'
(1941), which launched the concept of 'demythologizing', Rudolf
Bultmann seized on the kernel and husk model to accuse Harnack –
and liberal theologians of his type generally – of attempting to
reduce the gospel to a number of 'eternal, timeless truths' expressing 'certain basic religious and moral ideas'. To do this they
eliminate as 'time conditioned and inessential' what they regard as
'mythological representations'[15] – for example, talk about the
world as 'a three-story structure' where earth, in the middle, 'is a
theater for the working of supernatural powers, God and his angels,
Satan and his demons'.[16] Bultmann's protest is that such an
interpretation of the gospel abandons its heart as a proclamation of
the saving event of God in Christ and that it errs in considering that
some non-mythological elements in the New Testament presentation of the gospel can be separated from mythological ones. He
maintains instead that belief in an act of God is decisive for the
Christian understanding of salvation but that the New Testament's
presentation of this occurrence is wholly in terms of the mythological world picture. (So far as Bultmann's 'mythological' designates
the cultural position in which the New Testament authors found
themselves, Harnack would basically agree with the latter point.)
Since such a world picture is neither specifically Christian nor
credible today,[17] he asserts that 'the New Testament proclamation'
will only 'retain its validity' if it is demythologized.[18] To do this he

identifies the point of myth – to express 'how we human beings understand ourselves in our world'[19] and maintains that such self-understanding is now most adequately expressed in existentialist thought, particularly as developed by the contemporary German philosopher Martin Heidegger.[20] He therefore sets himself the task of outlining 'the dualistic mythology of the New Testament in existentialist terms'.[21] The end-product, he hopes, will be to make starkly clear both the gospel of God's offer of 'genuine human life'[22] and the scandal that this offer of salvation is possible – and only possible – because of an act of God in history, in Jesus Christ.[23]

Bultmann considers that by adopting such an approach we may grasp what the New Testament authors were seeking to express through the mythological world-picture. Basically this is possible because, while modes of expression and forms of understanding may differ considerably, the fundamental characteristics of human existence remain the same. Schleiermacher, Harnack and Bultmann – and most other students and practitioners of hermeneutics – are thus united in presupposing a common or universal humanity. It is a presupposition which has interestingly been called into question by Hans-Georg Gadamer. In his massive *Truth and Method* (1960), Gadamer criticizes Schleiermacher and Bultmann for not appreciating sufficiently the significance of the differences between ages and cultures. These differences, however, need not serve only as an obstacle to understanding texts from the past. Temporal distance may act as a critical filter which aids the interpreter to perceive what such texts are saying by drawing attention to the ways in which it contrasts with current thought. We should, therefore, approach texts from other cultures not by emphasizing their authors' similarities with us but by recognizing how our presuppositions and understanding differ from theirs. We should also recognize that we can never attain complete objectivity in interpreting a text because we can never become fully conscious of our own prejudices. What we grasp will always be affected to some extent by our own tradition and current interests. Texts only have meaning as interpreters come to them with questions and engage in dialogue with them.

The central notion of Gadamer's view of the hermeneutical process is that of 'the fusing of horizons'. By interacting with the text and, in particular, as a result of recognizing how its understanding belongs to a different culture, the interpreter creatively produces a novel 'horizon' of understanding which combines within itself the cultural world of the text and that of the interpreter. This comprehensive horizon is not something which interpreters develop before they begin the process of understanding nor is it something whose character can be established by metaphysical arguments independently of the consideration of particular cases. Rather, it both emerges with and provides the context for the understanding of the text. What, though, are interpreters seeking? According to Gadamer they should not see themselves as seeking to get into the mind of the author and recreate the processes that produced the text. Nor should they regard the text as a 'pretext' to be used as a source of inspiration for their own creative inventions. Interpreters are engaged in the task of discerning the significance and truth of what is declared in the text and of grasping it better than the original author. In understanding what is written, 'we are moving in a dimension of meaning that is intelligible in itself and as such offers no reason for going back to the subjectivity of the author'.[24] The proper goal of hermeneutics, therefore, is confrontation with the reality which the text seeks to identify and it comes about through respect for the integrity of the text. It is a process, furthermore, which is never complete, for there is no determinable end to the possibilities of illuminating conversation with a text, and which changes those who engage in it, for it opens them up to new insights. What is to be sought from a text, that is, is understanding as 'the genuine experience' of 'an encounter with something that asserts itself as truth'.[25]

Gadamer's response to the problems of cross-cultural under-standing raises in an acute way the question of what interpretation is seeking to achieve. The traditional answer is that it should aim to discern what the authors were wanting to communicate when they wrote as they did. This reply seems so obvious to common-sense that it may be odd to question it. People do not write at random: they write because they have something to say. Authors struggle to find the 'right' expressions because they want to help their readers to perceive accurately what they have to tell them. Readers interpret their writings correctly when they grasp what the authors intended them to grasp. If this is denied, the point of writing and the possibility of communication seem to be in jeopardy. It seems so obvious until we begin to reflect on literature generally. What is presumably the case with someone preparing an instruction manual for operating an aeroplane or drafting a statute – and with others who use such texts for flying that plane or implementing that law – may not be wholly the case with a novel or a sermon. Leaving aside, for the moment, the question of where the Bible is to be placed among the forms of literature, we will note some – but only a very few – of the insights into hermeneutics that come from literary criticism.

In the first place texts do not always say what they are intended to say. Judges sometimes have to point out to legislators that the form of words which they have passed, on careful reading, does not mean what they wanted it to mean. Students sometimes use an unfamiliar word or an unusual expression and their tutors say 'But is that what you really mean? – or do you mean . . . ?' Perhaps some readers will wonder at things written here. What such experiences indicate is that texts have an integrity of their own. Whatever was intended, the words and structures convey something particular because of their intrinsic character. It is because of this that authors wrestle with how to put things. They want the expression that says what they want to say. In this respect, therefore, hermeneutics may have to be on two levels: one identifying what the text says and another seeking to determine what the author wanted to say by it.

Secondly, though, it may be questioned whether the author's purpose is at all relevant to understanding what is written. In an essay on 'The Intentional Fallacy' W. K. Wimsatt and Monroe C. Beardsley suggest that 'judging a poem is like judging a pudding or a machine. One demands that it work.'[26] Whereas Goethe had claimed that criticism must consider what the author set out to do, whether the plan was reasonable and whether the author succeeded,[27] these modern critics maintain that the evaluation of a 'work of art remains public; the work is measured against something outside the author'.[28] It is arguable that in some literature at least this is true of the determination of the meaning of the text as well as of the judgment of its quality. In the case of many texts the author's meaning can, in any case, only be guessed at from an existing understanding of the text. Is it important? The fact – if it is a fact – that we do not know what Shakespeare himself had in mind when he wrote Hamlet or a particular speech in the play is probably irrelevant to finding meaning in it. To argue that 'because this is the meaning we find in it, therefore this must be what Shakespeare had in mind; and because Shakespeare had this in mind, this must be the meaning of the text' is to engage in a circular and pointless exercise. The important thing is that it speaks to us and what it says to us. Questions about an author's intentions only become significant if that author is held to give authority to what is written.

Thirdly, if a text is a public matter whose meaning is determined by its words and structures, how important is it to appreciate the background to the text? Those who produce commentaries on texts describe their cultural background and explain what are taken to be allusions in them. Often such notes are helpful. They expand our appreciation of what is written as they draw attention to riches in it which otherwise might have been missed. The question arises, however, whether there are any legitimate limitations to this process. In the case of 'allusions', for example, does it matter whether what is detected as an allusion was in the mind of the original author, consciously or subconsciously, or is a product of the interpreter's imagination? It is arguable that such a distinction is not important and, in most cases, probably cannot be implemented. What is important is that the elucidation of the supposed allusion adds to the value of the text as a source of insight. Another question is how far the background to a text needs to be appreciated before the text itself can be claimed to be understood. Many children, for example, recite 'Baa, baa, black sheep' without knowing that it is about the export tax on wool in 1275, and 'Hark, hark, the dogs do bark' without being aware that it expresses a dislike of Dutchmen who followed William III to England in 1688. It would be very odd, however, to claim that without this knowledge they could not 'understand' what they were reciting – and equally odd to say that the historical references were the proper meaning of those rhymes. What needs to be appreciated is that a text may have a number of meanings and be interpretable over a range of levels. In the case of texts which come to be held to have a high normative content (i.e., as providing a canonical standard for understanding and/or practice), the original background may be much less significant (even misleading) for its normative application than a knowledge of the background in which its normative status was established. For Christian exegetes, for example, the reasons why the Song of Solomon or Revelation came to be seen as canonical may be more revealing than their original backgrounds. In the end the criterion of legitimacy in the use of background material for interpreting certain texts may not be found through reference to some postulated original thought but, again, be a matter of balancing respect for the integrity of the text against what fruitfully extends our understanding – and that 'understanding' may be on various levels from concern with the language of the text itself to interest in the meaning of life!

A fourth insight into works of literature suggests that in certain cases the meaning of a passage cannot properly be expressed except in terms of that passage. Compare, for example, one of Aesop's fables with a poem by Keats. In the former case it is possible to follow the fable with a short statement of its meaning – its 'moral'. This is not possible in the case of a true poem. The poet in such an instance has not used the language and form of poetry as a pleasant way of communicating what could be put more directly. The language and form of the poem are intrinsic to what it expresses. 'The medium' may not 'be the message' but it is essential to it. Similarly the point of some stories may belong to those stories and is only properly disclosed in the telling of them. This is not because attempts to interpret them fall flat and are relatively uninteresting. The basic problem is that some stories are not translatable and reducible. If, then, the Christian faith is a matter of living by 'the Christian story', it may be that credal summaries and doctrinal statements are to be understood as shorthand reminders of the 'story' but it is the story itself that must be heard. Sallie TeSelle (now McFague) in her *Speaking in Parables* suggests accordingly that in the case of parables, we should 'let the story penetrate *us*, rather than look around for possible interpretations of it'. If we do this, we will find that 'we do not interpret the parable but the parable interprets us'.[29] So far as this is the correct approach, those who offer exegeses of what the stories 'really mean', however sophisticated their analyses, are in danger of fundamentally missing the point of this literary genre. It is an error which, in Christian history, began with the interpreters of the parables of Jesus whose efforts managed to be ascribed to him in the New Testament.

A fifth point to note from considering texts on literature is that exegesis begins by presupposing that a text is internally coherent. We thus seek to interpret one passage by relating it to other passages. Although, as we have noted, in the case of the Bible we are dealing with a collection of works, within each identifiably separate piece the principle holds. We are helped to grasp what Paul is saying in one place by comparing it with what he says elsewhere. One result of this approach is that when scholars find an apparently conflicting element in a text, they are liable to explain it as due to an editorial interpolation or a sign of inconsistent source materials. Frank Kermode, however, in *The Genesis of Secrecy* suggests that these may be the points for exegesis to concentrate on for it is here that we are challenged to probe further to find a meaning which leads beyond what we have previously perceived; narratives, like those of the Gospels, which are characterized by 'varying focus, fractured surfaces, over-determinations' and 'displacements' con-stitute 'a perpetual invitation to all inquirers after latent sense, a perpetual challenge to those more sober interpreters'.[30] It is not what we have made sense of – or, rather, think we have made sense of – but what troubles us by presenting problems which provokes us to new, deeper, more significant insights. For the believer concerned with the Bible such literary views remind us that a plain, 'common-sense' approach may obscure riches that a more sensitive, literary approach may uncover in the significance of the text as well as in the structure of a text.

Why study texts?

Finally, why do we study texts? When Sir William Hamilton posed that question in his *Logic*, he answered 'We read not for the sake of reading, but we read to the end that we may think. Reading is valuable only as it may supply to us the materials which the mind itself elaborates.'[31] A similar answer may be offered to the question 'Why do we interpret texts?' The value of hermeneutics may not be that it brings us closer to some supposed thought in the mind of an author but that it opens up for us new possibilities of understanding. It is the future application of a text that is important, not its past formation. William Golding, the Nobel prize-winning novelist, admits that his *Lord of the Flies* is a 'highly and diversely explicable' story which has evoked a great variety of interpretations. He does not consider, though, that as its author he has a privileged position in determining which interpretation is correct:

> I no longer believe that the author has a sort of *patria potestas* [that is, the total power of a human father over his children] over his brainchildren. Once they are printed they have reached their majority and the author has no more authority over them, knows no more about them, perhaps less about them than the critic who comes fresh to them . . .[32]

The task of the exegete is to lead readers of a text to fresh insights – and the exegesis itself is similarly to be so used in a process which should not end until those resources are exhausted.

What, though, is the significance of these points from literary criticism for our understanding of biblical hermeneutics? The conclusion to be drawn may be that not only is there no final interpretation possible but also no interpretation and no interpretative method that can claim to be the only correct one. There are various possibilities. What is important for exegetes is that they be conscious of which hermeneutical method they are following and that they evaluate their results accordingly. In particular they should recognize that they are responsible for their interpretations and for the truth of what they assert. The childish hiding behind authority – 'Teacher says' – is not an authentic stance for biblical exegetes. 'The Bible says' is not to be used as the introduction to a dictat but to a humble offering of an understanding derived from considering some part of it and as a prelude to providing grounds for holding that understanding to be true. Why, though, bother about the Bible? The answer finally lies not in its historic role as the source, guide and (in spite of its complexities and inconsistencies) norm of the cumulative tradition which is the Christian faith. Its authority – the recognition of its 'inspiration', perhaps – lies in its experienced ability to evoke profound understanding of God and humanity. Samuel Taylor Coleridge expressed this understanding of the Bible's significance in the first letter of the *Confessions of an Inquiring Spirit*. He has studied the books of the Bible and 'need I say that I have met everywhere more or less copious sources of truth, and power, and purifying impulses . . . In short, whatever *finds* me, bears witness for itself that it has proceeded from a Holy Spirit . . .'[33] In the final letter he comes back to this point; the authority and the value of the Bible resides in its ability to communicate 'objective truth . . . to the subjective experiences of the Believer.'[34] The biblical exegete today, deliberately employing the insights of hermeneutical studies, has the daunting task of using the biblical text to bring about such experiences. The expectation that it is possible is the result of its actuality throughout Christian history so far.

Chapter 5

Faith, History and Revelation

Christianity is often said to be a 'historical religion'. The description is not used to make the point that it is a religion which has a history nor that it is a religion which has had considerable influence on the course of human history for many centuries, although both points are correct. What is being asserted is the claim that the Christian faith generally understands itself to be derived from insights into God given in and through historical events and that it generally understands God as one who acts in a personal way in and upon the course of historical events. Every time the Apostles' Creed is recited as a summary of that faith these understandings are implied. The creed begins by describing the origin of all things as due to a personal mode of activity, it proceeds by referring centrally to events in the life of a person in the first century, it affirms that this person will eventually return as judge of all, and it speaks of the Holy Spirit – the current agency of the divine – and of the community of the faithful. In these ways it suggests the appropriateness and the complexity of perceiving Christianity as a faith which interprets the origin, present state and destiny of all things in their fundamental relationship to God in historical terms. In this chapter we are to consider the problems which face Christian thought because of the historical character of its faith. As in other chapters, however, we have room to introduce only a selection of the fascinating issues that arise.

History and historical judgments

Before we confront the problems of the relationship between faith and history, however, it may be useful to clarify what is meant by 'history' and what are the characteristics of historical judgments. The term 'history' always refers to personal activity and thereby is distinguished from 'nature' as the realm of non-personal activity. It may be used of actions of persons in the past or of the study of those actions. In the latter sense history is usually undertaken methodically. The study is an attempt to find answers to one or more questions. These may range from questions about what happened on a certain occasion or during a specified period, through questions about why things happened as they did, to questions about how far the character of those past events casts light on a contemporary situation and its future possibilities. To answer such questions historians investigate the records of the past which are contained in personal accounts and human artefacts, bearing in mind also the 'natural' context of what is recorded. The evidence available to historians is enormous. Their questions, of course, determine which is to be considered relevant – Wesley's journal is not going to be of use in determining the sequence of events in Luther's career although it may contribute something to understanding the social history of Bristol in the mid-eighteenth century. It is not enough, though, for historians to acquire relevant evidence. They have to assess its reliability and estimate its significance. In coming to their judgments, furthermore, they need to be aware of the complex interrelationships of factors which bring about events and of the ways in which human beings respond. Recent work such as that of Gadamer, which was mentioned in the previous chapter, has posed an important challenge to the traditional self-understanding of historical studies by questioning the legitimacy of presupposing a common humanity which renders the values and intentions of one person reasonably accessible to another in spite of their cultural and temporal distances. Many of the other problems and insights of hermeneutical investigations must also be recognized to apply to the historians' interpretations of records. As a result some historians deliberately avoid claims to be able to understand past individuals and concentrate their attention on the interaction of social, economic, political and psychological forces. The problem with such an approach is that in the end these forces are constituted by their embodiment in individual persons and have only a questionable mode of reality apart from such actualization.

Historical judgments, as judgments about what happened in the past and why it happened, are always problematic. In the first place the available evidence may create difficulties: it may be inadequate or, particularly in relation to recent times, it may be overwhelmingly enormous. What evidence there is may be inconsistent, either because of honest misapprehensions by those who recorded it or because of deliberate falsification. It is always biased evidence in that what people notice and how they apprehend it is controlled to a large extent by their cultural background. As evidence about past historical occurrences, it cannot be tested, in contrast to reports about natural events, by future experiments. Both the number of factors involved and the inclusion among them of human beings exercising their individual freedom makes it impossible to check theories about some historical event by repeating the processes which produced it. This brings us to a second difficulty with historical judgments. As the products of understanding they necessarily treat events according to general categories and in a comparative way. These necessary demands of understanding, however, make it difficult for historians to notice, let alone to appreciate, the significance of any unique characteristics of a particular event. Thirdly, historical judgments are problematic because their determination of the significance of the factors involved in producing a certain state of affairs is made after the event. Because of this unavoidable characteristic of their work, historians may 'make sense' of what happened at the cost of obscuring the perplexity of the participants in those events and of ignoring factors which at the time seemed important and which, but for some accident, might have considerably altered the course of events. It is, for example, very difficult for us to imagine what the start of Jesus' ministry may have meant to those present, granted that the gospel reports are basically accurate, since we cannot forget all that developed later from that beginning. Finally historical judgments must always be recognized to be provisional because they are inescapably controlled by the historian's own metaphysical presuppositions about what may happen, about what are to be deemed the marks of reliable evidence, and about what are plausible ways of understanding what happened. The history of thought warns us that while the presuppositions may seem self-evident to those who hold them, in time some of them have turned out to be relative, unwarrantable or misleading.

The relation of faith and history

Having, then, briefly outlined some of the characteristics of historical judgments, it is time to consider the relationship between history and faith. In principle the relationship involves three factors – events, the historians' perception of what happened, and faith. In practice, however, we can never get directly to the events themselves. As past they are apprehensible only as historical reconstructions from the evidence about them. If we leave aside mystical claims about the experienced presence of the risen Christ as a source of direction for Christian faith today, for such claims are notoriously difficult (if not impossible) to justify even though they may have profound influence over believers, the 'Jesus' whom that faith worships is a figure which has emerged (and changed) over the centuries as the community has responded to and interpreted the witness of the first disciples, eventually recorded in the Gospels, to what they had encountered. The question which arises, however, is whether there can be an intellectually satisfactory link between our grasp of what happened in certain past events and our faith in God. For Christianity the question is basically this: Can faith in God be based to a significant extent on our understanding of events in the past? In other words, can our understanding of some past event be so profound and so secure that it legitimately determines the basis of our lives and the criterion for all other understanding? This question, it should be noted, does not assume that theistic faith is wholly derived from how believers respond to the past. In most cases the supposed contribution of the evidence of history is to give concrete form and particular direction to a general theistic position whose foundations lie elsewhere. What the question probes is how far the use of history in moulding and augmenting faith about and in God can be justified. It is a problem whose fundamental aspects emerge in a paper which Gotthold Ephraim Lessing wrote in 1777, 'On the Proof of the Spirit and of Power'. Although the paper is primarily concerned to criticize J. D. Schumann's advocacy of the traditional argument that the fulfilment of prophecy and the performance of miracles proves the divine status of the Christian revelation, what Lessing says draws attention to two problems in principle which confront any attempt to base a theistic faith on historical events.

The first problem, and the one which subsequently has received the most attention, asks whether the inescapable uncertainty of historical judgments allows them to be regarded as a satisfactory basis for faith. A building, for example, will never be more secure than its foundations. A faith, similarly, that is built upon judgments that are essentially relative can never be less relative. Even though Lessing's own way of putting this, 'accidental truths of history can never become the proof of necessary truths of reason',[1] may be criticized because it presupposes (with a tradition in eighteenth-century German theology) that faith is the entertainment of necessary truths (i.e. truths which are either indisputably self-evident or can be demonstrated to be true), its basic insight can be applied to all forms of faith which see themselves as based on historical judgments. Is faith tenable when it relies on claims which may be the product of mistaken historical understanding and which may eventually be rebutted by later historical study? In the case of Christianity, for example, what would happen if later research into the career of Jesus showed that the accepted view of him on which faith rests (whatever that view might be) is substantially in error? Even if no historical research has yet convincingly shown this to be the case, can we risk our lives on a faith whose foundations are in principle always vulnerable to such disturbance? This is one problem which Lessing posed.

There are three major responses to the problem of the uncertainty of faith's historical foundations. The first points out that faith is not a matter of rationally demonstrable certainties. The use of the term 'faith' indicates that it is a commitment which, at least implicitly, acknowledges that it involves risk. Faith is assenting to the truth – in thought and in practice – of what cannot be objectively known to be such. For some the demand for such a commitment is existentially unavoidable and personally exhilarating. It is a challenge which gives zest as well as depth to our self-understanding. Others find it more uncomfortable. Tennyson expresses the experience of some when, in 'In Memoriam', he writes

> Our little systems have their day;
> They have their day and cease to be: . . .
>
> We have but faith: we cannot know;
> For knowledge is of things we see;[2]

and again

> I falter where I firmly trod,
> And falling with my weight of cares
> Upon the great world's altar-stairs
> That lead thro' darkness up to God
>
> I stretch lame hands of faith, and grope . . .[3]

Whatever the subjective experience of faith, however, its object is acknowledged to be at best only known to be highly probable. In view of this Lessing's problem is regarded as mistaken for it presupposes faith to be essentially other than it is. On the other hand it is possible that this response may leave faith as either unacceptably uncertain or, at worst, thoroughly irrational. Will people be prepared to give themselves wholeheartedly to Jesus as the Christ if they are aware that the next television series, newspaper article or learned research will show that he was not as they have considered?

A second response argues that while such historical scepticism may always be possible in principle, in practice the evidence is such that a highly reliable historical picture of Jesus can be established. Classical scholars tell us that there is much more acceptable evidence about the life and thought of Jesus in the New Testament (although there is very little useful non-biblical material) than there is for most of the other figures of antiquity about whom we have no doubts. It therefore seems unreasonable to be worried about what historical research *might* show when in practice its findings do not justify such worries. There are, however, problems with this response. On the one hand faith's assent to Jesus is of a different order to assent to judgments, say, about the location of Alexander's battles. Believers rest their whole being on the former; they may change their opinion about the latter without it disturbing very much else. Consequently, whereas the possibility of error in the latter case is not very disturbing, it may be worrying in the former case. On the other hand, the researches into the historical foundations of the Christian faith in the life of Jesus from H. S. Reimarus in the eighteenth century (Lessing published 'Fragments' of his work) to Don Cupitt on television have not presented a uniform picture. Reviewing the work to the start of this century, Albert Schweitzer, in *The Quest of the Historical Jesus*, showed how various have been the portraits. The situation has not changed. The 'Jesus' of E. Schillebeeckx or of C. H. Dodd may be much more comfortable for Christian faith than that of E. P. Sanders but it is far from clear that the former is more historically warrantable than the latter.

A third response maintains that the Jesus of history is of no concern to the Christian believer. The object of faith is the risen Christ and the gospel records are to be seen as reflecting such a faith. Rudolf Bultmann, for example, argues on the basis of II Corinthians 5.16 that Paul is not concerned with 'the human personality of Jesus – that would be "Christ after the flesh", who is dead', but with 'Jesus as *a historical event*' which 'brings in the new age and gives the possibility of new life'.[4] Christ has 'lost his identity as an individual human person' and 'has become a cosmic figure, a body to which all belong who have been joined to him through faith and baptism'.[5] Bultmann himself follows this Pauline understanding and accordingly is not worried at arguments which suggest that the historical Jesus is no longer identifiable: all that is consumed are 'the fanciful portraits of Life-of-Jesus theology'.[6] The authentic ground of Christian faith is 'solely the Word of proclamation (Romans 10.17)'.[7] While, therefore, Bultmann holds that this proclamation 'presents Jesus as an historical fact' which decisively conditions our existence, he denies that it is a fact which is 'verifiable by historical science'.[8] The Word is its own validation. It demands belief, not rational justification from us. This is a radical solution to the problem posed by Lessing but it is questionable whether many Christians would be prepared to accept it. Justifiably or not, it is generally considered that the Christian faith not only is founded upon the event of Jesus (which Bultmann affirms) but also finds its authentic form through a knowledge of the historical details of that event. How, though, do we move from the records of the life of a person who lived in a particular time and place to insight into the fundamental and universal nature of reality? It is this question that brings us back to Lessing.

Lessing's paper raises a second and much more disturbing problem for the Christian faith when it suggests that historical judgments and religious beliefs are quite distinct. There is no way of deriving the latter from the former any more than one can determine a portrait's aesthetic quality from the chemical composition of its paints or Katharine's moral reliability from her weight. The issues are unconnected. Lessing makes the point by referring to various historical judgments which may be regarded as acceptable and then asserting that it is quite another matter 'to expect me to alter all my fundamental ideas of the Godhead' because these judgments are historically acceptable.[9] Although Lessing's case is unlikely to be challenged when he cites Alexander's conquests, some may wonder if it is convincing when he includes reports that Jesus raised Lazarus, that Jesus rose from the dead, and that Jesus claimed to be the Son of God. His point, however, is that so far as they are historical, these reports simply state what happened – or is claimed to have happened. What they report may be commonplace or highly unusual but, so far as they are correct, that is what happened. Having heard them, we may legitimately respond, 'All right. That happened. So what?' If some of the events are puzzling, that is what they are. Neither their explicability nor their inexplicability as past occurrences correctly described in the records tell us about anything other than what happened. How do we get from there to faith? There is, said Lessing, an 'ugly, broad ditch' between historical reports and faith. He begged that someone should help him over it.[10] Unless it can be bridged, attempts to base faith on history are going to be essentially unsatisfactory.

Søren Kierkegaard recognized the significance of Lessing's problem. He points out the difficulty facing contemporaries of Jesus in deciding to be disciples.[11] They observe Jesus as a fellow human being – the stubble on his chin in a morning, the 'yawn' when tired, the dust and sweat of his feet after a walk, and so on. It is so much easier for us at second-hand who are presented with idealized pictures. Nevertheless, if we face up to the historical reality, the problem is the same. How do we move from the human person to faith in him? Kierkegaard's answer is that there is no rationally justified way of making the move. It is a matter of a leap of faith. Its occurrence is a miracle occasioned by the grace of God.[12] Understanding is what results from it, not what brings it about. The difficulty with this solution is that it leaves people basically irresponsible for what they believe through what they find to have happened in history. Whether they find God revealed in Jesus Christ is not up to their rational decision but to the work of grace upon them.

Another response denies that there really is a problem because both historical judgments and faith based on history are matters of interpretation of what happened. It is a mistake, therefore, to hold that they are logically distinct modes of understanding. Alan Richardson, for example, describes 'Christian theology' as 'a matter of the interpretation of history'[13] and maintains that in this respect there is a methodological unity in the 'knowledge of historical and theological truth'.[14] The unsatisfactoriness of this solution to the problem appears as soon as historical and theological treatments of an event are compared. Both of them are interpretations but they are distinct kinds of interpretation which seem to have very little, if anything, to do with each other. This can be seen if we consider interpretations of the death of Jesus. Historians will approach the reports of the event to discover what exactly happened – What would have been observed, when and where?, and why it happened – Who was involved and why did they act as they did? In the first place, therefore, they will be attempting to sort out the evidence to establish the 'facts'. There are, for example, problems in discovering the precise charge that was laid, the nature of the trials, the date on which the events occurred. Secondly the historians will try to discern the social, political, religious and economic factors and the personal motives that were involved in

bringing about what happened. As historians they will investigate
the issues in the same way as they would investigate the death of
Socrates or the execution of Charles I or the assassination of
President Kennedy. There are, furthermore, commonly recognized
procedures for checking their historical interpretations of the event
against the available evidence. Christian theologians have traditionally understood the event in a fundamentally different way.
They present it, for example, as disclosing God's judgment on sin,
or as revealing the limitlessness of divine love, or as performing 'a
full, perfect and sufficient sacrifice for the sins of the whole world',
or as making authentic life possible in practice. In seeing the event
in such a context and as concerned with establishing a relationship
between the human and the divine, theologians produce an
interpretation which is not verifiable by examining the records of
what happened at a certain time and place in the human past and
was observed by human beings. On reflection, then, the difference
between historical and theological interpretations emphasizes Lessing's second problem. What is significant is not that they are both
interpretations but that they are very different kinds of interpretation.

A third response argues that theological understanding of the
event of Jesus is justified by the resurrection. Biblical backing for
this solution is readily available. Paul, for instance, speaks of Jesus
as 'declared Son of God by a mighty act in that he rose from the
dead' (Romans 1.4). In contemporary theology Wolfhart Pannenberg affirms that 'Jesus' resurrection is the basis for the perception
of his divinity, that it means above all God's revelation in him'.[15] By
'the resurrection event' Jesus did not simply become what he
'previously had not been, but his pre-Easter claim was confirmed by
God' and his ministry was shown to have been 'divinely
authorized'.[16] Believers are thus provided by God with a sign which
both points to the religious significance of the history of Jesus and
justifies theological interpretations of it. Unfortunately, on examination, this solution also seems to be unsatisfactory. This is not
just because, as has been mentioned previously, it is far from clear
what the disciples are reporting in their records of the Easter
experience. The puzzling nature of the reports, though, do make
them of doubtful value for proving anything. What is more
significant for our purposes here is that the reference to the
resurrection as a justification for a theological interpretation of
Jesus' life in fact begs the question. The resurrection event as
understood by believers and theologians is a theological interpreta-

tion of some events or experiences which the earliest disciples encountered. Consequently it depends upon the justification of so interpreting events and cannot be offered as the justification for such a procedure. Bultmann, for example, holds that 'the resurrection itself is an object of faith'[17] and so is not to be regarded as 'an authenticating miracle on the basis of which a doubter can be secure in believing in Christ'.[18] Faith in the resurrection, rather, 'is nothing other than faith in the cross as the salvation event'[19] – the 'resurrection' in other words reports, not justifies, the disciples' conviction that Jesus is the one in and through whom God is disclosed.

Lessing's paper indicates a different solution to the problem. This holds that while historical events, or reports of them, may lead people to the Christian faith, that faith consists of truths whose status is intrinsically independent of past events. He suggests, in this respect, that if 'a very useful mathematical truth had been reached by the discoverer through an obvious fallacy',[20] the truth itself should not be denied – although, presumably, we would need a non-fallacious argument to prove it to be true. If this solution were adopted, the story of Jesus, as the heart of the Christian faith, would be important simply as a story. Its value would not depend upon its being an accurate report of the things that happened, any more than the value of the parable of the good Samaritan depends upon some such incident having actually occurred. Whether or not the reports were historically accurate would be incidental. The crucial issue would be whether reflection on that story did or did not evoke awareness of the ultimate truth about God and humanity. It should be noted, though, that this 'solution' cuts the Gordian knot by removing the historical element from the essence of Christian faith. However reasonable a position it may be in itself, to many Christians it is fundamentally unacceptable because it denies what they regard as a core conviction, namely, that God acts in history and did so supremely in Jesus. In that life 'the Word became flesh; he came to dwell among us' and the gospel is inescapably grounded in what was then seen, heard and handled.[21]

Lessing's suggestion, nevertheless, may indicate how the problem may be solved in a way that is more appropriate to the self-understanding of the Christian faith. In the first instance the historical reports are to be regarded as parables. Their significance does not lie in their historical accuracy. It lies in their ability to evoke an understanding of the divine-human relationship which is independently judged to be true. This understanding, however, includes views of God which suggest that it is appropriate to think of the divine as revealingly or savingly involved in the historical world. God's love, for example, is not the postulation of an abstract ideal but is to be regarded as an active care which affects the course of events for the benefit of humankind. Since, then, the events which evoked the initial insight into the nature and activity of God may be further interpreted as events in which the divine is so involved, it may be maintained that they are events which were influenced by God to produce the disclosure (or being about the state of affairs) which faith finds in them. If this be correct, the events did not have that effect purely accidentally. It was because of an involvement of the divine, although this could never have been perceived directly from observing the events as historical ones. The argument is circular in some respects and is complicated. It may, though, represent both how past events actually came to influence faith and a rationally coherent way of meeting Lessing's fundamental problem of the categorical distinction between judgments of history and judgments of faith.

The activity of God in history

This latter solution to the problem of how faith may be understood to be grounded in history includes the idea of divine influence on the course of history. It is an idea which is deeply rooted in theistic faith. Believers not only hold that the course of history (and therefore of human being as historical) has significance and meaning because it is the realization of a perfect purpose envisaged by God. They also find security in holding that the sequence of events is not out of divine control. Although what has happened has sometimes been horrifically evil, they have maintained that God can and sometimes has changed the pattern of events in order to exercise judgment and implement divine purposes in a particular situation. Which events, however, are held to be the locus of divine activity seems to be determined by the fact that they were of benefit to those who find God in them. The parting of the Red Sea was seen by the Israelites as a divine act but it probably was not similarly regarded by the Egyptians. The Bible contains a number of such claims. The Exodus, the Exile and the Return are presented as events in which God's agency was fundamental. John's Gospel claims that the life of Jesus is to be appreciated as an event in which 'God sent his son' into the world.[22] One of the arguments for the truth of Christianity which was popular in the eighteenth century was that its supposedly rapid spread from humble beginnings can only be explained by the intervention of God. The defeat of enemies and the success of conquests have often been ascribed, by the victors at least, to God's power implementing the divine will. It is comforting – God has 'the whole world in his hands'!

Claims about God acting in history, however, present problems when we try to make sense of what is supposed to be involved and to discover how such claims may be verified. In the first place, the claims are theologically suspect if they are to be taken as implying that God acts here and not there, to protect this group but not that, to effect his judgment on this person but not on that. It may be replied, of course, that how and where God acts is for God to decide. We must trust that it is always for the best. On the other hand the apparent selectiveness and puzzling non-intervention of the divine in certain situations raise doubts about whether this is a proper way to envisage the universal and perfect character of the divine. Secondly, it is apparent that what people judge to be results of divine agency depends upon their basic point of view. Jews are not likely to recognize 'the hand of God' in the spread of Christianity – but neither are Christians likely to see it in that of Islam. The danger is that while talk of the acts of God seems to point to events in which the divine is seen to be active and therefore those events are to be regarded as divinely endorsed, in practice it is rather the case that some events are held to be divinely supported because they accord with what is independently believed to be the will of God. Thus Schubert Ogden states that 'what is meant when we say that God acts *in* history is primarily that there are certain distinctively human words and deeds in which his characteristic action as Creator and Redeemer is appropriately re-presented or revealed'.[23]

A third problem arises when we consider how the agency of God is to be identified in historical events. The presence of other factors is recognized by the difference that they make – we decide, for example, whether or not it is likely that Churchill was involved in a particular decision by considering whether that decision has certain qualities which are characteristic of Churchill and not explicable apart from Churchill's activity. There seems, however, to be nothing which historians find explicable only if they include references to God's influence. Believers may claim that this is due to the methodological blindness of historians but the onus seems to be upon them to show the significance and justifiability of their claims about God's actions in historical events. One way in which this has been attempted is to hold that historical and theological ways of understanding events are complementary. They belong to different ways of looking at things (comparable, say, to psychological and physiological explanations of a person's behaviour) and each is valid in its own sphere of understanding. The problem with this view is how to show that the theological understanding adds anything to our appreciation of the events themselves and does not merely foist a vacuous pseudo-explanation on to the events or use them as ways of illustrating religious convictions. Another way is to suggest that theism, at least of the biblical form, is committed to seeing God as a kind of self within the world analogous to the dualistic view according to which our 'selves' are thought to 'inhabit' and express themselves through our bodies. Alternatively, and possibly more acceptably because it avoids the grosser notions of a 'ghost in the machine' which some philosophical critics of dualism find a stumbling-block, the cosmos may be viewed holistically as the embodiment of the divine selfhood whose reality is misunderstood when it is divided into mental and physical parts. So far as notions of the acts of God in history are concerned, the problem with this view, which Grace Jantzen has illuminatingly explored in *God's World, God's Body*,[24] is that either 'God' becomes a term which includes all agencies within the world (and so loses its significance as referring to a single purposer) or God is seen as the ultimate manipulator who, when so desirous, effects the divine will through unobservable controls. The former view of God is vacuous and the latter renders the divine unworshipful.

It may, though, be asked if the notion of individual acts of God influencing particular events for specific purposes is as necessary for theistic faith as has been widely presupposed. A more appropriate perception of God's activity may stress the utterly universal aspects of the divine being. God is not to be thought of as acting in one event more than or rather than in another but as directly present to and influencing all events. The divine is the omnipresent urge for creative love which is for ever disturbing the cosmos and, so far as we are concerned, rendering human being dissatisfying when it does not embody that totally accepting and responding love. Why is the divine activity, then, not more obvious? The reason is simply because it is universal. As A. N. Whitehead points out in *Adventures of Ideas*, the facts that are prominent in our consciousness are the superficial ones which are easily distinguishable from other superficial facts. The facts that are 'always securely there, barely discriminated, and yet inescapable' only flicker on the fringes of our consciousness.[25] They, nevertheless, are the universal states which ground and influence everything. The activity of God is perhaps most adequately understood as one of them.

Revelation

Consideration of the notion of acts of God in history raises the question of revelation. Although, according to Thomas Aquinas, some truths about God may in principle be discoverable by human reason, such discoveries are limited in his view to a few people who will only reach them after a long time and mixed with error. Other truths about God cannot be discerned by reason. Consequently, to make the former ones readily and accurately available and the latter ones known at all, God reveals them. Some theologians, such as Karl Barth, are more radical in their doubts about the competence of human reason in matters of divinity. They deny that any authentic knowledge of God may be attained through human reason. All must be revealed. Only thus do we properly acknowledge the sovereign freedom and otherness of God. Another argument, advanced from the religious perspective, holds that whatever may be the case with intellectual knowledge about God's nature in principle, awareness of God's personal mode of activity or the personal relationship of faith in God is only possible through divine self-revelation. What, though, is revelation?

Traditionally revelation has been understood as being a predominantly verbal matter. There are many biblical precedents for such a view. In Exodus the statement of the Decalogue begins 'God spoke, and these were his words',[26] The first chapter of Isaiah is typical of the prophetic announcement when it says 'Hark . . . for the Lord has spoken', 'Hear the word of the Lord', 'Come now, let us argue it out, says the Lord' and 'This therefore is the word of the Lord'.[27] In the story of the transfiguration the teaching of Jesus receives God's endorsement when 'out of the cloud came a voice: "This is my Son, my Beloved; listen to him"'.[28] Hebrews begins by affirming that whereas previously God 'spoke . . . in fragmentary and varied fashion through the prophets', he has now 'spoken to us in the Son'.[29] The result of such testimony is that revelation was considered to have a propositional form and the Bible was considered either to contain the record of God's narrative revelations or to be itself the medium of revelation.

Claims to present what God has revealed, however, need to be justified. The Bible itself warns us that there are false prophets as well as authentic ones. Using, therefore, the model of credentials by which the status of a messenger or a message may be verified, Christian theologians have put forward various arguments to justify their claims to a divine origin for the Christian revelation. Among the more popular in earlier times were the arguments from miracle, prophecy and the propagation of the gospel. In each of these cases it was argued that the Christian revelation was accompanied by actions which could only have been effected by God – the miracles which Jesus performed and the miracle of his resurrection, the prophecies which he made and were later fulfilled, the miracles worked by the disciples, and the power of Christianity allegedly to conquer the world from its obscure beginnings – were all seen as the divine way of endorsing the Christian faith with its essential component of claims about divine revelation in Jesus and, perhaps, through the Holy Spirit after Jesus' death. During the eighteenth century, however, it became obvious to many 'enlightened' minds that these arguments were fundamentally flawed – it did not seem possible to find a satisfactory definition of 'miracle' or convincing evidence for them as being more than unusual events, the supposed prophecies were either unspecific or suspected of being after the event, the spread of Christianity was perhaps not that amazing after all. If miracles were acceptable as a legitimate argument in principle, it was found that they could be cited to justify contradictory claims to revealed insight. As a result other arguments were advanced which rested upon the internal character of the revelation, especially as found in the teaching of Jesus. That teaching was held, for example, to be superior to what any human being could come to without divine aid. Jesus was held to have an exemplary character which warranted the truthfulness of what he said. Since his mode of behaviour was such that he cannot be regarded as mad or an impostor, he must be whom he proclaimed he was. These arguments, however, also turned out to be less than convincing. If we could recognize the superiority of Jesus' teaching, was revelation needed? Could not a sincere person be mistaken? Biblical criticism, furthermore, has indicated how the teaching of Jesus as given in the gospels is influenced both by contemporary forms of understanding which are no longer tenable and by the interests of those who recorded it.

Largely as a result of the difficulties with a propositional view of revelation, many modern theologians have adopted the view that revelation is given in and through events. The Bible – especially for

Christian theology, the New Testament – is accordingly seen as the record of the revelatory events and of faith's recognition of their significance. Jesus' teaching is thus important as a part of his whole life and it is that which is held to manifest the divine nature and will – as, in a large way, does the history of the whole people of God.

Two problems arise with such a view of the locus of revelation. In the first place, how are the events of Jesus' life (or the total event of that life) to be interpreted as revelatorily significant? In the case of the story of Jesus at the well of Sychar,[30] does it show his humanity (he was 'tired' and thirsty), his percipience (he was aware of the person's character), his need (he could not draw water for himself), or his significance (he is the Messiah), and what is its proper revelatory importance for us today? This question is hard to answer. Throughout Christian history preachers and theologians have used incidents in the life of Jesus to press home various points but it is not clear how any particular use is to be justified as the correct one. On the other hand if it is accepted that a story can be used to express various revelatory messages, in what sense is it held to be revelatory? Its value seems to depend on its interpreters. What happens with individual incidents in the life of Jesus applies also the understanding of his life as a whole. As has already been mentioned, studies of the life of Jesus have presented a wide range of portraits of the one who is to be regarded as the disclosure of the divine. Norse converts rejoiced in a Jesus who came not 'to bring peace but a sword' and 'to set fire to the earth';[31] Anselm saw him as providing the perfect satisfaction for God's honour; for Abelard he presented converting love; in the eighteenth century he emerged in some quarters as a teacher of sound morality; some Victorian portraits made him out to be a figure who would have been quite acceptable in polite drawing-rooms; Barth saw him as a figure of judgment; Teilhard de Chardin as a cosmically creative being; for some recent decades he has been hard to distinguish from the latest revolutionary cult-figure; for John Robinson he was 'the man for others' and for Küng's *On Being a Christian* in effect the odd man out. It is very confusing for those who look to revelation for clear guidance for their faith today.

The second fundamental problem facing the view that revelation is given in events has two major forms. One of them takes up the distinction which philosophers have discussed with reference to the so-called 'naturalistic fallacy'. This holds that it is not possible to infer a moral obligation ('ought') from a bare statement of what is the case ('is'). It is a problem which will be reviewed later when we consider the relationship between faith and morality. As applied to the question of revelation it challenges the validity of deriving divine commands from historical events. The other form of the problem is one that has been discussed earlier in this chapter – the problem of bridging the gap between reports of past events and insight into the divine. Further consideration of this issue suggests that the distinction between 'natural' and 'revealed' theology, which is frequently made in Christian thought, is not a distinction in kind. This is not because all genuine theology is 'revealed', as Barthian thought would maintain, but because supposedly 're-vealed' insights turn out, on examination, to have basically the same structure as those of so-called 'natural' theology. In both cases believers or theologians consider a range of evidence found in the observable world, either of nature or of history or of both, and become aware in it or through it of disclosures of the fundamental character of reality in the nature and will of God. These disclosures, however, are not to be verified by further consideration of that evidence, for they go beyond its ascertain-able character as recording states or events in the empirical world. They are justified by showing that the disclosures themselves provide an understanding of the divine which is internally consis-tent, coheres with reality as we find it, is universal and appropriate to that which is intrinsically the proper object of worship. The difference between 'natural' and 'revealed' theology, then, is not a logical one: it basically refers to the extensiveness and type of evidence which is used to evoke the disclosures. There is no way in which theologians can avoid the demands of truth-testing for their fundamental claims by reference to 'revelation'. What they take to be revealed is their interpretation of events and they must justify it.

Such a view of revelation may be judged to be unsatisfactory because it apparently omits any reference to divine initiative in providing revelation. In contrast it may then be asserted that the verb 'to reveal' as used in religious contexts describes an inten-tional activity by God, not the kind of situation in which David unwittingly 'reveals' his attitude by an unpremeditated gesture. We have already noticed how difficult it is to locate divine agency in specific instances and that it may be more plausible to think of that agency as a general influence on the course of events. Even if this is so, it is possible to regard that general influence as luring individuals to actualize in their being the creativity of love which constitutes the divine being. If individuals may be so lured, it is presumably also at least possible to hold that a particular individual has so fully responded to that lure that the character of that individual's life offers a normative revelation of the divine being since it incorporates total empathy with the divine love.

The divine initiative in revelation, furthermore, cannot be restricted to influence on the events in which the revelation is perceived. For a revelation to occur through an event, someone must perceive the revelatory significance of that event. Thomas Gray makes the point, although perhaps in a sentimental way which has now lost some of its original force, when he writes

> Full many a gem of purest ray serene
> The dark unfathom'd caves of ocean bear:
> Full many a flower is born to blush unseen,
> And waste its fragrance on the desert air.[32]

It is a truth which authors have to recognize when they see piles of remaindered volumes or visit the dusty depositories of great libraries! The life of Jesus would have had no revealing significance if he had made no lasting disciples or if they had not eventually begun to perceive the peculiar status of the one whom they were following and to communicate their insights to others. If the Christian faith is based upon the event of Jesus as the Christ, it is equally based upon the recognition that Jesus is the Christ. So far, then, as divine initiative in revelation is to be expected, it may be looked for in the perception of the significance of the revelatory event as well as (or even instead of) in the bringing about of the event itself. What is important for Christian understanding of God and creation is not some claim that the historical event of Jesus of Nazareth was somehow divinely engineered and manipulated but the perception that through considering that life we may attain insights into the concrete reality of the divine-human relationship.

Why, though, is the event of Jesus so significant? Most people in the world find the focus of their living faith elsewhere. So far as it is a religious faith, some find that focus in a tradition of teaching and practice which has no recognizable origin. Others, such as Buddhists, Jews, Muslims and Sikhs, find it in instruction given by (or through) some more or less historically identifiable figures. Christians, however, while sharing a general theistic understanding with others, are distinctive by their commitment to Jesus – and not simply to the supposed teachings of Jesus. It is the whole event of Jesus that for Christians is the key to the authentic self-understanding which is faith. Why, though, do they pick on Jesus? In most cases the answer in the first instance is cultural. Jesus of Nazareth happens to be the person whose life-story provides the focus for faith in the culture in which they find themselves. If they had been born into another culture, their faith would most probably have been formed by reference to something or someone else. Because of their background, however, their theistic beliefs are moulded by Christian applications of the story of Jesus – and it is God as so conceived that their atheistic co-culturalists deny.

This cultural answer, however, does not satisfy. While reminding us that there are social and historical factors which determine why most of those who are Christians have come to be such rather than Buddhists, Hindus, Jews or Muslims, the question 'Why Jesus?' presses the matter beyond such accidental issues. It wants to know why Jesus (or the story of Jesus) initially attained that significance and whether, in a multi-cultural and multi-faith world such as we find ourselves to be in, that significance can survive critical scrutiny today. The convincing answer to this question does not lie fundamentally in claims about what Jesus did or taught – nor in reports about what happened to him. The convincing answer is an existential and pragmatic one. Jesus' significance ultimately resides in the effect which he – or the story of him – produced in some of his followers and which has continued to the present as others have been told about him and thereby found themselves captivated by a faith focussed on him. A rough outline of this answer to the question 'Why Jesus?' starts by pointing to the witness of the first disciples that, in some way or another, they found through their contact with Jesus, a quality or qualities of experience which may variously be referred to as 'salvation', 'wholeness', 'fullness of being', 'abundant life' or 'deep harmony and rightness'. It was a profoundly satisfying experience which they did not find, at least not so completely, elsewhere. In order to express what they found in or through Jesus as much as to try to make sense of it, they took up various models from divine and human relationships which were later developed into doctrines of atonement ('at-one-ment'). While some of these ways of apprehending the quality of life made possible through Jesus were generally useful in the cultural situation in which they arose, in other contexts they may seriously misrepresent it, especially if they are misunderstood as literal descriptions. It is important, therefore, to see that they point to and their significance is justified by an existential reality in human experience. The significance of Jesus, both when people first were attracted to follow him and today, is that through him people find that human being becomes finally and profoundly whole and satisfying. The contemporary answer to the question 'Why Jesus?', if it is to be significant for human living today, must therefore be in effect the confession which Peter is recorded as having given when Jesus asked the disciples if they were going to give up, 'Lord, to whom shall we go? Your words are words of eternal life' – except that in the post-Easter situation, it is more easily recognizable that it is a response to the whole event of Jesus and not just his teaching that is needed.

If this existential and pragmatic assertion of the significance of Jesus is accepted, five points may be seen to follow from it. First, Jesus is held to be the Christ because and so far as people find 'salvation' through him. If he ceased to have such an effect, he would cease to be Christ – that is, the one on whom authentic faith focusses. Secondly, claims about Jesus' own person arise from attempts to develop and make further sense of the understanding of his effect on human life as expressed in the various atonement models. They are thus to be seen as possible implications of certain ways of apprehending that effect and not as necessarily significant apart from those ways. Thirdly, the way in which the event of Jesus and the figure of Jesus has been (and still is) open to so many different interpretations may, paradoxically, be one of the strongest arguments for affirming that Jesus is correctly understood to be the Christ. It shows that the multi-faceted character of the story of Jesus allows it to provide the authentic Christ for the distinctive needs of different cultures. Fourthly, it is quite compatible with such a view of Jesus as the Christ to hold that what is found in and through him by Christians may be found by others in and through other figures. As John Hick has suggested in *God and the Universe of Faiths*, there may have been different moments of divine revelation to different peoples,[33] especially considering the fact that not only do the basic self-understandings of people vary according to their culture but also because until relatively recent times a revelation in one culture would not have been effectively communicable to the members of another. Fifthly, the possibility of there being other figures and traditions which provide foci of insight into the divine does not show that the faith, the understanding and the wholeness found by Christians through Jesus as the Christ may not be normative for human existence generally.

Chapter 6

Faith, God and the Natural World

The natural world to which we belong is increasingly found by scientific investigations to be composed of strange and surprising forces. The more we probe beyond the scales of magnitude of which our sense experience is aware, the more we realize that things are not what they seem to be. There are great differences between the processes represented by quarks and bosons, by the genetic molecule DNA and the biochemical metabolic activities shared by all organisms, by quasars and black holes, and the familiar, reasonably orderly nature which we observe with its grasses and cows and milk, its rains and rivers, its apples and bees, its melting and boiling points, its predictable sun-rises and star positions. Scientific perceptions of the former orders of reality, furthermore, are changing rapidly. Whereas many theologians still consider it valuable to review, for example, fourth-century debates about Arianism and even more ancient views of the nature of God, a biochemist will expect an article published five years ago to be out-of-date and feel frustrated if the current research project has not opened up new discoveries in the past six months.

Both the rate of change and the quantity of information produced by current scientific thought is overwhelming. It is questionable how far our imagination can cope with them to produce a coherent and comprehensive understanding of reality. At times it seems that we are being showered with the separated pieces of what we expect to be an enormous jig-saw but we have to discover whether they do fit together and, if so, how and to form what picture. The situation is complicated by the fact that the pieces keep being changed and that we are told by some theoretical critics (for example, by those influenced by Kantian epistemology) that they are partly shaped by our own intellectual structures. If, therefore, we ever did manage to put together a picture from the pieces, we cannot be sure that it would tell us about the character of reality in itself rather than about the character of our thinking processes as they investigate reality.

Facing the situation in contemporary science and, in many cases, acknowledging their incapacity to comprehend what it is making known, believers and theologians may feel tempted to claim, with relief, that it is none of their business. Theology deals with God and, particularly, with the relationship between the human and the divine; the natural sciences investigate the empirical world. They belong, so it may be argued, to distinct domains of understanding and therefore do not (or should not) interfere with each other. Such a view of the relationship between science and religion has its attractions and we shall have to consider it in a little more detail later. It is not, however, an obviously satisfactory one when it is realized that theistic faith is generally understood to involve claims about the world.

The natural, empirical realm which scientists study is the same world which believers speak about as the product of divine creativity and in which many of them hold that the divine is active. Hymns provide some good examples of this aspect of traditional theistic faith. John Keble, for example, sees the natural world as a 'book' of 'heavenly truth':

> The works of God above, below,
> Within us and around,
> Are pages in that book, to show
> How God Himself is found.

According to Joseph Addison the 'spangled heavens' proclaim their 'great Original', Isaac Watts holds that 'clouds arise and tempests blow' at God's command, and John Wesley affirms

> Father, 'tis Thine each day to yield
> Thy children's wants a fresh supply;
> Thou cloth'st the lilies of the field,
> And hearest the young ravens cry.

Similar, if less poetic, views are to be found in the works of scientists and theologians. At the end of the seventeenth century, for example, John Ray published *The Wisdom of God Manifested in the Works of the Creation* in which he uses his extensive knowledge of the natural world to illustrate how it reflects the qualities of its divine Creator.[1] Just over a century later William Paley suggested in his *Natural Theology* that troubled believers should inspect an earwig since 'the hinges' in its wings and 'the joints of its antennae' are clear evidence of the care and benevolence of the Creator of all things.[2]

Such comments, however, belong to an era of understanding which is no longer credible. Although believers may utter such ideas in their worship and uncritically revel in the comforting picture of reality which they represent, the truth about the natural world, so far as we allow that scientists have been able to perceive it, is chillingly different. What is to be done? Have believers who accept the findings of modern science to become schizophrenics whose religious faith affirms a fantasy world which is cosy and supportive (an attempt to recreate the loving embrace of mummy) but whose scientific knowledge affirms an actual world which is unplanned and uncaringly neutral about personal welfare? It is hardly a recipe for a justifiable faith.

The problem posed by apparent incompatibilities between what faith has traditionally affirmed about the world as creation and current scientific understanding of it as empirically observed is an issue which came to the fore in theological discussions in the nineteenth century although it had earlier expressions in arguments over such matters as geocentricity and miraculous interventions. During the last century it became clear that what believers maintained about creation, largely on the basis of their reading of the Bible, clashed with what scientists were concluding from their investigations. The 'Genesis v. Geology' and 'Genesis v. Evolution' debates, with a few exceptions which remind us how some believers struggle to live in a dead world and refuse resurrection to new life, are now generally perceived to belong to the past. They had some value, though, in that they helped to establish a re-appraisal of the biblical materials which enhanced rather than evacuated our appreciation of their significance as religious documents. There are, however, other potential or actual conflicts between theistic beliefs and scientific understanding which pose important threats to the former. When, for example, Jacques Monod argued in *Chance and Necessity* (1974) that the processes of evolution are the product of unintentional genetic variations, he considered that his conclusions showed the untenability of any doctrine of divine superintendence.[3] Arthur Peacocke in *Creation and the World of Science* (1979),[4] Charles Birch and John Cobb in *The Liberation of Life* (1981)[5] and David Bartholomew in *God of Chance* (1984),[6] among others, have suggested how Monod's thesis might be challenged in ways that both do justice to current scientific thought and affirm the significance of theistic faith. We shall note how they seek to do this a little later in this chapter.

The relation of scientific theories and theological doctrines

Underlying the various debates over the clash between this religious doctrine and that scientific theory is the primary methodological issue of identifying how such doctrines and theories may be and should be related to each other. Various answers to that question have been offered. We shall comment briefly on six of them, starting with those that hold that scientific and theological (or religious) statements about the world are, to a significant degree, directly comparable because they belong to a common logic.

The first way of seeing the relationship between scientific and theological statements maintains that they are expressing the same truths about the world but in different forms of expression. Their differences are therefore only superficial. When correctly analysed they agree. It is feasible to hold, for example, that when Matthew (aged five) says that the liquid came up the straw 'because I sucked it' and Robert (aged sixteen) says that the effect was because 'Matthew drew air off the top of the straw, creating a partial vacuum which resulted in atmospheric pressure on the liquid in the vessel around the straw forcing liquid into the straw until the air pressures on top of the liquid inside and outside the straw were in equilibrium', they are expressing the same truth but using different ways of putting it. Similarly it might be (and has been) asserted that what the scientist reports about the appearance of the species and what we find recorded in the Bible are making the same point but in different ways and using distinct frames of reference which draw attention to different features of the process. Such attempts to equate scientific and religious claims, especially when the latter are derived from insights attained at a much earlier period in human thought, may be acceptable in some cases but are liable to be rejected in many other cases – and rightly so – when it is appreciated that the equation requires a radical reinterpretation of one or other claim. While, for example, only a pedant is going to dispute that when Jesus spoke of the sun 'rising' (cf. Matthew 5.45), he was expressing the same basic awareness as we might make in terms of the earth revolving in relation to the sun, it is hard to credit the claim that what the author of Genesis 1.27f. had in mind in describing the creation of human beings is basically what a contemporary biologist has in mind in describing the genetic developments leading to human beings.

A second view of the relationship between scientific theories and religious claims recognizes that they are not seeking to maintain the same points but, perhaps optimistically, holds that in certain fundamental instances the former both support the latter and need the latter for their own intellectual completion. Isaac Newton, for example, considered that while gravity and the first law of motion explain the greater part of the orbits of the planets, there are some irregularities which indicate continual divine interference. The orderliness of the system, then, witness to the skill of the creator and the exceptions to it witness to the reality of God as an active agent within it. In this way both what science makes sense of and what it cannot explain are held to support theistic faith. A similar kind of argument was used by Pius XII in 1951 when he claimed that cosmological investigations have confirmed 'with that conclusiveness which is characteristic of physical proofs' that the universe is contingent, was created 'in time' and hence is derived from a creator who, with a 'primordial *Fiat lux*' brought forth 'from nothing a sea of light and radiation'.[7] The problem with such arguments, as Newton's case indicates, is that the supposed support may turn out to be illusory. On the one hand the claim that God 'explains' the orderliness (or, in the case of Pius XII, the 'big bang') is vacuous – the reference to God in such cases may seem to refer to another, prior cause but in fact this 'cause' adds nothing to our understanding of what we are already aware of, namely, that events occur in this way. On the other hand, the claim that God's activity is needed to compensate for eccentricities is refuted when natural explanations are found for what occurs – in the case of the solar system by the postulation and discovery of other planets.

A third view sees scientific and religious views as making comparable claims but ones which, in some cases at least, are incompatible with each other. Since, however, it is a fundamental principle of logic – and of meaning – that contradictory propositions cannot be simultaneously true, it follows, where such conflicts occur between the claims of science and of religion, that one of them at least must be false. This was the principle that lay behind many of the battles between science and religion in the nineteenth century. The protagonists agreed, for example, that the doctrine that animals have developed over a long evolutionary process and the doctrine that each species was made as we now find it by divine command cannot both be true. Since they contradict each other, to hold one entails rejecting the other. Whereas, however, in the eighteenth century a John Hutchinson, in his *Moses's Principia*, might assert the supremacy of the divinely revealed Bible over the observations and calculations of Newtonian science,[8] today it is generally accepted that where conflicts arise between scientific and religious doctrines, it is the former that generally seem to be able to offer the more convincing evidence and arguments. Although it is a mistake to regard every latest scientific doctrine as necessarily correct – science advances too rapidly for such security – it will be by means of other scientific arguments that scientific claims will be effectively rebutted. In a relationship of conflict, therefore, religious faith is likely to emerge as the loser.

A fourth view maintains that there can be no genuine conflict – or mutual support – between scientific and religious doctrines because they belong to parallel but distinct ways of explanation, each covering the whole of reality. Each of these ways of explanation potentially offers a total understanding of what is the case. To illustrate this point, we might cite the way in which a behavioural psychologist might present a complete understanding of Katharine's conduct by reference to such factors as heredity, social environment, educational conditioning, past experience and the such like, in comparison to the way in which a moralist might claim to offer an equally complete explanation by reference to her moral values, sense of obligation, judgments on influencing factors, and personal freedom of choice. According to this view each 'explanation' depends upon presuppositions about intelligibility which form distinct structures of understanding. Consequently there can be no way of comparing them with each other and each may properly claim to be 'true' in its own intellectual domain. Similarly scientific and religious ways of understanding are incomparable but may each claim to be both true and complete according to their own way of perceiving matters. One difficulty with this position is that it is ultimately disturbing to be told that the one world in fact is *totally* explicable in utterly distinct ways. It seems in that case we are driven to accept that we are in a schizophrenic situation where we inhabit different intellectual worlds which do not merge. A more fundamental criticism is that on examination it is highly doubtful whether any of the supposed total explanations can claim to be satisfyingly complete. Their attempts at totality in practice seem to involve ignoring or treating inadequately points that other ways of understanding emphasize.

A fifth approach to the relationship between scientific and

religious doctrines stresses the inadequacy of either as a total explanation and asserts that they are to be seen as complementary positions. Each of them, so far as it is valid, identifies a particular aspect of the truth and total understanding requires that both of them be taken into account. Just as a total description of Robert involves physical and moral assessments, each of which is arrived at independently, so a total understanding of the natural world involves both claims about its physical structure and claims about its significance. A popular way of putting this position is that science answers questions like 'What happens?' and 'How does it happen?' in terms of empirically observable factors, and religion deals with questions such as 'Why does it happen?' and 'What is its purpose and end?'. Although there is much to be said for this approach, it is not without serious problems. It runs into difficulties, for instance, if answers to (scientific) questions about the structure of reality conflict with the answers to (religious) questions about its purpose. This would occur, for example, if science were held to show that all events, including human decisions, occurred according to strict causal necessity while religion held that the purpose of reality, in part, was to allow human beings to develop as creative and morally responsible free agents. The positions would then appear to provide contradictory rather than complementary doctrines. A fundamental methodological objection to this approach, furthermore, is that the attempt to keep the positions from clashing may result in religious claims being regarded as wholly about values and meanings and only scientific claims as being about what is the case. Such an analysis might help to prevent the respective doctrines clashing (although, as the previous objection has shown, it would not necessarily succeed in this) but it would do it at the cost of eliminating an essential element in theistic faith – namely, that God is the ontological ultimate (i.e., the being on which all else finally depends but which is not dependent on anything for existence) and that claims about God are about what is ultimately and universally the case in reality.

The five attempts to identify the relationship between scientific doctrines and religious theories which have been mentioned so far have presupposed that these two ways of understanding are to be regarded as initially independent of each other. As a result the problem of the relationship is one of mediating between two developed systems of thought. The presupposition may be justified by pointing to basic differences in what are generally regarded as the sources of their respective insights and in the logical status of their conclusions. In the latter respect the basic truths about divine existence are necessary and universal while scientific investigations deal with the contingent and relative. A sixth way of looking at the relationship between science and theistic faith rejects this presupposition. While it accepts that scientists do and should go about their studies without considering their significance for religious beliefs, it points out that believers are not only – nor, probably, even primarily – interested in very general truths about God's being as the ultimate ground and goal of all things. They are much more interested in what God does and how God is related to them. So far as the natural world is concerned, this means that they are concerned to perceive how the divine ultimacy affects how things actually are. What difference, for example, does the reality of God make to what has happened, is happening and will happen in nature? To answer that question, however, believers and theologians need to take into account what scientists report to be the nature of things as well as what the more traditional sources of religious insight suggest. Only so will their understanding have credibility. Otherwise what they purport to discern about the ultimate meaning and purpose of all things as grounded in the divine will be liable to appear as an illusion which is incompatible with the observed character of reality.

What this sixth approach does is to take seriously as a methodological principle the status of theology as 'queen of the sciences'. This status does not mean, as it has been erroneously thought in the past, that theology has privileged sources of insight which warrant it in 'lording' it over all other ways of understanding. What it does mean is that theology, because it is concerned with God, is committed to discerning how all valid insights into the nature of things combine to produce a single harmonious story which links together the Creator and the created. Theology, in other words, is to be seen as engaged in the task of achieving overall understanding. Hence scientific discoveries are to be regarded as part of the data which it has to examine critically and then seek to incorporate in that overall understanding, together with other data provided by more commonly accepted sources of religious insight.

God and the world

Consideration of the doctrine of creation highlights some of the problems which face theology as it seeks to produce such an integrated understanding. In the first place, it cannot avoid attempting to develop such a doctrine. The intrinsic ultimacy of the divine means that theism cannot coherently entertain a notion of God that does not include, at least implicitly, notions of being the ground and goal of all things. Although the actual character of the relationship may be hard – or impossible – to discern, theism entails that all things depend ultimately upon God for their being and significance. The doctrine of creation, hence, involves both ontological and valuative claims about God. Secondly, though, a credible doctrine of creation must be appropriate to what we are aware of as the character of the cosmos. Too often religious remarks about God's creativity apparently reflect a pre-Darwinian, even a pre-Copernican view of nature. The divine creative activity is talked about as if God were like a child modelling with plasticine – except that the divine skills were somewhat greater in that it could produce living creatures. The anthropocentricity of human understanding may be identified as the selfishness which is at the root of sin but it dominates most doctrines of creation. Human being is generally presented as the highest form of creation ('in the image of God') and as that to which all the rest is subservient ('master over all thy creatures' – Psalm 8.6). One of the great contributions of scientific thought may be that it has curbed this human pride. Since the time of Copernicus humanity has had to recognize that its home is not the centre of the universe, since that of Darwin that its nature is part of the animal world, since that of Marx and Freud that its rationality is subject to social and subconscious conditioning.

Today the search for a plausible doctrine of creation is confronted with the awesome task of discerning how God is to be perceived as creator of a universe whose extent is mysterious and in which earth is a planet circling a rather ordinary star in an undistinguished place in one of a huge number of galaxies. Earth, furthermore, has only finite resources and will eventually become barren because of developments in the sun, even if it has not previously become uninhabitable for human beings because of the exhaustion of its means of sustaining life, the evolution of a doom virus, or nuclear holocaust. In addition to coping with the extent of the universe, a mind-blowing problem in itself, a plausible doctrine of creation has to show how notions of divine activity and purpose can be significantly used in relation to what we know (or think we know) of the physical, chemical and genetic processes through which things have evolved into their present forms.

It is not clear whether our theological imagination can produce the understanding which is required. If it cannot manage it, though, theistic faith is jeopardized. So far as its understanding seeks to go beyond formal and abstract (and so rather empty) concepts of God, it cannot find it satisfactory to discover that the material significance of an essential component of the doctrine of God has to be consigned to the realm of mysteries beyond human grasp – a realm whose supposed contents may be illusions as much as realities for all that we can determine. On the other hand, where attempts are made to produce a plausible doctrine of creation, the result will be a vision of God which is very different from the wonder-worker who made everything as willed in a busy week in 4004 BC. In *Creation and the World of Science*, for example, Arthur Peacocke suggests that God is to be seen as a creator who constitutes the universe so that the randomness of molecular events has the biological consequence that the potentialities of the universe are eventually actualized in myriad ramifications through the operation of chance within the structures of necessity.[9] In this way God enjoys the unpredictable dance of creation as it realizes its possibilities and produces, on this planet, pterodactyls and humming-birds, influenza viruses and primroses, human beings and hippopotamuses – with ducks and penguins. Basically, though, the divine lets it happen rather than controls its processes. David Bartholomew, however, has recently argued in *God of Chance*, on the basis of the mathematics of stochastic processes (i.e. 'processes which develop in time, according to probabilistic, rather than deterministic, laws'), that the presence of chance in the processes of the universe is compatible with belief in the ultimate purposiveness and directionality of reality as an expression of the creative will of God. This is because mathematical analysis has shown, perhaps surprisingly to some, that 'a process whose law of development is a random one can have an entirely predictable outcome'.[10] According to this model, therefore, the divine could envisage what kind of things would eventually emerge from the freedom of cosmic and biological processes but not by what particular way. A third option which deserves consideration is that offered by theologians who have been influenced by the philosophical insights of Whitehead and Hartshorne. Although it is not possible in this study to explain how they come to the process view of reality, they perceive it as composed of discrete events, each having a brief duration and then being succeeded by a subsequent event which massively inherits the qualities of its predecessor but also has minute freedom to change that form in relation to possibilities presented to it by the divine. According to this model, then, the divine is continuously involved in the processes of reality but in a way that respects the integrity and appropriate autonomy of each entity. The processes are 'lured' towards the optimum goal rather than coerced.[11]

Doctrines of creation such as those which have just been referred to are principally concerned with divine creativity in relation to the ongoing processes of cosmic and terrestrial evolution. How, though, did the processes start? Classically theologians have spoken of God creating 'out of nothing' (ex nihilo). This notion, though, is misunderstood when it is interpreted either in terms of God being in effect a cosmic conjuror who magically produces a cosmos without the aid of a hat or in terms of the 'nothing' being a formless plasticine which God then shaped. It is also a mistake to equate the creation out of nothing with the primal 'big bang' of the currently preferred cosmological theory. The latter is an extrapolation backwards from the present expanding character of the cosmos to a theoretical point where all its constituents were packed into a singularity from which it erupted. Where the cosmic firework appeared from, however, may literally be a case of 'God only knows' but it is not made any more – or less – understandable by bringing in God. What references to 'creation out of nothing' affirm theologically is that the cosmos is not self-explanatory; that there is not an ultimate pluralism in reality but that all things ultimately depend upon God; that God is ontologically prior to the cosmos; that creation is an intentional act and so has a purpose; that the cosmos is neither an accident in the divine activity nor an automatic emanation from the divine. How these claims are to be linked with the actual genesis of everything is profoundly obscure in the present state of human understanding. Two things, though, may be recognized. The first is that theistic faith looks for the final explanation of things in personal rather than abstract terms. It thus seeks a satisfying story for reality by grounding it in values and purposes rather than in mere descriptions of physical relationships. Secondly, it is probably theistically mistaken to conceive of a beginning to the creation. While the current cosmic epoch may have a calculable first moment, the combination of everlastingness with love and aesthetic enjoyment as essential attributes of the divine imply that there can be no beginning and no end to divine creativity. This does not mean that God must always have been the ground of the present cosmic order but that God cannot coherently be envisaged as being without some creation to be the object of divine love and a source of divine joy and appreciation. The need for a 'beginning' to creation may be a consequence of our intellectual inability to achieve a satisfactory conception of an everlasting process -- as similarly may be our need for a sense of its ending rather than of a proper insight into the divine mode of active being.

How, though, is the ongoing relationship between God and the world to be envisaged? There are basically three possibilities which we may call classical theism (or deism), pantheism, and panentheism (or proper theism). According to the first of these, classical theism or deism, God and the world are to be conceived not only as radically distinct from each other but also as characterized by contrary qualities. God is predominantly thought of as absolute and unchanging. The eternity of the divine is a timelessness in which all events are simultaneously immediately present. The perfection of the divine is a state of completion which can never be affected by anything that happens. In contrast the world is marked by relativity, change, temporality, imperfection and the mutual interactions of its parts. Such a fundamental distinction between God and the world may at first seem to pay proper respect to the intrinsic otherness of the divine but, as we shall consider further in the next chapter, it results in a concept of God that is at odds with religious faith. In particular it denies any real, internal relations with the world in God. A being which is totally absolute, unchanging and impassible cannot be thought of as one who has intentions for, deliberately creates, acts toward, is aware of, and responds to the world in which we find ourselves. The divine on this view is an utterly transcendent absolute which is discontinuous with the world and which may affect what occurs in it only as an unaware, uncaring value that unwittingly attracts towards itself the contingent processes of the world.

Pantheism basically identifies God and the world. Its way of recognizing the absolute sovereignty of God is to deny that anything may be genuinely real which is other than God. The term 'God' in effect then becomes a cipher for the sum-total of the states or processes which constitute the world. The result is that either the world is seen as an emanation of the divine and therefore its constituents as having no real autonomy, or 'God' is denied to have any individual self-consciousness and therefore cannot coherently be conceived as having a will independent of the world. In neither case is it possible to produce a significant doctrine of creation as a matter of a relationship between God and the world: according to pantheism either God is all and there is no world to be created as a distinct reality or the world is all and there is no separate entity, God, to create it. Pantheism, however, should not be lightly dismissed. Irritating as it may be for classical theists, it arguably draws out the implications of their view of the absoluteness and total lack of any potentiality in the divine.

The term 'panentheism' is less familiar. It was coined by K. C. F. Krause early in the nineteenth century and has been used by Charles Hartshorne in contemporary philosophical theology to describe his analysis of what is required in a concept of God that is to be both philosophically and religiously appropriate to the divine. While, according to panentheism, the cosmos is ultimately dependent upon God (for God's existence is necessary and the cosmos is contingent), all that happens in the cosmos is influenced by and experienced by God. The divine is not an impassible, unchanging, unmoved and unmovable absolute but an actively caring love which participates fully in all events. God, therefore, is to be seen as embracing all things in the divine being. As a consequence nothing that is ever achieved is finally lost since it is everlastingly preserved in the divine awareness. At the same time, while the divine consciousness is totally aware of all that occurs, the divine is also aware of itself as a distinct centre of consciousness which can make decisions about what happens in the cosmos and seek to influence (while not determining) the other entities which constitute it in ways that are consistent with the purposes of creation. The result is a concept of God which recognizes that the divine has internal as well as external relations with the cosmos – that is to say, is affected by as well as affects what happens in it.[12] It is a concept which, far more than those of classical theism and pantheism, accords with the understanding of God central to biblical witnesses and underlying Christian faith in the loving Father of all – a God who, as Gordon D. Kaufman puts it, is thought of as 'personal or agential in character'[13] or, in less obviously anthropomorphic language, is 'the personifying symbol' (i.e. a word which represents something in personal terms) 'of that cosmic activity which has created our humanity and continues to press for its full realization'.[14] The panentheistic analysis of God, furthermore, provides the most accurate expression of the concept of God which has been intended in what is discussed here as 'theistic' faith and 'theistic' understanding. In effect, therefore, 'panentheism' is the technical term for what has been and will continue to be called 'theism'.

The intimate relationship between God and the world, which has just been suggested to be the most adequate way of thinking of God as creator, gives rise to two questions concerning the practical significance of theistic faith. These concern first the notion of special actions of God in the natural world, that is to say, the question of miracle, and secondly the notion of the general providence of God as creator and the problem of natural evil. To conclude this chapter we shall briefly consider these two issues in turn.

The problem of miracle

Although the more percipient forms of panentheism, for example as developed by Charles Hartshorne and those influenced by his thought, hold that the divine is not to be seen as a sole agent which totally determines the course of events, the idea that God does sometimes decisively intervene in the natural world to correct what is going wrong, to prevent what threatens disaster, and to bring about what would otherwise never happen is an idea which comforts many believers. Although such actions may not occur very often, their possibility means that people are not utterly subject to the unconscious forces of the natural world. When difficulties and dangers arise, it is worth praying that God will step in: 'Ask, and you will receive' (Matthew 7.7). The idea of miracle also meets what in many people is a deep desire for the out-of-the-ordinary and wonderful. This may be due to a justified disenchantment with the predictable world of dull daily routines and the tatty products of secular technology. It may, though, also be due to a misdirection of the sense that human being finds its fulfilment in relation to the transcendent and holy. These two aspects of the nature of 'miracles' are reflected in the words which are used in the New Testament to refer to such divinely occasioned events – 'sēmeia' which are signs or marks (of the divine) and 'terata' which are marvels or wonders.

In theistic understanding references to miracles have three main functions. In the first place, as was noted in the previous chapter, they have been seen as providing authenticating marks for a divine revelation. A messenger or a message is shown to be from God by being accompanied by supernatural powers. According to Acts 2.22 Peter claimed in his speech to the people in Jerusalem on the day of Pentecost that 'Jesus of Nazarath' was 'a man singled out by God and made known to you through miracles, portents, and signs, which God worked among you through him'. Secondly, miracles may be seen as providing evidence of the divine nature and will. This view is noticeable in John's Gospel where Jesus' miracles are 'signs' which not only reveal the glory of Jesus and 'led his disciples to believe in him' (John 2.11) but also convey in dramatic form the significance of his ministry. Converting water into wine illustrates how the Christ turns the dull water of existence into the intoxicating wine of life, healing the blind man marks how he is the light of the world, and so on. Thirdly, though, miracles may be held to attest the current reality of God as an effective agent working in particular ways in the world in which we find ourselves. The identification of some such activities, it may be argued, is necessary if faith is to be justified in considering the divine as a living God with an individual will and practical significance so far as the natural world is concerned.

Unfortunately, while theism may seem to invite a concept of miracle, fundamental problems arise once we attempt to define and to identify a miracle. If a 'miracle' is defined as 'a happy surprise, an unexpected event which has fortunate results' – like a bootlace breaking while we walk under an overhang and, in stopping to fix it, we miss being hit by a rock-fall – we may 'wonder' at what happened but there is nothing in it to make us consider that the event either is unnatural or involves the agency of God. The facts that the lace broke when it did and the rock fell where and when it did would appear to be naturally explicable. The coincidence of the events was fortunate for us but it may be plausibly maintained that such lucky cases do occur and there is no reason to bring in God to explain them. Another possible definition of a miracle is 'an act in which a person becomes aware of the divine'. This, however, is too general to be satisfactory. Some people may become 'aware of God' by contemplating a flower or a baby's birth, events which in no way are unusual in the natural world, as well as in (maybe more than in) exceptional events. Without denying that any event may (and perhaps legitimately may) act as a medium by which God is disclosed, this definition may be held to fail as a definition of 'miracle' because it does not provide any basis for distinguishing miraculous from non-miraculous events by considering the character of the events themselves.

A third definition holds that a miracle is 'an event contrary to the laws of nature which occurs because of the agency of God'. The fundamental problem with this definition is that the notion of being 'contrary to the laws of nature' is inherently problematic. The so-called 'laws of nature' are general rules of expectation based upon observation of what normally occurs. There is no certainty about them. What seems to be a case of them being 'broken' may be an exception to what is usual which regularly occurs in certain definable but previously unnoticed circumstances. In earlier times especially it was also pointed out that we may be ignorant of many of these so-called 'laws'. Consequently we cannot be confident that an unusual event has broken one or other of them rather than being the result of the interplay of regular factors which have not yet been identified clearly. In more recent decades, furthermore, numerous scientists have come to hold that at the level of fundamental 'particles' or 'events' there is not merely a methodological indeterminacy which restricts the extent of our possibility of knowing the states of these things but also a real indeterminacy which means that there is a degree of randomness at the basic level of physical processes. A further defect with this third definition of 'miracle' is that it is not made clear what characteristics in an apparently irregular event require it to be attributed to God. At times it seems as if events are held to be due to divine agency simply because their consequences are regarded as surprisingly beneficial.

A different attempt to define a miracle avoids the dogmatism of the previous one by describing a miracle as 'a surprising event, contrary to what we expected, and taken by us to be due to divine agency'. This definition recognizes the element of wonder in miracles and their attribution to God but avoids making claims about the breaking of 'laws of nature' and about an identifiable intervention by the divine. It is unsatisfactory because it makes the recognition of a miracle dependent upon an individual's response to an event and not upon some defining elements in the event itself. An event which is thoroughly 'surprising' to people in one culture may be banal to those in another. This view of 'miracles' also has the grave disadvantage that it makes it clear that the attribution of divine agency is not something that is justifiable by clear criteria but is a personal or group assessment of why what has occurred has so occurred.

Besides the definitional difficulties, there are two other basic problems with claims about miracles. One is the difficulty of securing reliable evidence about any alleged miracles. Cultural factors also seem to be much involved in claims about miracles for reports about supposed miracles largely arise from those who believe such things happen. It may be that only believers can recognize what is happening (or that God only so acts where there is the right faith) – but it is also more than possible that such believers may be reading their faith and expectations into events rather than discerning what is happening in them. Consequently it is arguable that the recognition of a miracle is not a cause of faith nor a justification of faith but a product of faith in God as one who actively intervenes in natural processes. The other difficulty with claims about miracles is a fundamental moral one. If God is to be held to intervene in some events to change the course of what is happening, the actual cases of such intervention seem so relatively few and partial that great doubt is cast on the benevolence of God. At times it seems as if God may be compared to a doctor in a hospital full of patients in agony who chooses to relieve only a minute fraction of them although quite capable of healing them all fully. In reply it may be argued that we cannot know all the factors and circumstances and so what seems arbitrary to us may be seen to be right by God. The problem with this answer is that it is an argument from ignorance which suggests that we may not be justified in making any claims about the activity of God or the character of what we trust to be divine benevolence. Overall the evidence of human needs, let alone the torments of the non-human, suggests that while in principle God may be able to work 'miracles', in practice it seems unlikely that they occur – for otherwise their apparent incidence suggests that, so far as we can judge, the divine acts in an unworshipfully capricious and restricted manner.

The hope for miraculous interventions by God in itself points to a further question: Why should such actions be necessary if God is the creator of all? This is the problem of natural evil – and of the positive significance of faith in the general providence of God.

The problem of natural evil

In dealing with the so-called problem of evil, it is important first of all to recognize that it covers at least two distinct problems – the problem of natural evil and the problem of moral evil. We shall discuss the latter of these in a later chapter on faith and morality. Here we are to consider how the suffering which is due to natural processes can be reconciled with belief in God as a benevolent creator. One way of putting the issue is by reminding ourselves of John Welsey's confident lines which were quoted earlier,

> Father, 'tis Thine each day to yield
> Thy children's wants a fresh supply

and then ask whether it would be more than an incitement to blasphemy to sing them in a village in a country devastated by years of drought and invite the starving inhabitants to worship that Father. Alternatively, might it not seem cruel as well as giving rise to false expectations to read Jesus' teaching that we 'have a Father who knows' what we need and so if we set our minds upon his kingdom 'all the rest will come' to us 'as well' (Luke 12.30f.) in such a situation or in a third-world country ravaged by earthquake or in a community stricken with a plague or in any other of the numerous places where people are dying in torment through no ascertainable human fault?

The problem of natural evil arises because theistic faith is confronted by an apparent contradiction between its belief that the world was created by an all-powerful, all-wise and benevolent God and its awareness of the presence of suffering and waste in the natural world so created. It is a problem which has long troubled believers. An early Christian apologist, Lactantius, quoting Epicurus, put it thus:

> God either wishes to take away evils, and is unable; or He is able, and is unwilling; or He is neither willing nor able; or He is both willing and able. If He is willing and is unable, He is feeble, which is not in accordance with the character of God; if He is able and unwilling, He is envious, which is equally at variance with God; . . . if He is both willing and able, which alone is suitable to God, from what source then are evils? and why does He not remove them?[15]

Various attempts have been made to solve the problem.

One line of attack has been to point to the mysterious otherness of God. This is the kind of response which is found in God's encounter with Job in Job 38ff. To question the propriety of God's actions is foolish for they are 'too wonderful' to be grasped by human understanding. The authentic theistic stance is silent, obedient acceptance that all is for the best even though we cannot see how this is so. A similar response which stresses the need for faith is found, for example, in Søren Kierkegaard's *Gospel of Suffering*: 'It is said of faith that it can move mountains. Even the heaviest suffering, however, cannot be heavier than a mountain . . . But if a sufferer really believes that the suffering . . . is for his good, then he moves the mountain.'[16] Such responses, however, do not solve the problem of natural evil so much as affirm that there is no intellectually satisfying answer available for the human intellect.

Among other 'solutions' which are really no solutions so far as theistic faith is concerned are those which hold that God is supremely powerful but is either sadistic or careless about suffering in the created world, and that God is opposed by an evil agent which produces evil in the natural world and which God has not (yet) been able to defeat. The former of these proposals is theistically abhorrent because it denies the intrinsic perfection of the divine. The worshipfulness of God, which is an identifying characteristic of what theistic faith understands by God, is not dread of a vicious tyrant – a cosmic Hitler who needs to be appeased for fear of what might follow. It is the adoration of that which – or the one which – has total worth. As for the latter proposal, it either denies that God is the ultimate creator of all (because it posits another, contrary power in opposition to God which is independent of the divine), or it holds that the natural world has partly fallen under the control of one of God's creatures ('Satan') who has exercised God-given freedom to become evil, or it transfers the problem of natural evil from the created order to a transcendent realm. In none of these cases are theists at all likely to consider that their faith in God as a perfect creator has been justified.

Another attempted solution suggests that suffering may be a punishment for sin. It is a response that lies behind the question which sufferers frequently ask, 'What have I done to deserve this?'. People apparently feel that what is happening to them will make sense if it can be shown to be moral retribution. At the individual level, however, this solution to the problem of natural evil collapses because there seems to be no recognizable correlation between what happens to persons and their moral character – too often the (relatively) innocent writhe in agony and the wicked pass away in luxury after a long and comfortable life for us to be able to maintain that suffering in the world expresses the righteous judgments of God. As for the view that human beings suffer for the sins of others and, in particular, because of inherited guilt, this too seems morally unacceptable. A God who punishes children for the sins of their forefathers is not worshipful. Nor does it seem morally acceptable to hold that pains in this life will be compensated for in a future existence. The unsatisfactoriness of such a solution, that is, does not arise from its postulation of a future life but from its presupposition that anything could justly compensate some people for what they suffer in this world.

Some have responded to the problem of natural evil by holding in various ways that it is not really evil. While claims that suffering is an illusion which proper faith will dispel generally seem unconvincing (for the illusion itself is painful enough), other suggestions seem more plausible. In his *Philosophical Theology*, for example, F. R. Tennant argues that we should not try to justify individual cases of suffering but try to show that pain in general 'is either a necessary by-product of an order of things requisite for the emergence of the higher goods, or an essential instrument to organic evolution, or both'.[17] In particular he attributes a great number of physical ills to the world being created, according to a loving purpose, to be a suitable context for the development of 'intelligent and ethical life.'[18] This kind of argument is developed further by John Hick in *Evil and the God of Love* when he admits that some suffering is not only 'undeserved' but also 'unjust and inexplicable, haphazard and cruelly excessive'. It 'challenges Christian faith with its utterly baffling, alien, destructive meaninglessness'. Nevertheless, its very irrationality contributes 'to the character of the world as a place in which true human goodness can occur and in which loving sympathy and compassionate self-sacrifice can take place'. The world is as it is because it is intended to be 'a divinely created sphere of soul-making'.[19] While, however, such an argument may fit the world of random processes as described by Bartholomew, it is not likely to appeal very much to those who are to be the objects of sympathy and compassion. It is also hard to see how the case can be justified by appeal to what happens in the world in view of the great amount of evil which both crushes its victims and arouses little good in others.

The difficulty of showing the appropriateness of the created order by empirical observation was faced by Baruch Spinoza and Gottfried Wilhelm Leibniz. The former sought to overcome the problem by arguing, in his *Ethics*, that we are in error when we judge things according to whether 'they delight or disgust human senses, or according as they are useful or useless' to human beings.[20] The limited nature of human understanding prevents us perceiving the genuine perfection of all things and 'hence it follows that if the human mind had only adequate ideas it would form no notion of evil'.[21] Leibniz argues from the supreme perfection which is the defining characteristic of what is meant by God both that God must necessarily exist and that 'in producing the universe he has chosen the best possible plan'.[22] Accordingly 'the perfection of the Supreme Author' is established prior to and independently of any consideration of the nature of the universe and entails 'that the order of the whole universe', both as a whole and as reflected in each of its constituents, 'is the most perfect that can be'.[23]

At this point, however, we have come back to our starting-point. Spinoza in effect is holding that human limitations prevent us from understanding the true character of reality and Leibniz that we must hold that the creation is perfect in spite of how it appears. Unfortunately the problem of evil persists in troubling theistic faith because we cannot stop trying to understand (and so we cannot accept the Job-Spinoza criticism of our presumption), and because there seems such an enormous gap between what faith in God as creator leads us to expect and what we find to be the case in the world (and so we cannot trust the Job-Leibniz affirmation of the perfection of God). In the end even the faithful may feel some sympathy with the protest implied in John Stuart Mill's comment:

> We have not to attempt the impossible problem of reconciling infinite benevolence and justice with infinite power in the Creator of such a world as this. The attempt to do so not only involves absolute contradiction in an intellectual point of view but exhibits to excess the revolting spectacle of a jesuistical defence of moral enormities.[24]

Is, then, the problem of natural evil insoluble? If so theistic faith in a worshipful God is fundamentally threatened because two central doctrines in that faith, namely that God is to be regarded as perfect and as creator, seem to be contradicted by the state of the universe as what has been created.

There may, however, be a partial solution to the problem of natural evil – though not the kind of solution that theists look for! It lies in recognizing that at present we are probably not in a position to pose the problem properly. The justification for this somewhat paradoxical remark lies in the presuppositions of the problem. The basic difficulty does not lie where Spinoza found it – namely, in our inability to perceive the qualities of things as God perceives them. It lies in our lack of any satisfactory idea of what in material terms is to be understood as the divine activity of creating. While at a formal level we may agree with the traditional formulation of the problem in holding that in some way or other God, as creator, is the ultimate ground of all, it is no longer credible to hold at a material level that each structure, each relationship and each object is exactly as it is because God has so made it. The amount of cosmic radiation that falls on the surface of this planet, the stresses in the plates which constitute its surface, the meteorological factors that control its weather, the kinds of viruses that are around, the potential failure-points in the organism that is the human body, and everything else – from ducks to adders, from supernovae to the dandelions in the lawn – is as we now find it because of an immense number of incredibly long series of minute physical interactions and evolutionary developments. It is not at all clear to what extent the current state of affairs can be attributed – either for praise or for blame – on divine agency. And yet this is what is presupposed in the formulation of the problem of natural evil. It is taken for granted that things are as we now find them because God has so willed. Starting, then, with this pre-scientific, certainly pre-Darwinian and probably pre-Copernican view, it seems reasonable to ask why God did not act differently and produce what would seem to us to be a better (i.e. a less stressful and less painful) order of things. The question, though, is absurd because its premise is absurd. Before we can pose the problem of evil we need to determine what it means in material terms to hold that God is the creator. If, though, we could attain a satisfactory understanding of the actual nature of divine creativity, we would probably discover that the problem of natural evil has ceased to trouble us. It is likely that it only appears as a problem for those who insist on holding in their religious faith to a view of creation which is fundamentally at odds with the evidence of the natural world. What, however, a significant doctrine of creation would be like for this developing and vast cosmos is not something which is currently obvious. It is a task that challenges the theological imagination.

Chapter 7

Faith and the Attributes of God

In the preceding chapters much has been said and more has been implied about the concept of God. Before we proceed further, therefore, we need to consider directly what is meant by 'God' and how the divine attributes are to be understood. To start with, however, we should note that some religious writers have deep suspicions about such investigations. John Robinson (the pastor to the Pilgrim Fathers in Leyden, not the recent stimulating theologian of the same name), for example, complains that

> Some ambitious, and curious wits, but not able (& no marvail) to raise up, & advance their notions to *God* his infinitenesse, for the comprehending of it; have laboured to depresse, & pull him down to their dwarfish conceptions of him: and have indeed rather made him some great, and giant-like man, or Angel; then (as he is in truth) an infinite *God*: allowing him an essence, power, and wisdom hugely great; but not properly infinite, and immence: as though *God* could not be that, which they cannot conceive of him.
>
> The essence of *God* is *known* onely to himself; but is undiscernable to all men, and Angels: partly by reason of its infinitenes, which therefore no finite understanding can comprehend; and partly, for that, no voice, signe, or form can sufficiently expresse it either to sence or reason.[1]

What Robinson says is a salutary warning against what is to follow in this chapter. At the same time it is important to recognize that what he is unhappy about, so far as it is the inevitable result of human attempts to think about God, is also unavoidable for theists. Because God is the object of their faith, theists cannot avoid attempting to identify the attributes of the divine. It is not a mere whim to satisfy their intellectual curiosity that provokes them – though that would not be an improper motive. The nature of faith compels it to seek understanding because believers need to know the one on whom they believe if their faith is to be expressed appropriately in their lives. Although intellectual beliefs about God's reality can never be a substitute for the religious commitment of a living faith in God, 'faith in' presupposes and is orientated by 'beliefs about' God. Consequently, while theists should not forget that the deity of the divine means that all their concepts of God can never be more than approximate and relatively appropriate apprehensions of the ultimate and divine reality, they cannot, if they take their faith as seriously as it demands, avoid trying to discern the proper character of the divine attributes.

Faced with the labyrinthine arguments of some theological works, believers may seem to be justified in responding that they have – or desire – a 'simple faith'. They have no reason to be interested in the supposed answers to such questions as 'Whether only the sin of pride and envy can exist in an angel?' and 'Whether the Father and the Son are one principle of the Holy Spirit?' which Aquinas discusses in the *Summa Theologiae*.[2] Their concern is 'simply with belief in God' – or so they may claim. Unfortunately for them, the concept of God shows itself on reflection to be a fundamentally complex one because it incorporates – and necessarily incorporates if it is to represent the divine – a number of diverse notions. Simply because it involves God, the understanding of theistic faith cannot be simple.

In the first place, as has been mentioned earlier, God is to be thought of as the proper and compelling object of worship. The divine is that which elicits adoration: encountering the divine we are 'lost in wonder, love and praise'. There are no qualifications and approximations here. We are confronted with what intrinsically has utter worth or value. Only such a reality is intrinsically worshipped. Anselm accordingly defines God as 'that than which a greater cannot be conceived'.[3] This definition, however, indicates a second characteristic of God, namely, that God is that which is ultimate in being, value and rationality. Although in the previous chapter it was noted that there are serious problems with discerning the material content of the notion of what God is as creator, it is a necessary entailment of belief in the reality of God that all else, in some way, depends for its being upon that reality. Furthermore, God's intrinsic perfection provides the standard by which all else is to be finally judged: our knowledge is correct to the extent that it agrees with God's knowledge; our love is pure so far as it coincides with God's love. As the ultimate in rationality, God's purposes and responses determine the authentic meaning and satisfaction of all that occurs. In these ways, therefore, the divine reality actualizes in its own being the principles (or 'regulative ideas') by which all understanding ought to be orientated. 'God', that is, does not merely denote these principles of understanding; 'God' names that ontologically independent reality which incorporates them among its fundamental attributes. Thirdly, though, God is intrinsically holy. The sacred is not to be tampered with nor treated lightly. As Rudolf Otto brought out in his classical study, *The Idea of the Holy*, there is a mysteriousness here which produces dread and fascination. A fourth quality that most believers regard as central to the divine reality is that of saving grace. The divine is that which brings wholeness, harmony and fulfilment to the distorted, broken and corrupt expressions of life. Fifthly, the divine is not an abstract principle or an impersonal agency but a reality which is most adequately understood in terms of the personal. It is, for instance, because the divine is envisaged as being self-conscious and purposive that the processes of reality can be held to be meaningful; it is God's awareness of it that gives each achievement of value in those processes everlasting significance. The personal mode of being of the divine, it may further be argued, is the only justification for holding that being has a point. We shall return to the notion of God as personal later in the chapter. Finally, the concept of God (as distinguished from the reality of God) is what we are able to produce by means of our human imagination and reflection. We are not supplied with a polished concept like manna from the skies. Our understanding of what God is has to be developed through the trial and error of human thought as we seek to discern a concept which is intrinsically coherent and appropriate to the nature of the ultimate and divine reality. When we become conscious of the different qualities which a satisfactory concept of God must include, we may wonder if a coherent concept is attainable. Theistic faith, however, demands that we do not stop trying to discover it.

Talk about God

Some believers have responded to their awareness of the divine by asserting that God is 'utterly other' or that the divine is 'ineffable'. Taken literally these claims would put an end to all theistic understanding. If God is utterly other than anything we can experience or imagine (like the sound of one hand clapping or an extentionless seven-dimensional colourless purple smiling clone), then it follows that we could not even know what is referred to by 'God' sufficiently to appreciate that the divine is 'utterly other' – we just could not be aware that anything of that kind existed. Similarly, if something is strictly ineffable, it cannot be spoken of (for that is what the term means). It is therefore hard to envisage how the reality of such a being could be apprehended and, if there were some kind of awareness of it, nothing could be said about it. Theology would come to a sudden and final stop so far as it is concerned about God. On the other hand, comments about the divine being 'utterly other' and 'ineffable' may be interpreted as valuable reminders that talk about God is to be taken as pointing to the nature of the divine rather than as providing direct descriptions of it. There are various ways in which theologians have explored this characteristic of their language.

A classical way of understanding the proper nature of descriptions of God is to hold that they are analogical. When, for example, Thomas Aquinas considers how we express the attributes of God, it is 'evident' to him that the differences between God and the creatures prevents a term being applied univocally (i.e. as having one and the same meaning) to both. On the other hand, if language is to be able to convey information, terms cannot be used equivocally (i.e. as having quite different meanings in different contexts). His solution is that 'whatever is said of God and creatures' is said 'in an analogous sense'.[4] The nature of such analogical usage can be variously understood. It may be held that there is a kind of proportionality which underlies it so that when we speak of God being 'wise' we are involved in an implicit calculation. We think, for example, of what is meant by acknowledging that Lesley is 'wise' and then we extend that quality to apply it to God by multiplying it according to the proportional difference between the intrinsic nature of God and the intrinsic nature of Lesley – according, that is, to the relationship between being a creator and being a creature, or between being an unlimited cause and a limited effect. The difficulty with this approach is that either the basic proportionality seems unascertainable or it is so ridiculously enormous (as becomes apparent if the relationship between God and Lesley is said to be that between the infinite and the finite) that notions of a calculation seem absurd. More plausible are approaches which involve a less rigid understanding of analogy. The 'way of eminence' suggests that when a term is used to describe a quality of God, we must endeavour as far as possible, on the one hand to eradicate from our perception of its meaning all that arises from the imperfect and limited forms in which we experience it and, on the other hand, to discern its pure and complete form. Unlike Lesley's wisdom, that is, God's wisdom is an unrestricted, faultless and final appreciation of everything. Later, though, we shall consider some of the problems in discerning what may be meant by attributing to God such a quality as that of eminent 'power'.

Other ways of attempting to establish the possibility of describing the attributes of God take up the way in which language uses symbols, models, metaphors and parables to express what is difficult or impossible to describe more directly. In *Symbolism and Belief*, for example, Edwyn Bevan explores how we use things from our everyday experiences as symbols to convey 'knowledge of things beyond the range of any human experience.'[5] He considers, for example, how ideas of height and light are used to express the transcendence of God. The notion of symbol is critical for Paul Tillich's theology although his treatment of it is not without problems. In *Dynamics of Faith* he holds that since 'the true ultimate transcends the realm of finite reality infinitely', nothing from 'finite reality can express it directly and properly'.[6] Symbols, however, are able to open up 'levels of reality which otherwise are closed for us'. They are able to do this because there is an ontological link between a symbol and what is symbolized – symbols 'participate in the reality of that to which they point'.[7] It is, therefore, only by means of symbols that we can express the ultimate[8] and 'the language of faith is the language of symbols'.[9] Using his knowledge of science, where models are frequently employed to gain insight, Ian Ramsey investigated the ways in which the function of analogue models sheds light on the possibility and nature of religious language while Sallie McFague has more recently considered the importance of parables and metaphors as a way of theological illumination. Good metaphors shock our existing perceptions by bringing 'unlikes together'[10] in order to produce 'basically a new or unconventional interpretation of reality'.[11] Here again, therefore, theology is understood to use the familiar to describe the unfamiliar in ways that are not to be taken literally nor definitively.

The above remarks are only a brief indication of a long debate about the possibility of describing God in indirect ways and the necessity for so doing. Three points, however, need to be made about the issue. The first is that the bogey of the accusation of anthropomorphism needs to be exposed for what it is – an insubstantial spectre which will evaporate under the sun of rational reflection. Some theologians seem to have been so frightened of being charged with constructing their concept of God in their own (human) image, that they have gone to inordinate lengths to try to show how unlike the divine is to anything human. The result has been that it is doubtful if their resulting remarks about the nature of God have any significant content. To some extent, it should be admitted, their desire to avoid the charge of anthropomorphism is justified. Descriptions of God are to be found that are crude and primitive in their use of human (and other) qualities – like discussions of God's awareness which imply that he 'sees' things in the same kind of physical, limited and perspectival way that we do. The proper way to respond to such naiveties, however, is not to attempt to avoid all anthropomorphisms, for that would make it impossible to say anything significant about the consciousness, appreciation, values, and purposes which structure the divine being. Since the human mode of being is the highest that we are acquainted with (it seems intuitively superior to that of a stone, a carrot, a computer or a virus, and we do not seem to have any clear ideas of a kind of being that would be superior to our own), it is inevitable that we use its qualities to express the divine as the supreme mode of being. There is nothing higher that we can refer to. What we should seek, therefore, are appropriately qualified and warranted anthropomorphisms – for by them we will discern the nature of the divine according to the highest qualities available to our understanding.

The second point that needs to be made about the attempt to speak of God in indirect ways is that the inadequacy of what is regarded as a 'literal' use of language has been misunderstood and overplayed. In the first place it is important to recognize that if indirect means of talking about God are employed they need to be accompanied, implicitly or explicitly, with at least one statement about God which can be treated more or less literally and which specifies what we are talking about. Only so will we be in a position both to identify what is referred to as 'God' and to appreciate how the indirect descriptions of 'God' are to be interpreted. It makes a great deal of difference to our understanding of what is meant by describing something as 'friendly' if the object is a kind of dog, a type of computer, a rock-climb or a climate. If, though, one reasonably direct statement about God has to be possible if theistic understanding is to have an identifiable referent, perhaps more than one is possible. Secondly, it is a mistake to lump together as indirect descriptions of God statements which are manifestly nonliteral, as when God is described as a 'mountain refuge', having 'ears', smoking 'from his nostrils' and riding 'on a cherub' (cf. Psalm 18), and more sober claims which hold that God is 'the ground of being' who 'knows and understands all things' or that God is 'reliable' and 'gracious'. It is closer to the truth to recognize that descriptions of God cover a wide spectrum of types from the highly pictorial and allusive to the attempt to be as direct, precise and accurate as possible. At the latter end of the spectrum the use of language not only approximates to but actually is in many cases what is meant by a 'literal' use of it (for no language, not even the most 'literal', is without some degree of looseness in its application). In the case of God, therefore, it is preferable to hold that some statements about God are meant more or less literally rather than to regard all talk about God as indirect and, hence, to be unsure whether or not it conveys any significant information. While we must always acknowledge that the intrinsic nature of the divine exceeds our comprehension, the statements that are to be regarded as literal are attempts to provide the most directly applicable descriptions of the divine which it is possible for us to apprehend. They are to guide our interpretation of the more indirect descriptions of the divine.

Thirdly, it is arguable that the reason why some theologians have come to stress the indirect nature of talk about God is because they have found great problems with some of the traditional claims that are made about God when taken literally. The answer to their situation, however, is not to keep repeating the problematic statements about God while attempting to escape fundamental criticisms by holding that the statements do not really mean what they appear to say. The solution lies in a fresh analysis of our understanding of God and, consequently, a re-appraisal of the correct way to describe the divine. A major contribution to philosophical theology in this century has been provided by Charles Hartshorne's development of such a solution.[12] What follows in the remainder of this chapter is much indebted to his studies.

Intrinsic problems with the concept of God

When we consider what some major Christian theologians have said about God we find some surprising assertions. Anselm, for example, apparently assumes that it is self-evident that God must be 'passionless' and unable to feel sympathy. Accordingly when he treats the divine compassion for the wretched, he finishes in the

unsatisfactory position of holding that the wretched may 'experience the effect of compassion' but that there is nothing in God's own
experience which corresponds to that feeling.[13] It seems an odd way
to describe a God who is held to love until it is remembered that
God is held to be perfect and the perfect is held by him to be
essentially unable to change – for any change would be to relative
states of imperfection. As intrinsically perfect, therefore, God must
be unable to suffer any change – that is, be impassible. A similar
oddity is found in Thomas Aquinas when the nature of God is held
to be 'altogether immutable' and without 'any potentiality'. Since,
then, 'it is impossible for God to be in any way changeable',[14] the
relationship of God to creatures 'is not a reality in God, but in the
creature'[15] – in other words creatures, being drawn towards the
divine, may understand themselves as related to the divine but there
is no reciprocal awareness in God. This, though, seems an
unsatisfactory way to think of the God whom believers, on the basis
of their religious tradition and in some cases of apparently
confirming religious experiences, hold to be characterized by
creative and responsive grace.

How do these oddities arise? They are not peripheral quirks in
traditional theological thought but reflect a fundamental tension
between what believers understand that their faith declares about
God and what theologians judge to be demanded by rational
reflection about God. The basis of the difficulty lies in some
apparently self-evident and fundamental attributes of God. As the
proper object of worship and as that which is instrinsically ultimate
in being, value and rationality, it seems that we must describe God,
in formal terms, as being absolute, necessary, unchanging, infinite
and eternal. A being which lacks any of these primary qualities
seems intuitively to be essentially other than what is referred to as
being God. To assert, for instance, that 'God' is not absolute would
presumably entail that 'God' is not ultimate, either because there is
no final reality or principle – all is relative, or because 'God' is
subordinate to some superior reality or principle. In neither case
would what we call 'God' properly qualify to be regarded as such.
The former case would in effect describe an atheistic reality and in
the latter case the 'superior' would qualify as God if it were
authentically ultimate. Similarly to attribute change to 'God' as if
'God' could choose to be divine or to resign the position is absurd.
God never became God nor ever will cease to be God: being God is
not a post which entities may compete for, nor is it a case of being
top but always liable to be dethroned by another. Such ideas are

absurd. God is God unchangingly. The same kind of arguments can be advanced to show the untenability of holding that God is not necessary (as if the divine were dependent on something else), not infinite (as if anywhere were beyond the divine), and not eternal (as if there could have been or will be a moment when God does not exist).

What has been maintained so far seems a proper appreciation of what is involved in speaking of God. Grave difficulties, however, have arisen for theistic understanding when theologians have developed what they have taken to be the inescapable implications of holding that the divine must be held to be absolute, necessary, unchanging, infinite and eternal. For each of these qualities, though, there is an opposite which refers to a contradictory quality – relative, contingent, changing, finite and temporal. Furthermore, by the principle of non-contradiction it is not possible to assert contradictory qualities of the same object in the same respect without rendering the assertion meaningless. Traditionally, therefore, theologians have held that because they must assert that God is absolute, necessary . . . , they must deny that God is in any way relative, contingent . . . The result may seem to affirm a view of God which is intellectually satisfying until we begin to investigate the implications of the denials.

Let us consider, for example, the quality of love. It is a fundamental claim in Christian theism that 'God is love' and that in loving we incorporate the divine in ourselves.[16] According to I John 3.18, furthermore, love is not a matter of talk: to be genuine it must show itself in action. What, though, is it to love? To love someone means to be selflessly concerned for the fullest enrichment of their lives. In practice this means continual adaptations to that person's states in order to respond in the most fruitful way. When, for example, Vaughan is over-the-moon about a rave review of his latest book, it means sharing in his joy; when he is burdened with essays to mark, it means being sympathetic; when he is worried about a hostile reception to his honest sermon, it means being supportive; when he wants to talk, it means being ready to listen long and attentively. To practice love, that is, is not to sit beaming benignly while complacently unaware of what is happening. It involves a profound capacity to sympathize, for genuine love means sharing fully in the joys and hopes and sufferings of the loved ones. It also requires an ability to respond to those states in an appropriate manner. No such possibilities, however, are open to a being that is in every respect unchanging. To love and to be totally unaffectable (i.e. impassible) are incompatible modes of being. If, therefore, God must be described as utterly unchanging, it follows that the divine cannot be aware of and appropriately responsive to the states of others. Hence the attribution of love to God is either meaningless or a misleading way of expressing some such claim as that relationships are most fulfilling when they are motivated by love.

Reflection on the nature of love thus suggests that there is a fundamental conflict between what rational considerations have traditionally been understood to require theologians to maintain about God and what actual theistic faith wishes to assert about the love of God. Similar problems arise with numerous other claims contained in theistic understanding. A being which is wholly absolute cannot coherently be said to create, for such a being cannot be envisaged as having either potentiality or other entities to be related to. Such a being must be all that there can be. A being which is wholly necessary cannot enjoy either the freedom to choose or the capacity to be aware of the choices of others. Reality in its case must be wholly determined. To live is to participate in and to be affected by processes of expression and enrichment: it is the dead, the past and the abstract which are unchanging. To speak of God, therefore, as living and as wholly unchanging is incoherent babbling. To be something means to be identifiable as being this and not that, and to be a personal being involves self-consciousness of this identity through differentiating relationships with others. Neither possibility is open to that which is strictly described as unqualifiedly infinite in every respect, for the boundlessness of such infinitude would prevent both self-identity and the being of others distinct from the infinite. Finally, a being that is wholly eternal in the sense that no temporal distinctions could be significant for that mode of being must be unable to choose, will, create and achieve fulfilment, since all those activities entail temporal distinctions between states of 'before' and 'after'.

The possibility of a coherent concept of God

Is there any way out of this problem or do we have to accept that theological understanding of God is always going to be unsatisfactory because the demands of rational reflection and of theistic faith are fundamentally at odds with each other? One solution is to allow the supposed insights of philosophical reason to take control. Where this happens religious affirmations about God as loving, creating, sympathizing, and responding are dismissed as pious but untenable claims. God is perceived as an unconscious and unalterable ideal. Having thus abandoned some of the vital tenets of religious faith, theological understanding presents a kind of metaphysic. The opposite solution is to allow religion to control theological understanding and to ignore the demands of reason where they are in conflict with religion. H. L. Mansel, for example, in his *Limits of Religious Thought* argues that since the rationally required attributes of God result in contradictions, we should recognize that such matters are outside our intellectual competence. Our theology should not depend on reason but be wholly derived from God's revelation. Neither of these solutions, however, is satisfactory. The former divorces theology and faith; the latter is liable to result in both theological understanding and faith deteriorating into extravagant fantasies as the checks of rational reflection are cancelled. A third solution is to refuse to take theological descriptions too seriously. Assertions are made about God but not all their implications are accepted. Believers and theologians thus baptize their contradictions as paradoxes and maintain, for example, that it is then possible to claim that God is both loving and impassible. Like other attempts to 'have the bun and one's penny as well', the procedure is discredited as soon as it is recognized for what it is. Unless the clear implications of statements are to be accepted as part of their meaning, there is no way by which we or anyone else can discover what they mean. The principle of non-contradiction cannot therefore be evaded in this way.

For a very long time sensitive theologians have judged that these three solutions are the only possible ones – and none is attractive. In recent decades, however, the brilliant insights of Charles Hartshorne have identified a different solution. He has developed what he calls the 'dipolar' concept of God in such works as *Man's Vision of God*, *Philosophers Speak of God* (with W. L. Reese), *The Logic of Perfection*, *Creative Synthesis and Philosophic Method*, and *A Natural Theology for Our Time*. The notion of 'dipolarity' brings to our attention that certain descriptions imply a correlate. A magnet cannot have only one pole – its 'north' must be balanced by a south; a lover requires a beloved; a cause must have an effect. Hartshorne applies this notion to the concept of God and shows that an adequate theistic understanding must be 'dipolar' in that it needs to treat the attributes of the divine reality as being, on the one hand, absolute, necessary, unchanging, infinite and eternal and, on the other, as being relative, contingent, changing, finite and temporal.

It may do this, furthermore, without any risk of condemnation from the principle of non-contradiction if it is realized that these two sets of qualities describe distinct aspects of the attributes of the divine mode of being and that traditional theological thought has been unwarranted in claiming that the former set wholly and exclusively qualifies all descriptions of God in every respect. Instead, the former set – absolute, necessary . . . – is to be recognized as identifying the abstract characteristics of the divine mode of being (what God is in principle), while the latter set – relative, contingent . . . – specifies the concrete characteristics of the divine mode of being (what God is in actuality). Such methodological remarks, though, may leave readers bemused. The best way to grasp what Hartshorne has perceived is to consider some examples of its application to the attributes of God. We will start by looking again at the claim that God is love and then by considering divine knowledge.

In principle God's love must be considered to be absolute in that in every instance it is never anything other than pure, and unadulterated. It is necessary because out of the three possible relationships with others, love, apathy and hatred, the second is imperfect and the third is finally self-destructive. The only possible relationship of the divine to the creation is therefore that of love. Furthermore, love is intuitively recognized to be the highest value and so it must be love which characterizes the divine as the proper object of worship. The divine love is also to be thought of as being in principle unchanging in the sense that the divine response to every situation is completely one of love. Nothing deflects, compromises or weakens God's appreciation of all that is and God's will that each situation be treated as the ground for eliciting the fullest aesthetic satisfaction that is attainable. God's love is infinite in that there are no bounds to it, and it is eternal in that it always has been and always will be the divine attitude. All these descriptions, however, are abstract descriptions of what God's love is in principle in any situation. When we turn to considering how the divine love is actualized in concrete forms in particular cases, we find that other qualifying terms are appropriate. The concrete expression of God's love, that is, must be relative because what it is to love in a situation depends on the character of that situation. Love for Jackie when an experiment has failed again means solid encouragement; love for two-year old Claire on a cliff-top means taking a firm grip on her hand; love for eighteen-year old Katharine means letting her go rock-climbing! The concrete expressions of love are also contingent on what is there to be loved – I cannot love my third child or my brother because none such exist. Similarly God cannot love them. The divine love is restricted to what happens to exist. In its concrete expressions God's love changes as the situations change – the love that once encouraged Jackie later turned to sharing her delirious joy when the project succeeded. The actual form of love in a particular case is finite in that it is limited to what is the relevant optimum desire for that case, and it is temporal in that it is conditioned by what is the state of affairs at each moment. In other words, the appropriate way to describe the divine love in principle as an abstract quality and the appropriate way to describe the actual concrete expressions of that love require us to use different, formally opposite, sets of qualifiers.

The description of divine knowledge requires similar treatment. In principle God's knowledge is absolute in that it is totally comprehensive and accurate – God knows whatever is to be known; necessary since ignorance of anything at all would render the divine less than perfect and other than the totally adequate object of worship – and so would mean that it was not authentically divine; unchanging in that divine knowledge is never other than totally comprehensive and accurate; infinite in that its capacity is limitless – God could never suffer from storage problems; and eternal in that whatever God comes to know is never forgotten. All these descriptions, however, describe the abstract aspects of divine knowledge – implications of the claim that in principle the divine must be conceived of as knowing all that is knowable. When, however, we consider what God actually knows, we find that it is relative, contingent and finite in that God can only know what is there to be known. God's knowledge of the real does not, therefore, include knowledge of what has not yet existed (although so far as something may be conceived as potential, it will be known by God as belonging to the range of what is possible) nor of what is impossible (such as the shape of a round square). The divine knowledge is enormous but it is limited – God does not know as real stars that have not existed or persons that have never lived, although God does know every star that has come into being in the cosmos and every person that has ever been born. The concrete state of divine knowledge, furthermore, changes and is temporal, for the contents of that knowledge are continually increased as new things come into being from moment to moment. Last Wednesday God did not know as real what I experienced last Thursday: on Thursday those experiences occurred and so became part of the divine awareness, everlastingly to be cherished for their value. Such temporality and change must, indeed, characterize the concrete state of divine knowledge if it is to actualize what in principle includes perfect knowledge of a processive reality.

Hartshorne's dipolar structure for correctly analysing the attributes of God is to be seen as a formal one by which the material attributes of God – reality, love, knowledge, activity, passivity and so on – are to be understood. It is accordingly somewhat misleading to use the formal qualifiers as direct descriptions of God and to assert that God *is* absolute or *is* temporal, even if it is also pointed out that these terms apply to different aspects of the divine. It is clearer to put it that the divine reality in principle is absolute, or that the divine activity is temporal in its concrete expressions. It is a disastrous misunderstanding of the dipolar view of deity, furthermore, to hold that it means that all contraries are to be predicated of God – that God is to be described as wise and foolish, good and evil, loving and hating. What the dipolar view maintains is that in the case of all the material attributes that are appropriately predicable of God (wise, good, loving and so on), they are to be seen as having abstract and concrete aspects and to be understood accordingly. Which these material attributes are may be a controversial matter in some cases (Is humour or strict justice or delight in orderliness to be included?), but generally it seems intuitively clear which are the appropriate material qualities to be used in describing the divine.

Perfection and other attributes of God

One of the descriptions of God which is not open to dispute is that God is perfect. Only a perfect being may be the proper object of worship and ultimate in value. The nature of the divine perfection, however, requires careful analysis if the notion is not to create difficulties for theistic understanding. Traditionally the notion has been understood in relation to God according to the interpretation of it found in classical thought. Here the fundamental idea is that of completion: the perfect is that which needs nothing more, which has accomplished the fullest possible expression of its own nature, which is finished in every respect. Accordingly what is perfect is held, as such, to be unable to change, since any change must produce in it some degree of imperfection. Something that is a hundred-per-cent cannot (logically cannot) be, do or become any better.

In consequence of this view of what it is to be perfect theologians have been trapped into making two claims about the divine nature which are theistically inappropriate. The first is that God has all possible perfections. When, for example, Anselm asks 'What good, therefore, does the supreme Good lack, through which every good is?',[17] it seems obvious that the answer must be 'None'. The divine must be conceived to be 'whatever it is better to be than not to be'. Such a notion, however, is incoherent. This is because not all qualities are compatible with each other: one cannot be simultaneously brave and fearless (because to be 'brave' is to overcome fear, to be fearless is not to experience fear), in bliss and compassionate with those who suffer, in total control of all events and respectful of the freedom of other agents. In thinking of the characteristics of the divine perfection, therefore, it is necessary to see that it does not embody all possible values whatsoever. The divine is to be conceived, rather, as that which embodies what is intrinsically the highest possible combination of values.

The other inappropriate claim is that the divine perfection means that God must be thought of as 'actus purus' – as pure actuality without any potentiality for change at all. This, of course, follows directly from the view that to be perfect is to be complete. It is, furthermore, a view of perfection which is appropriate to an engine or a painting or a multiplication table or a ball-bearing. In such cases, if the object is perfect, nothing needs to be done to it. It is finished. This is not, however, the model of perfection that is appropriate to a lover or an artist or a creator. In all those cases to attain a state where there is no potentiality for change would not be to reach perfection but to die. If, therefore, God is to be thought of as being more like a lover, an artist and a creator than like an abstract idea, a formal principle or an impersonal object, the guiding models for divine perfection need to be selected accordingly. The divine perfection is not to be regarded as a total lack of potentiality but as an infinite capacity for loving, artistic, creative activity. God is not an exhausted producer nor an empty notion: for authentic theistic understanding God is a living God, ceaselessly seeking to provoke in the creation novel realizations of aesthetic enrichment.

Hartshorne has described the proper perception of divine perfection as a matter of 'dual transcendence'.[18] On the one hand the divine essentially transcends all else. Nothing does or could rival God. The qualities of all other beings are to be judged finally by comparison with the 'unsurpassable' being of God. On the other hand, though, the divine is 'self-surpassing' in that the aesthetic riches which God embraces at one time and which contribute to his concrete reality at that time will be surpassed by those that the divine incorporates at a later time. This is because in the intervening period values will have been actualized and so the divine experience, which never loses anything by forgetfulness, will have been further enriched.

One implication of the perfection of the divine is that God must be conceived as being totally aware of all that occurs. The argument for this is that in respect of awareness, there are only three possibilities: to be totally aware of all, to be aware of some things but not all, to be aware of nothing. The latter, the state of utter ignorance, seems inappropriate for the divine. The state of merely partial awareness is manifestly defective. Hence the divine must be aware of everything. This, though, in turn means that the divine cannot be regarded as at all impassible or, in a cosmos where there is suffering, in a state of untrammelled bliss. To be totally aware of a state is to participate sympathetically in it. Such a conclusion should not be surprising to a theism which finds a key symbol to its understanding of the divine in the love and suffering of Jesus, but it is a view of God which has been and still is strenuously resisted by many theologians. Their assertion that the divine enjoys a state of unalloyed happiness which is unaffectable by any pain is both a confusion of their own ill-considered view of what is ideal in a personal mode of being with the divine mode of being and a failure to take seriously the claim that God genuinely loves.

As well as being affected by all, the divine must also be seen as affecting all. This brings up the question of how the power of God is to be understood. Often the divine is described as being omnipotent. This word means 'having all power'. It seems an appropriate quality to attribute to the ultimate until it is realized that it is a self-contradictory notion. The notion of the exercise of power only makes sense in the case of relationships between entities which each have a relative degree of power of their own. For one being to have power over another means that the former is able to influence or coerce the latter into conformity with the former's will. Such an effect, however, is only possible because the latter has some degree of independence or autonomy of its own which may be overcome by the former. A being that was supposed to have a complete monopoly of power (i.e. was strictly 'omnipotent') would really have no power for there would be nothing over which to exercise it. It could also be a being that could have nothing to relate to and so could not be a creator.

A more coherent understanding of divine power is as supreme power. It seems plausible to hold that nothing could ever destroy the divine (for the ontological ultimacy of the divine implies that God must necessarily exist) and that nothing could ever defeat the divine purpose in ways that the divine does not finally will to permit. It is the notion of divine will, however, that is the clue to appreciating the practice of divine power. So far as it is a deliberate act, the exercise of power is a matter of choosing how to use the power that is available. Given John Wesley's diaries to handle, the important thing is not my power but how I will use it – to protect them or to mutilate them. In the case of divine activity the power available is, presumably, potentially overwhelming but its exercise will be governed by the divine purposes. If the divine will is to create, where creation means the emergence of entities with an independence and autonomy of their own, the exercise of divine power will presumably be restricted by that will so as to ensure that the creatures are not coerced in ways that destroy their intended status. In the case of human beings it may accordingly be suggested that the divine power is most satisfactorily understood as a form of 'luring' whose origin is profoundly obscure (for otherwise people would have little choice about responding to it) and which may be trusted to respect individual freedom. God, that is, is considered to act only by 'attracting' others into willing conformity with the divine will. The divine neither coerces people like a cosmic Svengali, hypnotizing them in ways of which they are unconscious, nor presents them with lures that are so attractive that they are compelled to conform.

Some such notion of divine power and activity is plausible but it is very speculative. In theory the ultimacy of the divine may be held to imply that God's power must be supreme and God's influence on events, both natural and historical, universal. In practice, as the previous two chapters have indicated, the ways in which the divine power is exercised are not manifest. It is then arguable, as has been suggested already, that the divine activity must be largely, if not wholly, hidden in order for creatures to be relatively free to fulfil the divine will, that they may be in their own way responsible, autonomous and genuinely creative. In this way, therefore, believers may be justified in holding that God has supreme power and that the use of that power is governed by God's purposes as creator. It is also arguable, however, that the religious concern (at times 'obsession' might be deserved) with divine power is due to mistaken human views of what it is to be 'God'. Because so often we want to control rather than to love, to dominate rather than to respect, to coerce rather than to cherish, to manipulate rather than to create and to allow creativity, we tend to assume that God will be the same. 'If I ruled the world' becomes our guide for understanding God and the result is a picture of a cosmic dictator. We are then baffled when the divine does not act as we would expect. Perhaps instead of worrying about divine power – its extent and its form – we should look again at the image of God suggested by 'the brief Galilean vision of humility' and consider whether the inspiration of creative loving rather than the power to coerce which we (sinfully?) desire is the proper way to understand the divine.

Another attribute of the divine which has been the source of some discussion is that of being personal. The 'personal' is distinguished from the 'impersonal' by the presence of a number of over-lapping qualities such as self-consciousness and awareness of others, intelligence, will, appreciation of values, relationships with others, ability to choose between possibilities, capacity to respond to situations, and responsibility for what is decided and done. Personal being may be described as a unity in continuity of knowing, willing and caring. So far, then, as a decision is to be made between attributing impersonal and personal notions to the divine, a theism which regards God as a conscious agent who is affected as well as affecting will find it appropriate to speak of God as having a personal mode of being. Some theologians, however, have been worried that such attribution is unwarrantably anthropomorphic since the personal tends to be identified with human personal being. They have therefore suggested that God should be said to be 'supra-personal' – more than personal. Such a description may seem to do due honour to the deity of the divine but unfortunately it is probably a compliment without content. We are aware of the impersonal and of the personal but not of any other distinct mode of being. If the notion of the 'supra-personal' is to have any content, it can only be by purifying the notion of the 'personal' of the identifiable limitations and distortions that belong to human cases of it. In that case it is probably less misleading to speak of the divine simply as 'personal'.

A contrary response to the alleged unsatisfactory anthropomorphism of regarding God as personal is to deny that any such qualities are to be attributed to the divine. The adoption of this view, however, leaves the divine as a supreme principle, an idea which should regulate understanding and conduct, or a fixed point of reference but also as something whose reality is hard to make sense of. Principles, ideas, points of reference do not exist independently but only as they are envisaged by some mind. To be a mind, however, is the essence of personal being. Furthermore, to hold that the divine is not in some appropriate way to be regarded as personal is to imply that there is no conscious purpose and awareness of value at the heart of reality. Understanding God as personal seems to be a necessary condition of holding that the process of reality is ultimately significant.

It may be suggested, though, that it is contradictory to hold that God is both personal and perfect. The former quality implies having freedom to choose while the latter implies always doing what is the best. Is it, therefore, coherent to think of the divine as personal (and hence free) if in any situation God cannot, because of the necessary nature of deity, do otherwise than make the optimum response? This is an interesting conundrum but it does not seem to be insoluble. In the first place, the divine may be held to have some freedom to choose between equally valuable but incompatible options. The problem with this answer, though, is that it prevents the choice being a rational one – there can be no reason to choose one rather than any of the other options if they are strictly equal in potential value. A more promising move is to recognize that as the perfect (in will and in understanding), God may be thought to have no desire to choose other than the best. Just as believers may properly recognize that 'perfect freedom' is found in serving God, so they may also hold that God's conformity to the perfect is not a limit on divine freedom but a perfect expression of it. Such puzzles, however, are valuable, whether we solve them satisfactorily or not, because they warn us against assuming too much for our understanding of the attributes of God.

The notion of divine eternity is another attribute which has been widely misunderstood. In order to give what is thought to be a proper recognition of the 'otherness' of God, it is often claimed that God is 'outside time' and that all moments (past, present and future) are immediately and simultaneously present to God. Furthermore, as creator, God is said to create time. On reflection, however, these apparently appropriate views of the divine nature turn out to be seriously defective. They prevent the use of any significant notion of God as creating, responding and acting for all such notions presuppose a temporal mode of being – a 'before and after' situation. They imply that reality as we know it, namely as processive, is utterly other than how God knows it. For the divine all is simultaneous and there can be no future. If such is reality for the divine, it is absurd to consider the divine as engaging in the personal relationships which doctrines of grace suggest. Ultimately this view of divine eternity means that temporal reality is an illusion. God cannot even coherently be said to create time, for the activity of creating itself presupposes a 'before' when there was no time and an 'after' when time had been created – which is to say that talk about creating presupposes the state which its activity produces.

Is there, though, any other appropriate way of speaking of the eternity of God? One suggestion is to hold that it is to be understood as an everlasting temporality. The difference between the divine and all other entities is that the divine necessarily had no beginning and will have no end. Whatever has been a present moment was present then to God and whatever will be a present moment will be present then to God. This does not mean, of course, that the temporal sequence is experienced by God as we experience it. For one thing the passing of time is a threat to us since we know that times will occur when we will not be there, at any rate not in our present form. God, in contrast, is not so threatened. However long it may be before something is actualized, its actuality will become part of the divine experience. The past, furthermore, is never lost by God as it is lost by us. Although past achievements can never be undone, whether they are for good or for ill, the memory of them rapidly fades with us. In God they may be presumed to be preserved in the divine memory in all their freshness and vitality as when they first came to be. As for the criticism that the everlastingness of God implies that God did not create time and so is not ultimate, it is arguable that time is not something that is 'creatable'. It is to be understood, rather, as the way in which the relationships between actions and events are ordered. Time is not a 'thing' to be created. It was neither produced by God who existed 'before' it nor found to be there by God when the divine came into being. Instead of trying to make sense of such absurdities it is more appropriate to regard time as ultimately the description of the ordering of divine experiences and actions.

But if though, the divine is everlasting – if God will be for ever and ever – what is the point of the future? Without an end, can it have a purpose? The notion of unending activity may be a terrifyingly exhausting prospect to human beings because they are limited in their capacity and become tired. Eventually they wear out. This, though, is not an appropriate way to think of God. The divine capacity for creative activity and the divine zest for aesthetic enrichment is limitless. The goal of divine activity is not to be seen as the final accomplishment of a predetermined plan – as the complete fulfilment of the blue-print of the kingdom of Heaven. If such were God's intention and if it were ever achieved, that would be the end of everything, even for God. Activity would cease. Death would have the final victory – although no one, not even God, would be conscious of it. It is a horrific prospect. Such a prospect, however, is the result of thinking of the purpose of reality too much in terms of models of engineering design and construction. A better model is that of the artist who ceaselessly seeks to produce novel expressions of aesthetic delight. God's 'goal' in that case is not the material one of a particular state of affairs: it is the 'formal' one of a desire for the endless proliferation and enjoyment of values produced through aesthetic creativity. Each achievement in the process of reality is enjoyed for what it is and is then used as the basis for novel adventures. It is not a 'goal', furthermore, which could be frustrated by human destructiveness. A nuclear holocaust which eradicated life on this planet would only be the termination of one line of development in the cosmic creativity provoked and enjoyed by God. This is a God who never dies – but whose demands that we too should live creatively shatter any hopes for God-given rest.

Chapter 8

Faith and the Existence of God

Theistic faith is grounded upon belief in the reality of God. So far in this study it has generally been assumed that a belief of this kind is justified, in order that attention may be directed to questions about how the divine nature may be discerned and what its character may be. The belief, however, is not universally accepted. Within modern Western thought, for example, it has been attacked. Holbach, Feuerbach, Marx and Schopenhauer, among others, strongly maintained that there is no God. Nietzsche even asserted that the 'death of God' – the declaration that theism's God is no more – is a matter for rejoicing since only when God (or, rather, belief in God's reality) is abolished will human beings perceive their responsibility for life and the significance of their freedom. It is a view which Jean-Paul Sartre shares. In his existentialist interpretation of humanism, he declares that theism not only is 'an out-of-date hypothesis which will die away quietly of itself' but also must go if human beings are to live authentically. Only with the denial of God will they perceive that they are 'at liberty', 'left alone, without excuse' and 'responsible for everything' they do.[1] More recently Jacques Monod in *Chance and Necessity* has argued that scientific understanding now reveals to humanity its 'fundamental isolation': it lives 'on the boundary of an alien world . . . that is deaf' to its music and 'indifferent' to its hopes, sufferings and crimes. Humanity 'is alone in the unfeeling immensity of the universe' out of which it has 'emerged only by chance'.[2] Others have preferred to advocate an agnostic position.[3] They judge that the lack of logically satisfactory evidence makes it impossible to reach justifiable conclusions about either the existence or the non-existence of God. Many more do not explicitly assert either atheism or agnosticism but their thought and conduct, by ignoring any significant reference to the divine, shows that they consider reality to be *de facto* atheistic. Whatever they may profess in answer to questions, a large proportion of the population in the contemporary Western world fall into this category. Can theism, though, offer any significant arguments to justify its foundational belief in the reality of God? Various attempts to show that it can have been and still are made. In this chapter we are briefly to note the more interesting ones. Before we consider the arguments themselves, however, four preliminary points need to be made.

In the first place it is important to recognize that the question of the existence of God and questions about the nature of God are not independent of each other. In principle the question of God can be tackled in two ways. One way is to specify what is meant by 'God' and then seek to establish whether there are grounds for holding that something exists which has that nature. The problem with this approach is that there are serious disagreements about the fundamental characteristics of God. Is the basis of theism justified if it is found to be possible to prove the reality of an 'unmoved mover' (such as Aristotle described as being an eternal, separate, impassive and unalterable substance), or is it necessary to find reasons for affirming the reality of a self-conscious, purposive, agential ultimate reality, or of a perfect being which is a proper object of worship, or of a transcendent, mysterious Thou, or of some combination of these and other characteristics? If, furthermore, the initial description of God is mistaken, the conclusion may be reached that there are no good reasons to hold that 'God exists' whereas in fact what the investigation properly shows is that there are no good reasons for holding that the being misdescribed as the divine exists. The other way of approaching the problem of God's reality seeks to avoid this difficulty by starting from a very formal and abstract definition of 'God', for example, the ultimate, and then attempting to determine the nature of that which is ultimate in reality. A basic problem with this approach is that it presupposes that we are in a position to identify clearly what actually is ultimate and then to determine its characteristics. This presupposition, however, is not supported by what we find as we investigate the issues. The nature of the ultimate is obscure and mysterious. Consequently what seems to be involved in producing a convincing argument is a mixture of the two approaches. This results in a complex interaction between reasons which indicate that reality is grounded on that which we think of as 'God' and perceptions of the fundamental nature of reality which indicate how we should conceive of the nature of God's reality. Since, therefore, the question of what God is and whether there be a God are interdependent, it is always important to consider at the end of any apparently satisfactory argument about the existence of God just what kind of a being has been shown to exist.

Secondly, though, is the question, 'Does God exist?' a proper question? J. J. C. Smart, for example, holds that it is not. He suggests that just as the question 'Do electrons exist?' does not meaningfully arise in physics because the notion of 'electrons' is presupposed in that way of understanding, so religious faith presupposes the reality of God. On the other hand, just as the notion of electrons makes no sense outside the realm of the understanding of physics, so the notion of God has no meaning outside the religious context. Hence where the notion is meaningful, the reality of its referent is presupposed, and where that reality is questioned the notion is meaningless.[4] Alasdair MacIntyre presents another argument to the same end when he suggests that a particular religious belief is justified by showing that it has a place 'in the total religious conception' but the total religious conception cannot be justified by reference to anything beyond itself. In this, though, it is no different from science and morality for they, too, are fields of understanding 'defined by reference to certain ultimate criteria' which, since they are ultimate, it is impossible to go beyond.[5] These philosophical attacks on the principle of trying to justify belief in the reality of God have some theological and religious support. Theologically, for example, it may be argued that God is supremely a 'Thou' who is encountered, not a conclusion of an argument.[6] If God is met, there is no doubt about the divine reality; if God is not met, no reasoning about an object will ever be a substitute for the meeting. Religiously it may be argued that authentic faith is a matter of utter trust in God and that would-be believers are denying themselves the possibility of authentic faith by trying to justify its reasonableness to themselves and others. Rather than relying utterly on God they are trying to find security for their faith in their own rationality.

Although these objections to the legitimacy of enquiring into the reality of God have some significance, it is arguable that they indicate the nature and limits of the task rather than rule it out altogether. Arguments about the existence of God are not, for example, to be compared to investigations as to whether Gwyneth Owen ever taught at Ockbrook School or whether the yeti exists in Nepal. They are more like arguments to show that a particular way of understanding reality may be held to provide a significant perception of what is actually the case – that in relation to reality as a whole, for example, theism discerns the ultimate nature of things more appropriately than, say atheistic materialism, just as in relation to the interactions between substances modern chemistry may justifiably be preferred to alchemy and to hermetic teachings. Such arguments are never easy to establish for in the end they are always likely to be somewhat circular. In the case of theism, for example, the object of the argument is to show that the character of reality is such that it is reasonable to consider it as being fundamentally purposive, rational, and significant, since it is qualities like these which theism presumes must characterize reality if it is ultimately based on and derived from the being of God. The signs of purposiveness, rationality and significance that are found in it (and so have been held to point to God as the ground of its having this character) are, however, at least influenced by the fact that our understanding has probably been partly formed by an implicitly theistic attitude to what constitutes ultimate meaningfulness and so considers that things make sense only so far as it finds them to have such characteristics. The result is that our understanding tends to presuppose the presence of these characteristics by looking for them in what it investigates. While, however, its criterion of meaningfulness thus begs the question to some extent, what a satisfactory case for the reality of God will apparently show is that the theistic story makes more sense of the ultimate character of reality than other ways of viewing it. As for the theological objection, it may be replied that the aim of arguments about the existence of God is, in part, to show that believers are justified in claiming that there is a reality to be encountered, and that non-believers are mistaken in holding that such experiences must be delusory. The religious objection similarly may be countered by holding that investigations into the reality of God are intended to show that theistic belief is not open to dismissal as incredulous fantasizing, since it is reasonable to consider that whatever is ultimate in being is not simply a brute fact, an inevitable datum, but is, as theism maintains, a reality which it is proper to worship and trust. The conclusions of the arguments for the existence of God are not a substitute for encounter and faith. They seek, rather, to show that theistic understanding and theistic faith is a credible stance to adopt towards reality.

The third preliminary point is that enquiries into the reality of God are not merely seeking to establish that people talk about God. In a weak sense of the term, something can be said to 'exist' if it belongs to a form of discourse. Hence it is possible to say that economic laws, Winnie the Pooh, numbers, and the members of the Homeric pantheon 'exist' because there is a recognizable way of talking about them. At this level there can be no dispute that 'God exists' for people do make religious statements and 'God' is one of characteristic notions in such language. This, however, is not enough for the justification of theism as a way of understanding. As Dorothy Emmet remarks, 'religion loses its nerve when it ceases to believe that it expresses in some way truth about our relation to a reality beyond ourselves which ultimately concerns us'.[7] God for theism is not just an idea, not even an idea that is believed in: 'God' primarily refers to a real entity whose being is independent of any human recognition and response and which constitutes the ultimate basis for the being, value and final purpose of everything else. The reality of God is not the reality of a relationship between entities – as 'love' may be said to be 'real' although finally it is only 'real' so far as real entities constitute it by their relationship to each other. The reality of God is the reality of that which exists for itself as that which can have both external and internal relationships with other entities. When God is said to exist, therefore, it is in the 'strong' sense of the term where to say something 'exists' is to imply that it both can act upon other things and be acted upon by them. Although it is not necessary in this respect to accept the physicalist prejudice which defines existence in terms of having 'bulkiness' and 'endurance' (one of the recent professors of philosophy at Manchester once defined 'to exist' as 'to be kickable'), it is the way in which the table on which I write 'exists' rather than the way in which Pooh 'exists' which indicates what is meant in theistic understanding when 'God' is said to 'exist'. Better still, perhaps, it is the way in which I 'exist' for myself and you 'exist' for yourself which gives the basic content of the notion.

The final preliminary point is a reminder that while 'existence' is used in a strong sense when theism speaks of God's existence, the mode of that existence is unique. Paul Tillich went so far in this respect as to state that 'God does not exist. He is being-itself'.[8] By this remark he makes the point that God's mode of being is radically different from the contingent and finite mode of existence that everything else has. God's being is that on which all else depends and which itself is dependent on nothing prior. Charles Hartshorne has thus described the divine mode of being as a state of 'necessary existence' in that it is in principle a mode of being which cannot be conceived as either coming into being or ceasing to be, which is universal and omnitolerant in that it is present to and compatible with whatever else may happen to come to be or not come to be, and which is its own intrinsic ground.[9] The status of the divine as the source of all else is neatly expressed in a cartoon of a small child finishing the list of people to pray for with this comment 'And do look after yourself, God, for if you go, we are all done for' – but the prayer was unnecessary, for a proper insight into the divine shows that its reality could never end. The essential necessity, ultimacy and universality of the divine existence, however, render it extremely hard to establish. Since all else finally depends on it, without exception, its reality cannot be detected by straightforward empirical methods. Whereas we can discover the presence of titanium in a substance by discovering whether that substance shows, on analysis, characteristics which are found if titanium is present and are not found if titanium is absent, we cannot so test for the presence of God. Every instance that we could ever find depends upon God, if it is true that God exists. The reality of God produces no distinguishing marks which apply in some cases but not in others. In the end, therefore, the task of showing the reality of God is a matter of identifying the fundamental nature of everything actual and of everything that could ever possibly become actual.

It is time, however, to move from these preliminary consider-ations to look at some of the arguments which have been offered. We will briefly consider the cosmological, design, teleological, moral, experiential, existential, ontological and cumulative argu-ments. As elsewhere in this introductory study, it is important to remember that what is given is only a very limited outline of issues which have deservedly had whole books – and big ones at that – devoted to them.

The cosmological argument

The cosmological argument attempts to show, by various lines of reasoning, that the world in which we find ourselves must ultimately be derived from some primal reality – a 'first cause' – which is identified as God. Plato, for example, points out in the *Laws* that things in the universe move or change. Motion or change in one thing, however, is caused by motion or change in another thing which affects it, and that motion or change is caused in a similar way, and so on. From this he argues that the presence of motion or change in the universe is only explicable if we put an end to the apparently endless series of causes by perceiving that motion or change must originate in an initial self-moved mover or 'soul'. This soul is 'the source of change and motion' in 'all that is, or has become, or will be'.[10] Aristotle agrees that all movement is produced by something else but is not satisfied with the idea of a 'self-moved mover'. He considers that the 'movement' in what is 'self-moving' must be the product of something in that 'soul' which moves, and this in turn be moved by something prior to it, and so on. The series of movers, however, cannot be held to go back endlessly, for if there were no end, there would be no first mover; and if there were no first mover, the causal chain of movements would never begin. Hence the conclusion is drawn that all movement ultimately depends upon an eternal 'unmoved mover' which 'primarily imparts motion' but is itself 'unmoved'.[11] It can be envisaged as doing this by acting as a kind of lure (or 'final cause') which stirs other things by its value but itself is totally unchanging and even unaware of its effects on these other things.

So far as the classical forms of the cosmological argument consider motion or change in terms of locomotion, they are heavily influenced by the view that such movement is only possible through the constant action of a force. They accordingly declined in importance with the recognition of momentum as described in Newton's first law of motion. This suggested that the movements in the universe, especially in the heavenly bodies, could be satisfactorily understood without reference to something beyond the empirical world. The argument seems more plausible when it is put in terms of causality – of the need for a 'first cause' to initiate the causal chains which operate in the world now. What is generally considered to be the most significant form of the argument reasons from the contingency of things (i.e. from the fact that anything which we encounter in the world need not have existed: it is coherent to think of the possibility that its actuality might not have been realized) to the existence of a necessary being which is the ground of all reality. Once again the argument can be developed in various ways but it rests on two claims: that while some things exist (we at least exist), their non-existence is conceivable (i.e. it is possible that they might not have come to be), and that something real cannot be produced out of nothing (i.e. 'ex nihilo nihil fit' – out of nothing nothing comes to be). It is then argued that in a limitless sequence every possibility will eventually be realized; if therefore all things are contingent, at some time in the apparently endless past there would have been a state where the possible non-existence of everything occurred. From that state of 'no-thing', however, nothing could have been produced. There must, therefore, be a first, necessary, uncaused being which is the source of being in everything else. It is further argued that this being must have all the qualities found in the universe because of the principle that there can be nothing in a creature which is not first in its creator. Because this being is absolutely primary, it is also maintained that it will have these qualities in a supreme or perfect form. Hence the conclusion is reached that 'God exists'.

Various objections can be raised against this argument. Why, for example, must the causal chain (or the chain of contingent dependency) have a first point? Why could it not be an infinite series? To argue that if it did not have a first point, it would never have begun is to miss the point of regarding it as an 'infinite' series: an infinite series always, endlessly, is in operation and to think of it as having to have had a beginning is incoherent. The demand for a start to the process may reflect the limits of our ways of understanding rather than the limits of the essential character of reality. Again, the argument can be criticized for begging the question so far as it relies on the principle that everything must have a cause. Having used the principle to get to the 'first cause', it then, in an apparently arbitrary manner, asserts that this 'first cause' is a reality which has no cause. Why is not the sauce for the contingent geese also sauce for the divine gander? To say that it is 'its own cause' ('causa sui') is not to explain anything but merely to restate the problem. The criticisms, it should be noted, do not show that it is wrong to think of the divine mode of being as so characterized. What they do indicate is that it is not clearly legitimate to argue for the existence of God by means of these notions. Finally, even if the argument be held to have some validity, it is not at all obvious that it can establish that the God of theistic understanding exists. There is a huge gap between a first unmoved mover, a primary efficient cause, or a necessary being, and the conscious, value-appreciating, purposive, agential God of theism. The recognition of the evolutionary character of the natural world, both cosmologically and biologically, makes it far from self-evident that the 'first', even though absolutely prior, must have the qualities found in what depends upon it.

The argument from design

The last point raises the central issue in the second argument which we are to consider, the argument from design. According to this, consideration of the processes and contents of the natural world shows that they display clear signs of intelligent design. Such design, however, does not happen spontaneously. Consequently the character of the world provides strong evidence of the reality of a supreme, intelligent being which is responsible for the structure of its constituents. This being is then identified as God.

Those who have presented this argument have often plundered current scientific knowledge for examples of design by which to make their case. It is an argument which was especially popular in the early days of modern science. As people marvelled at what was being discovered, they found in it clear marks of the reality, wisdom, power and goodness of a divine creator. John Ray, for example, finds evidence of 'the Wisdom of the Creator' in the structure of the woodpecker's feet and tail-feathers which are convenient for climbing and perching on the side of tree-trunks.[12] William Derham holds that the orbits of the planets and comets 'demonstrate the planetary System to have been modelled by *Counsel*, and not by a *Necessity of Nature*, or left to *Chance*.'[13] He likewise sees 'the admirable Mechanism' of the stomach as 'manifesting the super-eminent Contrivance and Art of the infinite Workman'.[14] William Paley's *Natural Theology* discusses, among many other things, the mechanics of muscles and tendons, the hydraulics of the gall-bladder, the beauty of natural things, the composition of light, and the variety of animal appetites[15] in coming to the conclusion that

> The marks of *design* are too strong to be gotten over. Design must have had a designer. That designer must have been a person. That person is God . . . It is an immense conclusion that there is God; a perceiving, intelligent, designing Being, at the head of creation, and from whose will it proceeded.[16]

Paley was aware, though, that the argument was open to certain criticisms. He therefore points out that we do not have to understand every part and function of a structure to see that it is the product of design, that an object's ability to reproduce itself is a sign of a highly skilful original design, and that cases of imperfection and disorder in a structure do not disprove that it was designed.

Before Paley wrote, however, the argument from design had been severely mauled by David Hume in his *Dialogues concerning Natural Religion*. On examination the argument seems to be vulnerable at several points. How, for example, do we know that the order which is apparently observed in nature is not immanent in the system? What justifies us in thinking that our experiences of planning and constructing something, say a house, are a proper model for understanding the formation of an eyeball or a carrot or a universe? If we come across a house, we are justified in thinking that it had an architect and a builder because our experience has informed us that this is how houses in general come into being. We have no parallel experiences of either the formation of a universe as a whole or of the particular items within it. Indeed so far as we do now understand the way in which natural structures have emerged, the notion of design and its execution appropriate to the building of a house seems widely inappropriate to natural things. Furthermore, it is arguable that the perception of supposed design is to be dismissed as an imposition of our intellect upon what is presented to it (as we impose patterns upon ink-blots in a Rorschach test). If, however, it seems plausible to claim that there is a designer behind the world, where did that designer come from? Why would it be illegitimate to apply the design argument to the designer and postulate a prior designer for the designer, and then a prior designer for the designer of the designer of the world, and then . . . ? It may be less harassing to admit that while natural objects show amazing structures as if they were designed to fulfil the functions which they do fulfil, we have no justifiable way of moving in such cases from the 'as if' to saying that they are the products of design by a designer. If, however, the argument from design be accepted, all that it shows is that the designer of the universe is clever and powerful enough to have produced it. The argument does not show that the 'architect of the universe' is perfect. The extent of imperfections, deficiencies and break-downs in the natural world (eyes and ears fail, diseases destroy, weather-systems produce disasters, earthquakes and volcanoes demolish) suggest that the designer of the world, if there be one, is seriously deficient in power or wisdom or benevolence. As we noticed, however, in the earlier chapter on 'Faith, God and the Natural World', the view of creation which underlies both the argument from design and these objections to it is no longer at all plausible. The recognition of the evolutionary process which produced the present order of nature shows that it is no longer reasonable, let alone necessary, to think of an intelligent, purposive designer to explain the specific characteristics of particular species. The emergence of these characteristics can be adequately understood as a 'natural' consequence of the interplay of genetic accidents with the struggle for satisfaction in a world with limited resources and competing agents.

The teleological argument

The teleological argument is often treated as a form of the argument from design but it is preferable to regard it as a distinct argument. Whereas the argument from design concentrates on the apparent signs of intelligent manufacture exhibited by natural objects, the teleological argument considers in a much broader way whether the structure of reality indicates that it is fundamentally purposive. Its argument rests upon two claims. The first is that the general order and system of the world is manifestly appropriate for the realization of values. The second is that it is hardly credible that the world should have emerged with such a structure through a random interaction of blind forces. It thus concludes that the basic character of the world strongly indicates that it is the deliberate product of a conscious will that is intelligently concerned about values.

F. R. Tennant's *Philosophical Theology* provides a powerful statement of the teleological argument. He recognizes that the particular cases which are used as evidence in the argument from design may each be explained by reference to 'proximate causes' immanent in the natural order. The strength of the teleological argument lies rather in what Tennant describes as 'the conspiration of innumerable causes to produce, by their united and reciprocal action, and to maintain, a general order of Nature'. This order, furthermore, may reasonably be understood to be concerned with the realization of values.[17] There are five factors which Tennant considers to be especially significant in thus leading to the conclusion that theism offers the most probable hypothesis for understanding the world as being the outcome of divine intelligence and purpose.[18] The first of these is 'the mutual adaptation of thought and things' which makes nature an intelligible structure.[19] By this Tennant refers to the way in which the structures of our awareness and of thought turn out to be apparently compatible with the way things are so that nature is graspable by us as rationally understandable. The second is the overall 'progressiveness of the evolutionary process' and its general 'directivity'.[20] Thirdly there is the 'apparent preparedness' of the inorganic world to be 'a theatre' for the emergence and sustenance of life. 'Common-sense reasonableness' regards the likelihood that this 'apparent preparedness' was due to chance 'as infinitesimally small'.[21] The fourth factor is an aesthetic one. For Tennant the world is 'a bearer of values', not merely in the sense that things of value may be produced from it (in the way, for example, that a block of stone may be said to be the potential bearer of the value of a piece of superb sculpture) but in the sense that the natural world itself includes structures and entities whose 'beauty and sublimity' themselves give aesthetic delight. As such a bearer of values the world seems to have a basic 'affinity with beings' that have aesthetic appreciation.[22] Whereas the structure of the world may point to 'intelligent power', the concern for values which is intrinsic to the world 'alone can provide guidance as to the world's meaning'.[23] Finally Tennant considers at some length the significance of the fact that 'Nature . . . has produced moral beings, is instrumental to moral life . . . and is relatively modifiable by . . . moral agents pursuing ideals'. In his view, 'the whole process of Nature' may reasonably be regarded as 'instrumental to the development of intelligent and moral creatures'.[24] These five factors, he concludes, when taken together, forcibly suggest that the world is to be understood as the product of 'divine design'[25] and that design as concerned with a divine purpose involving 'the element of value, of desire and satisfaction'.[26]

Although Tennant is justified in claiming that the strength of this argument rests on the combined effect of these factors, analogous to the strength of a piece of chain-mail, rather than on the strength of the weakest item, like the links in a chain, the argument only convinces so long as the individual factors and their combined effect are regarded as significant. Some critics, for example, suggest that the characteristics of intelligibility and openness to value which Tennant finds significant are read into nature by human investigators seeking to find meaning and purpose in it. The link between inorganic and organic and the suggested directivity of the evolutionary process may be the result of considering nature from our human perspective rather than an appropriate assessment of its cosmic dimensions. As with the argument from design, the workings of chance and the presence of destructive forces ('dysteleology') in the natural world may be thought to count against the story of reality advanced by the teleological argument. With both arguments, too, there is the fundamental problem of whether they are based upon a justifiable view of divine creativity. Unlike the argument from design, however, the teleological argument does not concentrate on individual species and processes: it seeks to discern the character of the whole. From our human perspective, though, can we credibly claim to be able to perceive the significance of the whole? The argument finally rests on the credibility of the answer to this question. Tennant himself is aware of these problems and attempts to overcome them. The importance of the argument depends on the degree to which such answers are convincing.

The moral argument

Tennant's presentation of the teleological argument finds considerable significance in the way that the world may be held to provide an arena for moral development. Another group of arguments for the reality of God seeks to show, in various ways, that moral experience finally makes sense only in terms of divine existence. Immanuel Kant, for example, in his *Critique of Practical Reason* maintains that all people, as rational beings, recognize that they are under an unavoidable moral duty to seek the highest good. A duty, however, can only exist if it is possible to fulfil it – this is according to the moral principle that 'ought implies can'. I am under no obligation to feed my grandfather if he has died, nor is someone who is totally paralysed under a moral obligation to stand during the playing of the national anthem. This highest good, furthermore, is defined by Kant as a state in which the highest virtue is joined to the highest happiness.[27] The possibility of such a state (and hence of the moral duty to seek it) presupposes the existence of freedom, immortality, and God. Freedom is required if people are to be able to be morally responsible for their actions and so to be virtuous; immortality is required to give people time to fulfil the moral law; and God is required to ensure that in the end there is established 'the exact harmony of happiness with morality'.[28] This argument, however, can be challenged on the grounds that an ideal does not have to be attainable in order for it to be our moral duty to seek it. In any case, it only shows that the reality of God must be 'postulated' if our moral experience is to be rationally coherent. It may be, though, that our moral sense is an attempt to impose rational meaning on a reality which is intrinsically meaningless.

A different form of the moral argument maintains that the unconditionality of the moral obligation points to a transcendent authority which imposes it. In *Does God Exist?* A. E. Taylor holds that our experience of moral judgments shows them to be authoritative 'just because' they are apprehended as being 'not simply the pronouncement' of our own views 'but of one more august and universal'.[29] The voice of conscience is thus to be regarded as 'evidence of *fact*' which witnesses to 'the active reality of the living God'.[30] A. C. Ewing, in *Value and Reality*, similarly sees the authority of the moral law (which, in his view, cannot possibly be overstated) as indicating 'that it is bound up with the essential structure, the fundamental groundwork of the real'.[31] Its 'unconditionally compelling character' and 'objectivity' seems to be most readily explicable if its origin is attributed to 'the mind of the deity'.[32] The major defect in such an argument, though, is that some people claim not to be aware of any transcendent, unconditional moral demand and others find the experienced authority of the moral demand satisfactorily explained by reference to the social conditioning which occurs in the education of every individual to be a civilized person. Consequently, even if the fact of moral experience is allowed, it is not at all clear that it indicates the character of ultimate reality. It may just tell us about our moral sensibility as human beings.

A third version of the moral argument maintains that the essential independence of the moral ideal implies a divine mind where it is realized. In his *Theory of Good and Evil* Hastings Rashdall presents such an argument. It starts from the premise that 'the Moral Law has a real existence'. This is justified by the claim that however much individuals may disagree over a particular moral judgment, it is not disputable that 'there is something absolutely true or false in ethical judgments'. Since, though, the disagreements about moral values show that the moral ideal cannot be located in an individual human consciousness, it must be concluded that the moral ideal must exist for 'a Mind which is the source of whatever is true in our own moral judgments', a 'Mind', furthermore, 'from which all Reality is derived' and by which it is 'controlled'.[33] The objectivity of morality is therefore held to be sustainable only on the supposition of the reality of God as a transcendent mind which envisages it. The basic problem with this argument lies in its premise. It is not self-evident that the moral law has an objectivity and reality which is independent of human beings. The argument, indeed, may plausibly be reversed to hold that it is only where people already believe in some way in the reality of God that they find morality to have an objective, transcendent reality. In that case it is not the quality of moral experience which proves God, but the sense of God's being which determines how moral experience is apprehended.

The experiential argument

The most convincing way to establish the reality of someone whom one has been told about is to meet that person. Some philosophers and theologians accordingly argue that the reality of God is not something to be inferred from the evidence of other things. It is known by being directly experienced. For H. H. Farmer this happens in moral experience – the experience of unconditional demand and succour and the experience of God 'are given indissolubly and simultaneously together'.[34] Earlier in *Towards Belief in God* he asserts that those who have never experienced the awareness of God – and responded in worship – will never appreciate what talk of God refers to. He assumes, however, that 'the capacity to become aware of God is part of normal human nature like the capacity to see light or to hear sound'.[35] In the seminal *I and Thou* Martin Buber holds that God is pre-eminently personal. Accordingly the reality of God is not to be discovered by considering the implications of other things: 'God is the Being that is directly, most nearly, and lastingly over against us, that may properly only be addressed, not expressed.'[36] God is a pure Thou whose reality is only known through person-to-person encounter.[37] It is John Baillie, however, who deliberately offers an apologetic argument for the existence of God on the basis of experience. In *The Sense of the Presence of God* he asserts that faith is a 'primary mode of apprehension' which is self-authenticating.[38] As such it 'does not deduce from other realities that *are* present the existence of God who is *not* present but absent; rather it is an awareness of the divine Presence itself, however hidden behind the veils of sense'.[39]

There need be no doubt that for those who have these experiences, they are thoroughly convincing. The problem is to determine whether their theistic understanding of their experience is justified. Is it an experience of a reality which confronts us as an other or is it an experience of a quality, perhaps a projected or reified quality, of our own thoughts and feelings? To claim that the experience is self-authenticating as an experience of God may convince those who claim themselves to have the experience. It leaves those without it, those who are wanting to discover whether or not God exists, puzzled and suspicious. It seems that either they lack a fundamental mode of human awareness or other people have misinterpreted a quality of experience which they do recognize but do not see as necessarily theistic. The argument from experience thus seems to work for those who have had the experience in question (and so do not doubt the reality of God) but to be unconvincing for those who have not had it and wonder if there is a God. Furthermore, as in the case of the moral argument, it is arguable that the experience of God is a product of an existing belief in the reality of the divine rather than a mode of awareness which, by itself, is a proper justification of such belief.

The existential argument

The sixth argument for the reality of God which we are to discuss may be called the existential one. It starts from what is held to be the fundamental character of the self-understanding of human existence and argues that such self-understanding is only properly justifiable by reference to the reality of God. Therefore, either human existence is basically absurd or God exists. We noticed in chapter 2 how Schubert Ogden's essay, 'The Strange Witness of Unbelief', presents an argument of this type in response to Sartre's atheism. In the long paper which provides the title to the volume *The Reality of God*, Ogden points out that self-conscious human existence is always confronted by the question of its ultimate meaningfulness.[40] In the face of the threat of meaninglessness people seek reassurance and confidence. They can exist authentically as selves only where and because they have 'a confidence in the final worth' of their existence.[41] It is a confidence, though, which Ogden holds to be fundamental to human being. He describes it as 'ineradicable' and as 'original and inescapable'.[42] The function of religion, in its different expressions, is to provide people with 'particular symbolic forms'[42] by means of which, 'at the level of self-conscious belief',[44] they may affirm this fundamental faith in 'the meaning and worth of life'.[45] The notion of 'God' has a key role in such affirmations. It refers to 'the objective ground in reality itself' of this confidence in the significance of human existence.[46] Since, therefore, 'God' designates that which 'justifies' the trust at the heart of being human,[47] 'belief in God' is claimed to be 'unavoidable'.[48] Whether people explicitly recognize it or not, and whether they choose to express it in theistic language or not, the character of human existence means, according to Ogden's analysis, that 'everyone must in some sense' believe in God.[49]

A similar argument is advanced by Hans Küng, briefly in *On Being a Christian* and at length in *Does God Exist?*. He maintains that while belief in the reality of God cannot be guaranteed by means of the stringent proofs of an 'external rationality', there is 'an intrinsic rationality' which justifies trust in that reality.[50] This intrinsic rationality is grounded in the nature of human being. Although people who are self-conscious are aware that human existence is profoundly uncertain since it is possible that it may be, as nihilism claims, 'meaningless, worthless' and 'vain', in practice they may bring to reality 'not a fundamental mistrust, a basic lack of confidence, but a *fundamental trust*, a basic confidence'.[51] Accordingly they may regard reality, in spite of the threat identified by the nihilist analysis, as meaningful and valuable. The question of God's reality then arises as the question of whether such fundamental trust is rationally justifiable since, in Küng's view, only the existence of God would entail that reality has ultimate meaning and value. Since, however, the atheistic position is a real possibility, people are faced with an existential dilemma.[52] With their whole being they must decide whether they are to be fundamentally mistrustful or basically confident in their response to the ambiguous character of reality. What they discover, though, is that if they open themselves up to reality in trust and so seek to give themselves to its 'ultimate reason, support and goal', reality shows itself to be trustworthy and they become inwardly convinced that they are 'doing the right thing, in fact the most sensible thing of all'. In this way, then, Küng holds that the intrinsic rationality which justifies theistic faith is to be found in the existential experience that reality discloses its 'ultimate reason, support, goal, its primal source, primal meaning and primal value' to those who trust that it is so structured.[53] It is the practice of theism, the total commitment of actual faith, which confirms its truth.[54]

The significance of this existential argument for the reality of God depends partly on the correctness of its analysis of the fundamental character of human being and partly on its implicit assumption that what makes sense of that being must correspond to the actual character of reality. The correctness of its analysis is not easy to determine. Although the vast majority of people clearly have no desire to die and in desperate situations often struggle to survive with remarkable tenacity, it is not so clear that they are fundamentally confident about the meaning and worth of reality. While there are enough positively-directed people to make the analysis recognizable and even credible, there are others who seem fundamentally neutral. Basically these latter neither trust nor distrust reality. They avoid ultimate questions, for they see no point in troubling with what they regard as insoluble riddles, and they concern themselves with things at a much more superficial level. Their main aim is to be happy and, if that be not possible at times, to be as least unhappy as possible. It is, of course, possible to argue that such forms of being are inauthentic and that those who feel content with them are denying the intrinsic quality of human existence. The apparent actuality of such forms of being, though, raises some doubt about the analysis of human existence underlying the existential argument. The other basic question with the argument is the acceptability of the principle of rationality which it presupposes, namely, that reality ultimately makes sense. How, it may be asked in criticism, do we know that our human confidence in the meaning, worth and trustworthiness of reality is not an attempt to impose order and find security in a reality which is intrinsically absurd? It is not an easy question to answer – but, on the other hand, the assumption that reality is rationally intelligible is the principle which underlies all attempts at understanding. To deny it, therefore, is no mean matter.

The ontological argument

A very different kind of reasoning to show the reality of God is presented by the ontological argument. This argument starts from the concept of God and holds that the proper definition of God entails that it is self-contradictory to hold that God does not exist. If, though, 'God does not exist' must be false, it follows that God must exist. The classical statement of this argument is to be found in Anselm's *Proslogion* and in his *Reply* to criticisms which had been made of the argument by Gaunilo. Descartes and Leibniz both produced forms of this argument and in recent philosophical theology it has found a powerful advocate in the writings of Charles Hartshorne, especially in his *Anselm's Discovery*[55] and *The Logic of Perfection*.

The argument begins with the definition of God. Anselm puts it that God is to be understood as 'that than which nothing greater can be conceived'[56] while Descartes states that 'the idea of God' is 'the idea of a supremely perfect Being'.[57] This definition is held to be a coherent concept. It is then maintained, as intuitively evident, that it is better to exist than not to exist: an existing gold sovereign, for instance, is better than the thought of one. Since, therefore, existence is a quality which it is better for something to have than not to have, it is self-contradictory to think of God as not existing. If, that is, we tried to think of 'God' as non-existing, we would be thinking of a being that lacked at least one quality, namely that of existing; we could in that case then think of another being that had all the qualities of the former one but also had the quality of existing. The former one would then be inferior to the latter one and so the former one could not be 'that than which a greater cannot be conceived' or 'the supremely perfect'. Consequently it is argued that God, as the greater than can be conceived, must be thought of as existing.

A variant of this argument seeks to overcome problems with treating bare existence as a quality by holding that there are two modes of existence, necessary existence and contingent existence. The latter is the mode of existence which belongs to an object that happens to exist but whose non-existence is coherently conceivable. Such an object may not have existed at some time in the past and may not exist at some time in the future. Its existence is dependent on factors beyond it. Hence its existence is 'contingent'. Necessary existence, in contrast, is the mode of existence of that which cannot not exist – or, in other words, must exist at all times. It is self-contradictory to think of such an object coming into existence or being caused to be by anything other than itself and it is equally self-contradictory to think of it as being destroyed by anything other than itself or simply ceasing to be. When compared with each other, necessary existence is intuitively superior as a mode of being to contingent existence. Because of the way that the notion of God is properly defined, it thus follows that God must be conceived as having necessary existence as the divine mode of being. But, the argument concludes, what has necessary existence must necessarily exist; therefore God exists.

The ontological argument has fascinated many philosophers and theologians. If it is valid, it is an attractively neat and ingenious argument for its reasoning requires nothing more than a consideration of what is meant by 'God'. Unfortunately most of those who consider it are not persuaded of its validity. The central defect in it is its use of the notion of 'existence'. Existence is not in all cases a desirable quality, let alone a perfection, as anyone with an existing overdraft at the bank will appreciate! More important, though, is the recognition that existence is not a quality to be attributed to an object in the way that being 166 centimetres tall, weighing 57 kilogrammes, having an IQ of 140 plus and being concerned are qualities that may be attributed to a person, or being spherical, nine inches in diameter and made of brass may be attributed to part of a pawn-broker's sign. The function of the term 'existence' is not to add another attribute to the list of attributes by which we may describe an object. The point of saying that it 'exists' is to report the relationship between the concept of an object which we have developed through listing its attributes and the contents of the real world. So far, then, as the ontological argument treats existence as a quality which is to be included in the concept of a perfect being, it has fundamentally misunderstood the nature of the notion of 'existence'. Even if we could produce an exhaustive list of the divine attributes, we would still be faced with the question 'But does a being exist which corresponds to that description?'.

The attempt to avoid the problem by referring to the 'necessary existence' of God fails for basically the same reason. The concept of 'necessary existence' is not to be dismissed, as some philosophers have argued, by asserting that 'necessity' can only be applied to the relationship between propositions. Hartshorne has shown that there is a coherent use of 'necessary' in relation to existence as a way of referring to the mode of being of that which cannot not exist, is omnitolerant, endless and so on. What the notion of 'necessary existence' refers to, though, is a quality of the divine mode of being – and is directly comparable to descriptions of God as being 'eternal' and 'omnipresent'. If, therefore, we accept, as we should, that God must be conceived of as having 'necessary existence' as the divine mode of being, we are still left with the question 'But does a God conceived of as having this quality exist?'. The recognition that God is to be conceived as having necessary existence is an important appreciation of the special quality of the divine mode of being but it does not allow us to infer that because the concept of God must be so conceived, God must exist. There is no logically entailed step from concepts of objects to their reality, not even in the peculiar case of God ('peculiar' because it seems that 'necessary existence' is attributable only to God's mode of being).

The cumulative argument

Finally, and briefly, we should note what may be called the cumulative argument for the reality of God. What this argument does is to draw attention to all the other arguments which have been advanced to justify belief in the reality of God and to the various criticisms which have been levelled at them, and then to ask what, considered together, they signify. While none of the arguments on its own may be very convincing, it is possible that in combination they may show the reasonableness of theistic belief in the reality of God as a self-conscious agent who is ultimate in being, value and rationality. The strength of such an argument depends, however, on each of its constitutive elements having some degree of probability. If the criticisms of each of the arguments for the reality of God which it cites mean that the probability of its conclusion according to that argument is zero, there will be nothing to add together to produce a cumulative case. Zero plus zero plus zero, no matter how many zeros are included, never adds up to anything other than zero. On the other hand, while objections can be raised against each of the arguments, it is possible that, at least in some cases, those objections do not prove that the conclusion of the argument must have no significance at all. The argument may, in that case, indicate that there is something to be said, even if not very much, for regarding the ultimate nature of reality in the way that its conclusion suggests. The cumulative argument then maintains that theism provides a means of incorporating these different suggestions in a single way of understanding, and does so (it also claims) in a far more satisfactory way than any other way of understanding the ultimate nature of reality.

It is a mistake, though, to regard the cumulative argument primarily it terms of the mechanical addition of the probability-values of the conclusions of other arguments (or in terms of a resolution of the lines of direction of various 'pointers', if the cumulative argument is seen as one by converging probability). The argument is most usefully viewed as posing this question 'In view of the various considerations which the arguments for the reality of God draw to our attention, does theism provide the most coherent, all-embracing, fruitful and fitting view of reality that we can envisage?'. In the end, that is, the problem of the reality of God is to be solved by judging whether the story of reality which theism tells makes more sense of reality than any other story. Presenting the issue in this way admittedly begs the question to some extent for it assumes that reality is finally intelligible and that what appears to us to be the most reasonable story to make sense of it is to be accepted as the truth about it. This, though, is the choice that confronts us. Do we see reality as rationally intelligible and trust worthy – and so are drawn in some way to a basic acceptance of the reality of God, or do we regard reality as finally irrational and absurd – and so are committed to an atheistic view? Agnosticism is the refusal to choose at the intellectual level of self-conscious belief. Theism and atheism, though, are not just matters of intellectual decisions. They concern our appraisal of and response to everything. Their intellectual expressions are only convincing as they reflect a story which convinces us. The value of the arguments for the reality of God, if they have any value, is that they bring us to reflect on aspects of reality which we must take into account if the story which we accept is to satisfy us, intellectually and existentially. As I. T. Ramsey once put it in an article on 'Contemporary Philosophy and the Christian Faith', the function of the traditional arguments is '*not* to supply tight deductive proofs, but to provide talk by which, first, a cosmic disclosure may be evoked for a prospective believer, and secondly, . . . some guidance may be given . . . as to how to use the word "God"'.[58] Those for whom the phrase 'cosmic disclosure' may not appeal, may substitute for it 'a realization of the story that makes sense of everything ultimately'. The question is, Do the arguments help to evoke such an awareness? Only if they do are they important.

Chapter 9

Faith, Death and Immortality

The awareness of the temporal nature of reality brings with it an awareness of death. According to S. G. F. Brandon this is the clue to the nature of religion. In *History, Time and Deity* he reminds his readers that time not only threatens human beings with the 'vicissitudes of fortune' in their 'social or economic situation'; it also 'menaces' each of them with the warning of eventual 'disintegration' as selves – a menace which 'will certainly be fulfilled, whether its event comes soon or late'. The result is that the consciousness of time arouses in human beings 'a profound foreboding of ill' and evokes in them 'the instinct to escape, to find some abiding security from a destiny so sure and so dreadful'.[1] For Brandon this reaction to the consciousness of time 'constitutes a basic factor in all religions' and may 'even be described as *the* basic factor, or rather, the very source, of the religious intuitions and aspirations of our race'.[2]

Although it is disputable whether concern about death and post-mortem existence is as central in religion as Brandon maintains, it is an issue which has traditionally been important in religious understanding, not least in Christianity. Paul, for example, asserts that to say that 'there is no resurrection of the dead' is to render the gospel 'null and void' and to make faith empty: 'if it is for this life only that Christ has given us hope, we of all men are most to be pitied.'[3] In the Apostles' Creed Christians profess belief in 'the resurrection of the body, and the life everlasting' and in their hymnody proclaim such sentiments as

> Jesus lives! henceforth is death
> Entrance-gate of life immortal.

In some of the more affluent parts of the world today such concerns are not so pressing. People expect to have opportunity to use their potential in their life-times. Their major fear may well be not of death but of a death which does not come soon enough to prevent the embarrassments of senile decay. Indeed in some cases death may be welcomed – as it was by the minister who made a Freudian slip at a funeral service and invited the congregation to sing 'Rejoice for a brother deceased, his loss is our infinite gain'! (For those who do not know, the correct text of the hymn reads, 'our loss is his infinite gain'.) Death, however, does bring loss – loss of the physical presence and comfort of those whom we love. Is it the absolute end of such relationships? And death poses a question to each of us: 'What is my destiny? Do I live to die or is death but a transformation in the mode of human existence?' It may not be fashionable to discuss such questions and the bonhomie of funeral gatherings may reflect a desire to hide from them, but self-conscious existence cannot escape them. They are properly included in the self-understanding of religious faith.

Philosophers have been interested in such questions, both because they concern the nature and purpose of human being and because the notion of post-mortem existence raises some interesting puzzles. We shall first look at some of these puzzles and then investigate the two distinct notions of immortality and the arguments which are offered in connection with them.

Puzzles of post-mortem existence

The oddity of the idea of post-mortem existence is disclosed to some extent by the language which we use in discussing it. If, for example, we talk about 'surviving death' in this connection, we employ a notion whose normal usage is to refer to events where a person avoids death. 'Arthur was in the crash but survived' means that Arthur did not die. This suggests that talk about 'surviving death' contains within it the implication that death, as the extinction of a person, does not occur. On the other hand, when we consider the verb 'to die', it is easy to grant that the future, present and past tenses of the verb in the second and third person have a meaningful use as do the future and present tenses in the first person. The oddity of the verb appears when we consider whether it is meaningful to use it in the first person in the past tense. What would 'I have died' express? Could it conceivably be uttered? If it could be uttered, at least in a non-metaphorical way, would not others be inclined to say 'The fact you can say "I have died" shows that your statement is false. If you had really died you would not have been able to report it'? (In this respect the verb is interestingly comparable to the verb 'to be born' where the first person future is the puzzling one – 'I will be born' is not a statement that has an obvious usage.)

These linguistic points indicate that references to 'death' are ambiguous in certain respects. For those who deny immortality, 'death' refers to the end of one's being. It is not an event in one's existence but the end of all such events. For those who affirm some kind of immortality, however, 'death' refers to an event in one's existence – an event which presumably radically alters its state but still an event which one can subsequently look back at and say 'That happened to me!'. It is a view of death which has some intriguing implications – as indicated by the question posed in a paper by A. G. N. Flew, 'Can a Man Witness His Own Funeral?'.[4] It is also a view of death which raises some fundamental problems about the identity of the self before death with the self which is supposed to survive. We shall have to return to this question later but for the present it is sufficient to point out that there is at least an oddity in thinking of, for example, Joe witnessing Joe's funeral, for who is the 'Joe' that is observing and who is the 'Joe' that is being buried? And, crucially, how does the first 'Joe' identify himself with the second? The notion of the first 'Joe' as a disembodied spirit, released from the corpse of the second 'Joe', may have some credibility but such a dualistic notion of the human self is not easy to sustain when our only indubitable encounters with self-conscious selves is with embodied selves.

Two other oddities of the notion of immortality arise when we consider how claims about it might be rationally proved. In the first place claims about a post-mortem existence will never be empirically falsified. If our belief in immortality is mistaken, we will never discover it. We may, on the other hand, discover that our denial of immortality was mistaken. Death in this respect is an annoying prospect for if we hold one view about it, namely that death is the end, we will never discover if we were correct. Secondly, some arguments which purport to prove the reality of post-mortem existence may be held to be reversible so that they prove, equally well, pre-existence (i.e. a state of existence prior to conception). J. McT. E. McTaggart, for example, considered that there were such strong rational grounds for believing that we survive death that he republished his arguments on the matter to comfort the bereaved during the First World War. His study, *Human Immortality and Pre-existence*, is interesting not only as presenting a case for immortality from an atheistic position but also because its author confesses that he does not see 'how existence in future time could be shown to be necessary in the case of any being whose existence in past time is admitted not to be necessary'. He therefore concludes that 'any demonstration of immortality is likely to show that each of us exists through all time – past and future – whether time is held to be finite or infinite'.[5] At this point others may consider that the argument is proving too much – and see it as a signal that here, at any rate, reason shows that it is straying into issues beyond its competence. With this warning in mind, then, we shall consider what may be said for and against the notions of 'subjective immortality' and 'objective immortality'.

Subjective immortality

Subjective immortality is what is usually meant when people talk about 'surviving death' and 'post-mortem existence' or use the term 'immortality' without qualification. It signifies the belief that individuals continue as self-conscious subjects after the event of death. The experience of dying is consequently another incident in the course of personal existence, more dramatic perhaps than a first kiss or awakening from a post-luncheon nap but in the end just one more item to 'chalk up to experience'. Since this belief envisages that the individual self continues as a person after death, both as an experiencing and a responding subject, it implies that post-mortem existence is temporally ordered. No subjective selfhood would be possible in a state where all is 'at once' in a timeless eternity and where, consequently, there could be no significant forms of apprehension, response and activity. If, therefore, subjective immortality is to be described as 'eternal life', the notion of 'eternity' that is implied must be understood as a state of unending temporal successiveness or everlastingness (presuming that the immortal never ceases to be) rather than as a state of timeless being where nothing can ever occur. Only so can the 'eternal life' be an authentic form of living.

Some Christian theologians maintain that the Christian belief in post-mortem existence should be referred to as a belief in 'resurrection' rather than as a belief in 'immortality'. Their view is based upon a distinction between the two notions which holds that 'immortality' refers to a continuing state of being after death that is considered to be a natural (or quasi-natural) quality of human being whereas 'resurrection' refers to an event that occurs only through the agency of God. In the former case, that of immortality, we would discover that we are immortal if we could make a full analysis of the intrinsic nature of human being. The immortality would be found to be as characteristic of it as growth and ageing or a capacity for self-consciousness. In the latter case, though, that of resurrection, the knowledge that human beings are destined to be resurrected would only be known through a perception that this is the will of God for them. If, however, resurrection is a restoration to life which occurs because of the grace of God, it is conceivable that God may freely choose who is to be restored and in what form. At this point, though, considerable problems may arise about the identity of the post-mortem self with the previous self. If, for example, certain evangelical doctrines are correct in holding that the resurrected self is not merely a recipient of a new mode of being (in I Corinthians 15 Paul speaks of a person who dies having an 'animal body' and being resurrected as having a 'spiritual body') but is also immediately transformed into a sinless state, that self may have difficulty in recognizing itself as being identical with the one who died. In such a situation it is not at all easy to see how one can decide that the self which comes to be after death is not a new person who happens to inherit some memories of another self rather than a continuation, through transformation, of that former self. The more radical and sudden the transformation that occurs at resurrection, the less plausible is it to hold that a self who died has been restored to being. In this respect doctrines of purgatory which suggest that the self goes through a process of change from its sinful to a sinless state at least have the merit of making sense of the self-identity of the person involved. Perhaps, though, these are problems posed by a person who is so aware of imperfections that the idea of being identifiable as a perfect person is incredible.

What, though, are some of the arguments which have been offered to justify belief in subjective post-mortem existence, whether it be interpreted in terms of immortality or of resurrection?

Plato argues that the soul, which is to be distinguished from the body, must be held to be unchanging and immortal. In the *Phaedo*, for example, he reports a conversation in which Socrates argues that the nature of knowledge shows that the soul must pre-exist the conception of the body. Its knowledge of the reality of 'absolute beauty and goodness and an absolute essence of all things', which is the basis of the Plato's theory of knowledge in his doctrine of the Forms, does not and cannot come from our bodily sense-experiences. On examination it is found to be an 'inborn possession' which thereby shows that 'our souls existed before we were born'.[6] Furthermore, since the soul's proper nature is to be 'in communion with the unchanging' Forms in 'the region of purity and eternity and immortality and unchangeableness', it should be thought of as itself being 'in the very likeness of the divine and immortal and intellectual and uniform and indissoluble and unchangeable'. Consequently, whereas the body is changeable and dissoluble into its constituent parts and therefore mortal, the soul is indissoluble and immortal. When separated by death from the body, it 'departs to the invisible world' where it is 'secure of bliss and is released from the error and folly of men, their fears and wild passions and all other human ills, and forever dwells . . . in company with the gods'.[7]

According to this argument, then, the immortality of the soul is a consequence of its intrinsic indestructibility. It is not dependent either on the grace of God or on any moral or religious qualities in the soul. The conclusion of the argument, however, does not justify belief in anything that might be recognized as the self's continuing existence as a self-conscious subject after death. Even if the Platonic epistemology were acceptable (including its dualism) and its implications about the soul were granted to follow from it – and these are highly disputed matters, what it would indicate is the survival of a 'soul' which existed prior to a person's birth and persists after that person's death as an unchanging entity. Such an entity is hardly identifiable with what a person is conscious of as the being of his or her own self. Whatever it is that may persist as this Platonic immortal soul, it is not a self which is conscious of change and development through its experiences and interactions with others. It is a mistake, furthermore, to think that some such unchanging entity as this 'soul' is necessary in order to establish the identity of person as that person's selfhood passes through changing states from birth to death. A person's awareness of being a continuing self does not consist in the consciousness of possessing some unchanging substance which persists unaltered whatever may be done to and by that person. Although for some official purposes I may be identified as the individual with particular details on a birth-certificate, so far as I identify myself and am identified by others, it is as a person whose character in its present form is the product of past experiences and decisions, only a few of which are now remembered, and whose future forms will be the result of further experiences, responses and decisions. If, then, there is to be a subjective immortality as the continuing being of the person, it would seem to have to be the continuation of this ongoing and cumulative tradition of remembered and forgotten experiences, responses and decisions that must occur. The Platonic argument about the 'soul' fails to justify the belief that it does occur because this 'soul' is not identifiable with our self-conscious being as personal selves.

A second argument for subjective immortality maintains that the human capacity to experience 'the eternal' indicates that there must be something eternal in human being. So far as this argument is an application of the principle that nothing can be known which is not first in the knower, it is far from convincing. By the same principle it could be argued that all the qualities of the divine of which we are aware must also be possessed by us! Furthermore, it is not self-evident that we do have an actual experience of the eternal as such. It is arguable that what we are aware of in our experience is the contingency and finitude of our mode of being, and that our notion of the eternal rises from our envisaging the possibility of there being that which is not so limited.

What may be considered to be a more plausible form of the argument from religious experience maintains that unity with God is the proper destiny of human beings and that anticipations of this oneness with the divine are experienced, at least by some people, during their life-time. Since, therefore, the human is to become one with the divine, it must share eventually the eternity of the divine. It may be objected, though, that such experiences of oneness neither provide sound indications of a post-mortem state nor, if they did, would they necessarily show that we continue after death as subjective selves. Unity with the divine may involve the loss of individual selfhood through incorporation into the divine or it may be realized simply through God's everlasting memory of all the occasions of our life in the state of 'objective immortality'.

A third, Kantian, argument from morality holds that since the moral demand is only binding if it is possible to be fulfilled, our inability to realize the highest goal in this life requires us to presuppose subjective immortality. The argument's basis, however, rests on an understanding of morality which may be challenged. For one thing, it is possible to argue, as Reinhold Niebuhr does in *An Interpretation of Christian Ethics*, for 'the relevance of an impossible ethical ideal'. Although it seems to be the case that the moral standard of 'an ultimate perfection of unity and harmony' is 'not realizable in any historic situation', it does not follow that this moral standard should not direct and judge our activities.[8] If, though, we do not accept the Kantian 'I ought, therefore I can' as a principle of morality, we cannot use it to imply a state of immortality. Furthermore, as Charles Hartshorne maintains, it is arguable that morality should not be held to require 'post-terrestrial rewards or punishments' since the proper reward of virtue 'is truly "virtue itself"'. Our moral satisfaction does not lie in a future state but in the present recognition that we have loved and that God has participated 'indestructibly' and 'definitively' in the experience of that love.[9]

A fourth argument for subjective immortality which is presented by some Christian thinkers, usually in terms of a belief in resurrection, considers that the teaching and resurrection of Jesus justifies belief in it. Those who put forward such a case may cite, on the one hand, the Johannine Jesus, 'because I live, you too will live'[10] and, on the other, such Pauline texts as 'Christ was raised to life – the first fruits of the harvest of the dead'[11] and 'for we know that he who raised the Lord Jesus to life will with Jesus raise us too, and bring us to his presence'.[12] So far as this argument rests on the teaching of Jesus its significance depends upon our judgment both of the accuracy of the Gospel records of that teaching and of the authority of his remarks on the matter. In view of the apparent erroneousness of the apocalyptic ideas which the Gospels attribute to him, is his alleged teaching on these other eschatological matters to be relied upon as the product of privileged insight into the divine purposes? It is a debatable issue. Even less convincing is the argument that Jesus' post-mortem experiences are a guide to our fate. For one thing we clearly do not find or expect events after death to occur as they have traditionally, and probably mistakenly, been understood to have happened after the death of Jesus. When we have buried granny, we do not expect her calling in for a chat and a snack three or four days later. More significantly, the fact that certain things happened to Jesus after his death, whatever they were, is no reason for holding that similar things will happen to us. The Christian doctrine of the person of Christ makes such an argument at least problematic when it asserts the divinity as well as the humanity of that person. Furthermore, as we noticed in an earlier chapter, it is not at all clear how the reports of the resurrection of Jesus are to be understood. To argue about our fate on the basis of those reports is thus likely to be judged a matter of speculating about the unknown on the basis of the unclear.

Finally there is the argument for subjective immortality which infers its credibility from the love of God. On the basis of considerations of the nature of God, of Christian claims about the revelation of God perceived in Jesus, and of religious experience, it is maintained that God is to be understood as one who cares for each human being as an individual and establishes, as far as each individual will permit, personal relations with that individual. The argument then proceeds to claim that since God genuinely cares for each individual person and since God must be attributed the power to preserve or reconstitute the being of each individual after death, it is inconceivable that God would allow any individual (or perhaps any individual who responds to the divine love and enters into personal relations with the divine) to cease to be. Otherwise God's experience will be continually scarred by the loss of relationships with those who are loved. Why should God's joy be thus blemished by avoidable loss?

This is probably the strongest of the arguments for subjective immortality but it is still open to objections. Its basic understanding of God's love may be over-sentimentalized and so the supposed sense of divine loss when an individual ceases to be over-exaggerated. While love does imply care for its objects, it does not involve their irreplaceability. I discovered this when my daughter's first hamster died. Her sorrow was soon eased by the promise of a successor and the contributions of 'Hammy Two' to our entertainment soon made 'Hammy One' a happy memory. He had done his life and now another was presenting other enjoyments. Although human to human relationships are much more profoundly valuable, is it totally mistaken to consider that a similar thing may happen at a personal level? While we miss our personal friends when they die while the friendship still has creative possibilities, it is much less disturbing, even a relief, when the relationship has ceased to be aesthetically valuable. Perhaps, therefore, in the divine case, the relationship with any human individual should not be seen as everlasting. We may be making unwarrantable claims for ourselves if we assume that each of us has such an inexhaustible creative capacity that God will be deprived if our death is our final termination. Just as after the sadness of bereavement the healthy response is to find and enjoy new relationships, so it is arguable that the divine love should not be considered to involve grieving over what is not there. It is a love, rather, which cherishes what has been, enjoys what is there, and looks for further riches in a creatively inspired future. We have our place in the divine love as we contribute to the riches of the divine experience. While, then, there must always be objects of the divine love if God is to be regarded as essentially loving, there is no justification in inferring from this that each of those objects must be immortal. All that follows from the notion of divine love is that if its original objects cease to exist, they will be replaced by other objects which will in turn be recipients of divine love and contribute their particular riches to the divine experience.

These objections to the argument from divine love touch upon issues which raise doubts in principle about the notion of subjective immortality. If these doubts are justified, they suggest that the belief in subjective post-mortem existence should have no part in theistic understanding even though it has traditionally been regarded as a basic constituent of such faith. This conclusion does not follow from the difficulty (or impossibility) of finding convincing arguments to justify such beliefs. Our failure to discover how to prove something only allows a verdict of 'not proven': it does not show that it is false. What the conclusion does follow from is finding that the belief itself is intrinsically and fundamentally faulty. Before, therefore, we turn to the notion of objective immortality, we will briefly notice four reasons for considering that belief in and hope for subjective immortality may be unwarrantable.

In the first place it may be claimed that the desire for subjective immortality is a desire to be divine. The story of the Fall and the story of Babel suggest in rather unsatisfactory ways ('unsatisfactory' because they imply a jealousy and insecurity in God that is not compatible with divinity) that the heart of the human predicament lies in the refusal to accept the creatureliness and finitude of human being. The desire to try to 'be like gods',[13] though, is a powerful temptation. Faced by the inescapable mark of their non-divine status, namely their mortality, and unable by their own powers to prevent eventual physical death, it is arguable that people have attempted to deny its finality by resorting to belief in subjective post-mortem existence. The belief may then be criticized as a product of the human failure to accept that humanity is not divine. Authentic theistic faith and understanding, according to this point of view, acknowledge instead that the creaturely contingency of human being requires a recognition that we are temporally as well as spatially limited. Just as our location in one place prevents us being simultaneously somewhere else, and just as we accept that there were events which occurred before we were born, so we should accept that our limited mode of being means that there will be events that occur in the future at which we will not be present. The refusal of such a recognition may thus be held to indicate that we wrongly covet the everlastingness which belongs properly to God.

This objection is not totally conclusive since it is conceivable that God may choose to preserve individual human beings even though they are essentially contingent. The creatureliness of their mode of being is recognized in that case by acknowledging their dependence on God for their persistence in being. It is not wrong, then, for those who enjoy life now and have unfulfillable desires in this life to hope by God's grace for opportunities of fulfilment in its continuation after death. Such a hope, however, becomes less plausible when we take into account other aspects of human finitude. A second objection to subjective immortality is that if, as is generally the case, the post-mortem state is held to be unending, it implies that individual persons are beings with limitless capacities for personal being, whereas their finitude should be recognized to indicate that they have restricted potentialities. For them to continue for ever, therefore, would involve them in persisting beyond the exhaustion of their capacity for making and assimilating novel responses. In such a state they would have ceased to be creative and so would have ceased to be significantly living beings, even if they continued in some sort of sated equilibrium of an undisturbed and undisturbing peaceful relationship with God and other selves. On the other hand a divine grant of new potentialities and capacities would arguably be the creation of new persons, albeit with some inherited memories and dispositions from former selves. To grant me, for example, capacities in a later life which I do not now enjoy (like the ability to sing in tune and appreciate musical subtleties or to understand Japanese) would not be for the present 'me' to continue in being. As finite creatures we should perhaps accept that our creative powers – our essential capacity to 'live' – is limited. If this be so, it makes much more sense of human being to consider that its proper goal is to exploit its capacities to the full before death than to consider there will be an endless series of moments in which to actualize them – to and even beyond the point of bored and boring repetition when nothing novel is possible for us.

This argument was once developed in conversation by a rather elderly and distinguished philosopher who argued that he had contributed as much as he could to the subject and that others must now take on the task. He was clearly feeling worn out and his case had some apparent plausibility. A few years later, however, when he was around eighty-five years old, I was amused to note that his philosophical fires had not been extinguished for he published three books containing many rich insights. Perhaps we should not write off our potentialities too readily. This educational hope, however, should not make us too ready to think of ourselves as for ever developing new riches. It may be that we can eventually exhaust our potential as this or that particular self. On the other hand, if it is conceivable to think of a self as endlessly living, it should be appreciated that the future states of that personal being will not be a preservation of the present state of the self (nor of the state of being of that self which, at some future time, experiences death). The person that happens to exist at some point in post-mortem experience will be as little (or less) identicial with the self which exists now as a self which exists now is identical with the self which that person (who is now forty-nine) was at six hours or six days or six years or sixteen years old. Selfhood is an ongoing process of becoming, not the preservation of a self-identical substance through change. Just as I am relieved that I am not the same self in all respects that once bore my name (and doctrines of conversion are a religious reminder that there is hope all the time for each of us while we live), so I may hope that future states of my selfhood will have lost some of the embarrassing traits which now characterize me. In this respect, therefore, hope for subjective immortality is somewhat altruistic since it is hope for experiences to be enjoyed by later selves – though, admittedly, selves which will inherit and regard as more or less important my current memories and experiences.

This response to the objection based on the finite capacities of human selfhood gives rise, however, to a third objection which is not so easy to answer. Basically this objection asks who it is that continues in or returns to personal being after death. If I die as a confused, senile, arthritic old man with a bald head and a wooden leg, what comes into being after death? If it is to be the self that died, especially if the curtailment of powers in senility is irreversible, it would be preferable for death to be the end of me. If, on the other hand, it is a self at the peak of its powers, say 'me' at thirty-five (though even then bald!), what happens to the self that I became after that age? If what survives death is some 'real me' that persists as the same through all the changes from birth to death, that is not something which I have ever identified myself as being. An active, living, conscious self is in process: its continuation after any point in that process must be from what it is at that point. If, therefore, reversion to a previous or ideal state of a self is held to be involved in the notion of subjective immortality, however preferable that state may be to later states of the self, the supposed reversion makes the claim that the self that died continues to be at least highly puzzling and arguably contradicts it.

This third objection may be countered by arguing that it implies a far too physically based view of the human self. In this respect the notion of resurrection as suggested by Paul in I Corinthians 15 may be held to be helpful because it considers that the post-mortem state of the self is in terms of a new type of body – a 'spiritual' instead of a 'fleshly' one. Unfortunately this response is not without its own problems which present a fourth objection to the notion of subjective immortality. The notion implies that subjective existence may survive the dissolution of the body or transfer to 'another body'. In the latter case, though, we immediately face the problem of identity again. While we may claim that our own consciousness of our own identity involves privileged access to certain feelings and memories of feelings as being peculiarly our own, our awareness of being a self is also a product of our interaction with other selves. We are 'I's only so far as there are 'you's with whom we interact. Furthermore, our sense of identity is reinforced by the way in which people whom we met yesterday recognize us today as the person whom they met yesterday. They do this in terms of the distinctive (though slowly changing) bodily characteristics which we have. What would happen to our sense of self-identity if such recognition were withheld? It is likely that we would face a profound crisis of identity. A student once pointed out the bizarre consequences if, after an accident, her brain was transplanted into my body (as her body and my brain had suffered irreparable damage). The prospect was given added spice by the fact she was a nun. She thought her Mother Superior would be highly amused! Where would the 'survivor' live and who would the 'survivor' be? Although such fantasies are fantasies, they remind us that the idea of the 'transplant' of a self to another mode of being is not without problems even if a plausible way of thinking of the present self as surviving the dissolution of its physical body can be found.

These objections to the notion of subjective immortality are not overwhelmingly conclusive. In spite of the difficulties which have been considered the notion may still be judged to be coherent and belief in such a future state credible. Is there, though, any other way of thinking about immortality which avoids these difficulties and gives permanent significance to individual human being? It is arguable that the notion of 'objective immortality' fulfils both these requirements and provides a much more theistically appropriate way of envisaging human destiny.

Objective immortality

The notion of 'objective immortality' maintains that the experiences which each moment constitute our being are also experienced by God and as such are for ever preserved as 'objects' in the divine awareness. They thus become part of the divine reality and, albeit minutely in any specific case, contribute to the ongoing divine response to the world. Our past thus 'lives on' as it is incarnate in God in all future moments. Nothing is lost except the ephemeral experience of present immediacy as an 'I': while the movement from present to past is a perpetual process of perishing for our experiencing, all is retained in the divine memory. Immortality is thus perceived in a way that is God-centred and recognizes the essential finitude of human being. It is God that lives everlastingly, not finite creatures. On the other hand, as totally grasped by and contributing to the divine experience, every moment of each creature's existence has significance for it is incorporated into the everlasting life of God.

Various objections may be raised against the notion of objective immortality. In the first place the notion implies that God, as aware of contingent and temporal events, must be both passible and have a temporal aspect. Such ideas may initially seem unacceptable to those who have been persuaded by traditional doctrines of divine impassibility and eternity. On the other hand, as was noticed in an earlier chapter, such doctrines in turn imply that the divine cannot be regarded as significantly living nor as knowing anything besides unchanging essences. A God who is seriously to be considered to be aware of what happens in a temporally ordered reality and as lovingly responsive to it must be considered to be both passible and temporal in appropriate respects. This objection to objective immortality may thus be held to be only sustainable by implicitly denying certain fundamental convictions of genuine theistic faith.

This response, however, may itself be challenged on the grounds that it implies that the divine mode of being is not perfect. A second objection to objective immortality thus argues that if God is aware of everything, then the divine being will in some sense include within itself what it is aware of. If, for example, God is totally conscious of a person's selfishness and lewdness, the divine being will to some extent be tainted by those traits; if God is thoroughly aware of a person's pain and frustration, the divine being will also contain those experiences. There are, however, several ways of responding to this objection. A less than wholly satisfactory one is to suggest that the divine is only aware of the good in reality. By means of what is sometimes referred to as a 'negative prehension' or grasp of things, the divine is held to perceive and only to perceive in any situation what expresses positive values. Even an act of thuggery, for instance, may be seen as expressing in a socially perverted way a desire to affirm oneself, or a theft of a work of art as a socially disruptive way of fulfilling a desire to be surrounded by beautiful things. Such a view of the divine consciousness, though, implies that it is severely deficient in its awareness of the contents of this world. An awareness of me that was restricted to my good aspects would be only a fragmentary awareness. It would be ignorant of a great deal that constitutes my being. Such ignorance is not compatible with perfect love for me and with perfect knowledge in God.

A much more satisfactory response to the problem posed by this second objection to objective immortality is to point out that it highlights the cost and character of the divine love. On the one hand God is affected by the states of all things for the divine love is universal and love involves sharing to the full in the states of the objects of love. A lover cannot watch the agonies of a beloved without being torn by them – for love requires compassion – 'suffering with'. This implication of divine love should not, however, be surprising to a Christian theism which takes seriously its claim that the life and fate of Jesus manifest the nature of God. On the other hand, as Jesus suggested in relation to a different problem, it is not what goes into the person but what 'has its origins in the heart' which 'defiles' that person.[14] The divine is not to be held to be polluted by total awareness of the evil in the world. The perfection of the divine is to be seen, indeed, in the way that God responds to all the instances of evil in the most creative and fulfilling way that is possible. It is a vision of the divine which Whitehead expresses towards the end of *Process and Reality* when he speaks of God as exercising 'the judgment of a tenderness which loses nothing that can be saved' and 'the judgment of a wisdom which uses what in the temporal world is mere wreckage'. God thus 'saves' the world: 'he is the poet of the world, with tender patience leading it by his vision of truth, beauty, and goodness.'[15] God is not tainted by the knowledge of evil but rather shows the indefectibility of divine love by seeking to evoke from evil situations the highest good that is then possible.

A third objection to the notion of objective immortality claims that it is incompatible with divine love for people as individuals. According to this objection it is inconsistent for God to love an individual (and, it is often added, to seek personal relationships with that person) and to allow them to cease to be a living subject. This may seem to be a much more telling objection than the previous two until we remember what was suggested earlier about the essential finitude of human being. For God to preserve in being an individual who had exhausted all capacity for creative response and activity would, arguably, not be to love them any more than it is loving to keep a body functioning on a life-support system once the person's capacity for conscious selfhood has irretrievably been lost. The significance of this objection thus depends in part on the coherence of the notion of subjective immortality but this, as we have already discovered, is difficult to establish. It also partly depends on credibility of the view that our continuing being as individuals is of such importance to God that our ceasing to be as subjects would seriously impair the satisfaction of the divine love. The questionableness of the view will emerge as we consider another objection to the notion of objective immortality.

The fourth objection to objective immortality, which is the final one to be considered in this chapter, holds that it is a misnomer to speak of 'objective immortality' as a form of immortality because according to this notion the self does not survive death as an experiencing and responding subject. My objective immortality, that is, is not 'my' immortality at all. It is God and God alone who is to be regarded as immortal and everlasting. What of 'me' that survives death is a series of personally-ordered recollections of me in the divine memory. Although this memory preserves every item of my experiences without loss, I do not survive as a living 'I'. In that the threat of death is the threat of becoming an object totally in the power of others, an object to be looked at rather than a subject able to stand out for itself, death has finally conquered. Although belief in objective immortality may make death less than totally horrific in the sense that the object is never forgotten since all its achievements of value are everlastingly cherished in the divine selfhood, it is not the living 'I' that survives but God's memories of a past 'me'.

The strength of this objection to objective immortality depends upon the credibility of holding that our individual lives are so important that their continuation is a requirement of the rationality and meaningfulness of reality. To hold that they are so important is probably a natural assumption for us to make – for it is hard for us not to judge as well as to see everything from our own perspective. It is, nevertheless, an anthropocentric position which is put into question once we try to consider how things may be appreciated from a theocentric viewpoint. Hurtful as it may be to our pride, the significance and value of reality does not lie in its contribution to our corporate and individual well-being. What Copernicus made humanity aware of in relation to the physical world, namely, that the earth is not the centre of the universe, religion ought (but has badly failed) to make it aware of in relation to the purpose and value of reality, namely that humanity in general and individual selves in particular are not the ultimate centre of interest. Their significance lies in what they contribute to the richness of the divine enjoyment of the creation.

From such a theocentric position the fourth objection to objective immortality may thus be judged to be a product of human self-centredness rather than a warrantable appreciation of the divine nature and purpose. It may further be argued that the notion of objective immortality provides a properly God-centred view of the value and destiny of human being which ensures it everlasting significance. What more can either be wanted or justified? Each of us is immortal in that each moment of our being is embraced by and preserved in God, but we are finite beings who have only limited contributions to make to the divine being. Our aim in life must be to enhance our contribution as much as we are able and our satisfaction lies in knowing that nothing we achieve will ever be lost All will become part of the concrete reality of God. It is God, though, that lives everlastingly, not the creatures.

The notion of objective immortality thus places the ground for immortality in the nature of God. It does not depend upon any inherent or achieved quality in human beings. It depends wholly upon the fact of the divine awareness of all that occurs. If, on the other hand, the objections against subjective immortality are judged not to be conclusive, it is on the grace of God that its reality must also depend. Whether, therefore, we continue as subjects or not is not in our determination. The significance of our life now, furthermore, does not depend upon its future destiny but on its achievement of value at each moment of its being. It is the richness of our experience now – and so the richness of the experience which we currently contribute to the divine – that determines the value of our being.

The fairy-tales of childhood close with the words 'and they all lived happily for ever after'. Perhaps we would like to be children again and identify ourselves with the characters of such stories. Mature reflection, however, informs us that it is God who lives 'for ever after'. For the divine life there is no ending. Our everlasting continuation lies in our incorporation, whether objectively or subjectively, in that divine life.

Chapter 10

Faith, Morality and Experience

Theistic faith is lived out in an appropriate morality. The two are essentially united. This characteristic of its faith was recognized, for example, early in the formation of the Christian community when James asserted that if faith 'does not lead to action, it is in itself a lifeless thing'[1] and I John declared that it is by 'genuine' love in 'action' that 'we may know that we belong to the realm of truth'.[2] The point which these authors are here making is that faith involves more than intellectual assent to certain beliefs; it is also a matter of practice.

This aspect of faith is now generally accepted – as is illustrated by the way in which the nature of a person's real faith is held to be shown by how they act rather than by what they profess. There is, however, also a widespread conviction that the conduct of Christian morality can be practised and sustained without a correlative assent to the beliefs of the Christian faith. According to this point of view, Christian beliefs, if authentically entertained, involve certain patterns of behaviour, but those patterns of behaviour do not reciprocally involve assent to those beliefs. A Christian style of conduct can be followed by people independently of their views on the credibility of Christian understanding. It is a point of view which was condemned by Friedrich Nietzsche. In the course of an attack upon George Eliot in *Twilight of the Idols* he maintains that 'when one gives up Christian belief one thereby deprives oneself of the *right* to Christian morality'. Since the Christian faith is a '*complete* view of things', it collapses if any part of it is given up.[3]

Nietzsche concludes his comments by suggesting that 'morality is not yet a problem' for the English because the Christian position is so deeply embedded in their culture.[4] When he wrote, a century ago, this was probably a reasonable assessment of the situation. Today the situation is different. The moral capital of a social Christian inheritance has become depleted. The widespread abandonment of the theistic understanding at the heart of Christian faith is being found to be eventually followed by the decline of Christian morality as the basis for public and private conduct. The uncertainty and confusion about morality which characterizes contemporary English society (and elsewhere) agrees with Nietzsche's main thesis. Is there, though, an essential link between the two? The fact that A is followed by B does not prove that A causes B, although it may indicate (especially if it occurs frequently) that it is worth investigating whether such a link exists. Furthermore, even if it is possible to show that the abandonment of Christian belief leads to the loss of Christian morality, this does not make that belief credible. Any attempt to persuade us to believe something on the grounds that the results of not believing it are undesirable is a denial of reason. No matter how horrific may be the consequences of refusing to accept the truth of some position, those consequences of themselves do not show that it is true. Thus the truth of the Christian faith is not established by showing that its rejection has moral as well as intellectual and existential implications. If its truth cannot be shown to be credible, our understanding and conduct must seek another foundation.

The relationship between theism and morality

Can we, though, establish that there is a fundamental unity in theistic understanding between its beliefs about the reality of God and the morality which is considered to be their appropriate practical expression? Three arguments may be put forward to show that no such unity is coherently conceivable.

The first argument suggests that it is a mistake to look for such a unity or link between claims about God and moral principles because on analysis claims about God turn out to be disguised expressions of moral convictions. When, therefore, we consider that a full appreciation of theistic understanding requires a perception of the relationship between claims about what is the case with the fundamental nature of reality (as expressed in statements like 'God is love') and claims about what we ought to do (as expressed in statements like 'We ought to live in a loving manner'), we misunderstand the situation. There is no real relationship to be discerned because what are supposed to be the different factors to be related are really identical. The problem of their relationship disappears just as the supposed problems of the relationship between God and Allah, or between the Eucharist and Holy

Communion, or between taking physic 'lying down' and 'in a recumbent posture' turn out to be pseudo-problems when it is realized that they are different ways of referring to the same thing.

Such an argument might be advanced on the basis of a famous analysis of statements about God presented in Richard B. Braithwaite's lecture, 'An Empiricist's View of the Nature of Religious Belief'. Adopting as his principle of interpretation the view that the meaning of any statement is disclosed by the way in which it is used, he considers what is to be observed when a person makes a statement about God 'to express his religious conviction'. His conclusion is that its primary function is to express 'a moral assertion' – and that 'a moral assertion is used to express an *attitude*' of the person making it.[5] Thus 'a Christian's assertion that God is love (*agape*)' is to be taken 'to declare his intention to follow an agapeistic way of life'. To enquire about 'the connection between the assertion and the intention, between Christian belief and Christian practice' thus indicates a fundamental failure to understand what is meant by statements about God.[6] Basically the two are identical.

While, however, Braithwaite's assimilation of religious assertions to moral assertions may be the only way that the former can be held to be meaningful in terms of the empiricist principle of meaning which he adopts in this lecture, it is an interpretation of them which theistic believers may well regard as emptying their statements about God of an essential component. They may consequently consider that the analysis shows that its principle of meaning is inappropriate rather than that its results adequately identify what is being expressed when theists make statements about God. When they affirm that 'God is love' and that 'they intend to live lovingly', they do not regard themselves as repeating themselves. According to their understanding of their faith, the former statement expresses a state of affairs in the fundamental structure of reality, a thorough acceptance of which involves the behaviour policy described in the latter statement. When Christians sing 'Love so amazing, so divine, demands my soul, my life, my all', they are not announcing that *Agape* is their God. They are asserting that the ultimate reality is characterized by 'love' and that their loving conduct is their appropriate expression of their recognition of this state of affairs. Ian T. Ramsey, responding to Braithwaite's paper, puts it that 'when the Christian asserts, "God is love", he declares *primarily not* his commitment to *agape* or to an agapeistic way of life, but his commitment to certain "facts" somehow or other described in the Gospels: "When I survey the wondrous Cross".[7] It is these 'facts' about the divine, as manifested for specifically Christian theism in the event of Jesus as the Christ, which believers consider to constitute the heart of their faith and to explain its morality.

If, though, it is granted that theistic faith includes both claims about what is the case and moral elements, a second argument may be advanced to show that there is no coherent way of establishing a relationship between them. This argument is based upon what is called 'the naturalistic fallacy'. Although there are different ways of stating it, basically it alleges that it is fallacious to consider that purely factual statements (which state what *is* the case in reality) can imply moral judgments (which state what *ought* to be the case). For example, if I am presented with the picture of a child suffering from severe malnutrition, no moral requirement follows from that fact by itself than from the fact that the child is seven years old or from the fact that it has ten fingers. The moral conclusion, 'That child ought to be helped' (or, better, 'I ought to do what I can to help such children') only follows if we add in another, moral, principle such as 'children ought not to be left to starve' or 'starvation is wrong'. Again, no moral implication follows just from the statement of the fact that 'David is unhappy'. That is just a statement of what is the case – as are the statements 'David is alone in his room' or 'David is writing a book'. A moral duty only arises from this fact if we link it with a moral principle such as 'People who are unhappy ought to receive comfort'. Without such a principle, all we are told is what is the case and all we have to do is to decide whether we accept the report or not.

In the case of statements about God, it is thus argued that descriptions of God are just that – descriptions of God. No moral implications follow from such descriptions any more than they do from other descriptions of what is the case. Thus, so far as morality is concerned, the claim that 'God is love' or the claim 'God wills us to love' or even the claim 'God commands us to love' only report what God is, wills and commands. No moral obligation follows from those reports any more than they do from such reports as 'Marie is loving' or 'Marie wills us to love' or even 'Marie commands us to love one another'. In all such cases, so the argument runs, it is logically coherent to accept that the reports are correct – and leave it at that. Awareness of moral duties does not follow solely from the acceptance of statements about what is the case: it follows from the combination of the acceptance of such statements with the acceptance of relevant moral principles.

This argument, based on the naturalistic fallacy, against a coherent link between beliefs about God and morality only presumes to be valid if those beliefs are simply descriptions of what is the case in ultimate reality which contain within them no elements of moral evaluation whatsoever. On analysis, however, it turns out that, at least with the case of God, the argument is invalid. The reason for this becomes clear when it is recognized that many terms which we use to describe situations include moral evaluations of those situations. For example, to describe an event as one of 'murder' is not only to state that someone has been killed but also to express an evaluation of the event – that it was wrong; to describe a population as 'starving' not only expresses the view that they are suffering from a lack of food but also makes the point that there is a duty to help them; to say to twelve-year-old Robert 'Your father said you mustn't go out until you have finished your homework' is not only to remind him of what was said but also to remind him of what he ought to do. This is because notions such as 'murder', 'starvation' and 'father' carry moral as well as factual connotations. How these moral connotations are understood may be culturally relative – a relationship which is considered to impose a moral responsibility in one culture may not in another – but they remind us that in some cases at least descriptions of what is the case are only fully appreciated when they are understood to convey moral judgments on what is being described. For theistic understanding, as we have previously indicated, the notion of God refers to that which is intrinsically the proper object of worship. In the case of God, that is, we do not move in our recognition of the divine from an 'is' to an 'ought' by first deciding that a certain being exists and then, on reflection, concluding that it is a proper object of worship. The definition of God, the judgment that God exists and the awareness of God are only authentic when God is understood (or encountered) as the pre-eminently worshipful. Because of the very nature of the divine, there can be no question about the worshipfulness of God any more than there can be of the ontological ultimacy of God.

Descriptions of God are hence not merely statements about what is believed to be ultimate in being: they also state what, for that understanding, is essentially ultimate in value. There is, therefore, a fundamental error in trying to compare 'God is love' with 'Marie is loving' as if both statements merely and only describe the character of two beings, 'God' and 'Marie'. To refer to God is necessarily (according to theistic understanding) also to refer to that which must be the standard for all value-judgments. Consequently, while the naturalistic fallacy may identify some errors in moral reasoning, it is not applicable to the case of the relationship between God and value. Because of what theism means by 'God', descriptions of God essentially convey at one and the same time both claims about what ultimately is the case and claims about the values which determine what ultimately ought to be the case. The naturalistic fallacy is therefore not able to establish a real division between God and good.

A third attempt to show that it is not possible to conceive a satisfactory link between theistic belief and morality takes up the question of the relationship between God and good. It argues that it is not possible to relate these two notions to each other without denying the ultimacy which properly belongs to each of them. The argument is often put in terms of a conundrum which asks 'Is it good because God wills it, or does God will it because it is good?'. To choose either option has unsatisfactory consequences. In the former case what is good is what God deems to be such. This option thus protects the ultimacy of God but it is at the cost of making the nature of goodness finally dependent upon the arbitrary will of God – 'arbitrary' because according to this option there are not (and logically there cannot be) any standards superior to and independent of God by which the divine will may be directed. God is absolutely supreme: values and duties are the result of what God chooses to be such. While, therefore, God may have chosen that love ought to be the proper relationship between people, the divine choice could equally authoritatively have laid down that all people who write and all people who read books on philosophical theology are doing what is morally wrong. If the divine choice were such, we would be doing wrong just as much as if we were hating our neighbour: there could be no argument about its being wrong if that is what God has decided. In an attempt to avoid the implication that moral values are dependent upon an unrestrained and possibly capricious divine 'fiat', we may consider taking up the alternative option. This maintains that what God wills is always right because the divine will always chooses what is the good. The problem here is that the status of moral values is established at the cost of suggesting that God is not in all respects ultimate. According to this option, the divine will is good because it chooses to conform to the final standards of goodness. These standards would be such whether or not they were acknowledged by God. Such a being, though, would not properly be 'God' for, however praiseworthy its goodness might be, it would not be intrinsically adorable. The authentic object of adoration would be those values by which the goodness of all wills, including God's will, are ultimately to be judged.

In view of the problems posed by the conundrum, it is argued that no satisfactory relationship between deity and morality can be established. Either we must make one of them ultimate as the source of moral values and thereby undermine the status of the other, or we must accept that they are autonomous in their respective realms and thereby be faced with an uncomfortable dualism. The argument, however, depends upon the acceptance of the tacit assumption of the conundrum, namely that the relationship between God and good must be a relationship of dependence: one must be superior and the other derived. It is a presupposition which needs to be questioned. As in the case of the previous argument which we considered, a proper understanding of what is meant by 'God' discloses that the supposed problem is due to a fundamental failure to recognize the special character of the divine. The presupposition of the conundrum is inappropriate in the case of God. Goodness is neither derived from God, as a product of some act of divine creativity, nor independent of God, as a standard external to God by reference to which God acts. The essential ultimacy of the divine means, among other things, that perfect goodness is one of the intrinsic qualities of God. It is this which makes God the proper object of worship and of unconditional trust, for it means that God is necessarily incapable of acting in any other than an absolutely good way. Whatever God wills and what is good coincide.

The nature of divine goodness

If, though, the intrinsic nature of God requires that the divine be held to be perfectly good and so there is a coherent unity between theistic faith and morality, what is the character of that goodness? Is it primarily to be understood in moral terms or is morality to be seen as instrumental and so as justified by reference to a higher good? The answer to these questions will throw more light on the nature of the relationship between beliefs about God and morality.

Under the influence of the image of God as one who lays down commandments the divine goodness has been widely interpreted in fundamentally moral terms. It is an image which is powerfully presented in parts of the Old Testament and has been liturgically reinforced by the tradition in some churches of writing the Decalogue on the wall behind the altar and of reciting either those commandments or their summary by Jesus in the worship. It is also an image of God which accords with the way in which, during and after the Enlightenment, widespread doubts about doctrine have been accompanied by firm convictions about the morality which religion requires. Philosophically the foundations of the arguments for the existence of God may be threatened but in the thought of Kant and some other modern philosophers God is affirmed, whether as a reality or as a symbol, in relation to the categorical imperative of the moral demand. In spite of Rudolf Otto's perceptive analysis of holiness, it is still commonly identified with moral goodness.

This interpretation of the divine goodness as fundamentally moral goodness may be challenged by considering the question 'Why be morally good?' If moral goodness is genuinely ultimate, this will be a pseudo-question for there will be no way to answer it beyond asserting some such tautology as 'You must because you must' or 'Moral goodness is its own justification'. According to some thinkers, that is the only correct response to the question. In that case the identification of God in some respects with moral goodness is a correct perception of what ultimately happens to be the case: the fundamental nature of things demands – morally demands – that we be morally good. There is no way of justifying the demand by reference to something external to the demand. It is just how things are.

There is, however, another way of tackling the matter. This way considers that the question 'Why be morally good?' is a proper question and that answers to it can be given which are not either obvious or disguised tautologies. According to this position moral goodness is not an end in itself but a means to an end. It is to be seen as instrumental in the production of that which is intrinsically good, and moral rules are justified to the extent that they lead to the realization of the intrinsically good. What, though, is intrinsically good? It is that which is utterly satisfying in itself, that which is its own justification. It is probably most adequately perceived as the beautiful, for beauty is good in itself. Keats speaks of it thus:

> A thing of beauty is a joy for ever:
> Its loveliness increases; it will never
> Pass into nothingness; but still will keep
> A bower of quiet for us, and a sleep
> Full of sweet dreams, and health, and quiet breathing.[8]

This, however, is a static perception of the beautiful. It is an appropriate description of an object which is to be adored with unending delight, of the beatific vision. It is not wholly appropriate as a description of the beauty which is the goal of living, whether divine or human, for to live is not to persist but to create. Whitehead perhaps points the way to a more adequate understanding of the beauty that is the goal for living when, in *The Function of Reason*, he suggests that the role of reason is 'to promote the art of life'. Whereas 'the art of persistence is to be dead' – only 'inorganic things persist for great lengths of time',[9] the art of life is *'first* to be alive, *secondly* to be alive in a satisfactory way, and *thirdly* to acquire an increase in satisfaction'.[10] The goal of living which is ultimate and self-justifying is the pursuit of ever more satisfying experiences through richer and novel forms of aesthetic creativity. This is the good which is to be sought as good in itself. Hence it is this good which is characteristic of the divine. It is an aesthetic good which is identifiable as love, not love as a grim-faced, teeth-clenching condescending charity but love as the spontaneous joy of creatively loving and being loved, as the tireless delight in appreciating what of value has appeared and in producing fresh forms of value. It is a love which is undemanding and unthreatening because it both enjoys to the full all that has come to be and seeks to evoke from it ever deeper experiences of satisfying value.

If, though, the good which is an end in itself is the creating and experiencing of beauty, the answer to the question 'Why be morally good?' is that it is such behaviour which enhances our ability to produce and to enjoy aesthetic satisfaction. Honesty, for example, is a moral good because it provides the ground for that openness between persons which allows them to enjoy each other's being. Care is a moral good because it is in the supportive community of caring persons that individuals can find the confidence to be creative selves. Respect is a moral good because it fosters the appreciation of values both in persons and in objects. On the other hand, since morality is justified because it is instrumental in producing states that are intrinsically good, its tenets are also to be judged by their effectiveness as such instruments. Moral rules, however sanctified by traditional culture and religion, are always open to be challenged if it appears that they hinder rather than foster the intrinsic good that is characteristic of God's being and purposes.

Such challenges are not to be made lightly. It is always possible that objections to traditional rules arise from a selfish desire to pander to individual interest rather than from a genuine perception of what will lead overall to greater aesthetic satisfaction and creativity. It is also possible, though, that some traditional rules reflect human failings rather than a proper perception of the divine goodness. Consider, for example, the traditional understanding of the commitments of theism and of marriage. In both cases Christian morality has laid down that a person's most important relationships with God and with another person must be exclusive. This accords, among other things, both with the view that God is a jealous God and with human possessiveness. Is such restrictedness, however, a proper perception of the conditions for expressing to the full the love that characterizes the divine goodness? It is possible to argue that this restrictedness is a product of human insecurity and selfishness which has been projected on to the nature and will of God, rather than an appropriate apprehension of the outgoing delight in others that properly marks the goodness of God. If this argument can be sustained, it may be that exclusiveness is an idolatrous worship which God rejects and that the enjoyment of all that is good is the true worship since all that is good is shared, embraced and affirmed by the divine. On the other hand, it may be argued that we are such fickle, weak and limited beings that the traditional rules of monotheism and monogamy are necessary to prevent us from damaging ourselves and others. The divine love may be boundlessly free but ours has to be kept within strict limits to restrain its possibilities for perversion into harmful, destructive expressions. Which is the correct understanding of morality must be determined, however, by reference to the intrinsic goodness of God and to what will best contribute to the creation and enrichment of aesthetic satisfaction for ourselves, for others and above all for God. The actions and relationships that are to be endorsed are those which arise from love, express love and lead to richer love. In this divine will and human fulfilment coincide. The test – the enormous responsibility – that is left to each of us is to decide before God how we are to find and express that love.

In deciding what we are to do and, even more, in considering the actions of others, we should bear in mind what Whitehead says about God and love towards the end of *Process and Reality*. He points out that genuine love does not seek to impose itself in coercive rule, that it is affected by the state of those who are loved, and that 'it finds its own reward in the immediate present' rather than in the future. He also suggests that 'it is a little oblivious as to morals'.[11] God is not to be thought of as a scrupulous – and pathetic – inquisitor, fussing over every minute fault in our conduct and punctilious about every detail of the moral law. Such an image is the expression of an insecurity and fear of life whose negative attitudes pervert the goodness of God into its opposite. The divine goodness is a positive zest for living – for living where joy and satisfaction flourish. We are most truly moral when our behaviour leads to such flourishing. Morality in general and moral rules and their observance in particular ways are justified if and where and because they provide the conditions for such satisfyingly exciting living.

The problem of moral evil

What, though, is to be said about moral evil? In chapter 6 on 'Faith, God and the Natural World' we discussed the problem apparently posed for theistic faith by the suffering due to natural processes but we postponed to this chapter consideration of the suffering resulting from morally wrong human actions. Although some of this suffering, as in the case of the horrific deaths in Kampuchea following its 'liberation', may be the result of the perverted application of policies aiming at future good, most of it is the product of human ill-will. From the appalling events in German concentration camps to the sadistic acts of a child-abuser, and from the general carelessness of the wealthy for the deprived to the hurts so often casually inflicted in personal relationships, human beings show themselves capable of inflicting enormous suffering. Faced with these situations theists may ask, Why does God allow it to happen? Why does God not prevent this evil? Why does God not make people so that they are incapable of such cruelty?

   The usual answer that is given to such questions is that the possibility of such evil is the regrettable price of human freedom. In moral terms it may thus be argued that if people are to be morally responsible for their actions, then they must be free to choose whether they do what is good or what is evil. They can only be accounted morally good where they have the possibility of being morally bad. In more general terms it may similarly be maintained that people can only be capable of creativity if they have the possibility of destroying as well as of producing what is of value. Creativity involves a spontaneity and an openness to novelty which can only be found where there is also the opportunity for spoiling what already exists. The value of freedom, however, is of such significance that it is clearly better for human beings to be free (and hence capable of evil) than for them not to be free. The problem of moral evil is thus held to be overcome by what may be called a 'free-will defence'.

Although many theists consider that this is a satisfactory (even if rather depressing) response to the problem posed by moral evil, some thinkers have challenged it by arguing that a genuinely benevolent and omnipotent God would have created people so that they could choose to do only what is good. In a paper entitled 'Divine Omnipotence and Human Freedom', Antony Flew argues that 'there is no contradiction in suggesting that Omnipotence might so arrange his creation that all men in fact always would freely choose the right'.[12] To support this position he holds that the only view of creation which would take God seriously is one which presents God, so far as human beings are concerned, as 'the Great Hypnotist with all his creatures acting out, usually unknowingly, his commands'.[13] Another example of this rejection of the 'free-will' defence is provided by J. L. Mackie. In 'Evil and Omnipotence' he argues that since 'there is no logical impossibility in a man's freely choosing the good on one, or on several occasions, there cannot be a logical impossibility in his freely choosing the good on every occasion'. Consequently God did not have to choose between 'making innocent automata' and creating beings who were free but would 'sometimes go wrong'. God had 'the obviously better possibility of making beings who would act freely but always go right'.[14] Since this option was clearly not taken up – as the evidence of moral evil demonstrates – it follows that there is no benevolent and omnipotent God.

Unfortunately the limits of such an introduction as this does not permit a detailed discussion of the various and sometimes subtle arguments by which the rejection of the foundation of the 'free-will' defence is held to be justified. Overall, however, the rejection is itself open to serious criticisms. In the first place it is far from certain that we are sufficiently clear in our apprehension of the nature of divine power to be able to warrant the implications from the notion of 'omnipotence' which are made in such arguments as those of Flew and Mackie. Speculations about what the divine could have done if the will to do it were there imply a transcendental understanding which it is hard to render credible – though, in justice to such as Flew and Mackie, it should not be forgotten that it is a presumptuousness to which theistic believers and theologians are prone. Secondly, in spite of the counter-considerations which are offered, it is still arguable that it is incoherent to hold that persons would be significantly free if they were incapable of doing evil or being destructive. It would be odd, for example, to regard them as able to live morally significant lives when they had no option to do what is evil or to refrain from doing what is good – it would be as pointless as praising Arthur for having a heart or blaming Lesley for having hay-fever. It would be evaluating them in terms of something they could not avoid being. Moral responsibility does seem to require the possibility of doing evil – and to say that persons could have the choice but could be made so that they would never choose it, is in fact to change the 'would never' into a 'could never' that denies the possibility. So far as moral responsibility is concerned, good and evil seem to be polar concepts: the meaning and possibility of the one entails the meaning and possibility of the other.

Thirdly, the way in which the problem of moral evil is posed, the traditional 'free-will' answer to it and the objections to this answer are all subject to the same basic criticism which we saw earlier to apply to the problem of natural evil. They all presuppose a picture of divine creativity which is hard, if not possible, to warrant in view of today's understanding of how things have come to be. Attractive as it may be at times, it is not credible to think of God as considering how to make human beings – deciding in the process what capacities to give them and what to prevent them having – as if the divine were designing a drinks-dispenser. What human beings are now is what they have come to be after a long process of natural and cultural evolution. To what extent the divine is to be held responsible for how things have turned out is far from clear. Accordingly it is probably not possible to pose in a justifiable fashion, let alone to attempt to solve, the problem of moral evil as a problem about theistic understanding of divine creativity.

On reflection the problem of moral evil is most fruitfully approached as a human problem. So far as it is useful to try to discern the origins of evil and its continuing influence on human life (the problem of 'original sin'), it is probably to be attributed to a combination of natural instincts and imperfect self-consciousness which results in a wide range of misapprehensions of what is truly good for human being. Instead, however, of regarding human being as 'depraved', having 'fallen' from some supposed idyllic state, it is more appropriate to regard it as having risen, through expansion of its self-consciousness and awareness of values, to a point where it is aware of some of its imperfections and is troubled about them. It is arguable, for example, that in spite of all the current evils of humanity today people are more troubled, both individually and socially, about the condition of those who do not belong to their immediate society than was the case in the past. The problem posed by moral evil is the problem of how to continue the process of individual and social awareness so that the good may be more adequately perceived and its intrinsic attractiveness may more strongly influence human behaviour. In such a process love will increasingly be distinguished from possession: to love will be undemandingly to seek the enrichment of the other. The pursuit of the good will similarly be separated from the search for one's own security and prestige. It is a process in which Christian theism sees God as deeply involved, both as one who experiences utterly all the suffering produced by human evil and as one who seeks by love to draw people from perverted conduct arising from their sense of unimportance into acts of creative love made possible by the self-respect that comes from knowing their total acceptance by God.

Conscience

The complexity, ambiguity and unpredictability of situations in which we often find ourselves sometimes makes it difficult to determine by rational reflection what we ought to do. In a specific context both the appropriate material goods to seek to realize and the morally permissible means by which to realize them may be unclear. In such situations – as in those where reflection is not so troubled by obscurity and confusion – we may be told that we ought to be guided by our 'conscience'. If we follow our conscience, it may be claimed, we will do what for us is right; to go against our conscience can never be morally justified. John Henry Newman, for example, describes conscience as 'the aboriginal Vicar of Christ, a prophet in its informations, a monarch in its peremptoriness, a priest in its blessings and anathemas'. He concludes his *Letter to the Duke of Norfolk* on papal infallibility by asserting

> Certainly, if I am obliged to bring religion into after-dinner toasts (which indeed does not seem quite the thing), I shall drink – to the Pope, if you please, – still – to Conscience first, and to the Pope afterwards.[15]

These are powerful claims for the authority of conscience. Can they be justified?

As with many such questions the answer partly depends on what is meant by 'conscience'. The term may refer to our rational judgment of the situation before us, based upon our apprehension of the factors involved in that situation and the values and principles of conduct which have captivated us as being normative. In this sense the dictates of our 'conscience' are in fact the final conclusions of our understanding of the matters at issue. As Samuel Taylor Coleridge puts it, conscience is 'no other than the mind of a man, under the notion of a particular reference to himself and his own actions'.[16] It is then obviously right for us to follow these dictates because they are our rational decisions about what is to be done. They are properly to be treated as authoritative for us since they express what we have decided to be right for us to do in the circumstances. Even if our judgments may later be recognized by us or by others to have been mistaken, at the time when they are made they are morally binding upon us: what I believe in my conscience to be right, that I ought to do.

This view of conscience may be challenged on the grounds that the guidance of conscience is immediate. Since, that is, conscience is experienced as telling us directly what we are to do, it may be held that it is wrong to treat it as if it were based upon a process of reasoning and its deliverances as the expressions of the conclusions of such reasoning. In answering this objection, it must be admitted that our experience of conscience is not an experience of an explicit reasoning process leading eventually to a conclusion. Our consciousness of conscience is that as we consider a situation we become deeply and convincingly aware of what we ought to do. The error in this objection, though, is that it assumes all our reasoning processes are conscious and explicit. As John Henry Newman points out in *The Grammar of Assent*, this is not so. The reasoning which is most significant for us is not conducted by explicit stages but occurs largely, if not wholly, unconsciously. Newman thus speaks of us as having a natural reasoning faculty – he calls it 'an illative sense'. It is 'a sort of instinctive perception' by means of which 'we reason without effort and intention, or any necessary conciousness of the path which the mind takes in passing from antecedent to conclusion'.[17] So far as we are conscious of it in ourselves and in others it may appear, because of its immediacy, to be a kind of 'simple divination';[18] in fact its conclusions are the products of a 'multiform and intricate process' of unconscious reasoning by which we take into account the cumulative significance of a range of probabilities which are 'independent of each other' and 'too fine to avail separately, too subtle and circuitous to be convertible into syllogisms, too numerous and various for such conversion, even were they convertible'.[19] This process of reasoning in any particular case is impossible to express in the 'cumbrous' apparatus of verbal reasoning'.[20] Its conclusions, nevertheless, are the product of reasoning and, furthermore, they are very much our own conclusions 'because they are in great measure made by ourselves and belong to our personal character'[21] and apply 'our own principles'.[22]

If, then, by conscience we refer to our awareness of the conclusions of such an unconscious process of reasoning, it is not only legitimate but also necessary for us to regard them as authoritative for us. They declare what we fundamentally assess to be our duty. To go against them is to go against our best judgment. At the same time, we must not forget that these conclusions – and so the deliverances of conscience as so understood – are only as sound as the reasoning which produces them. Because that reasoning may be partly based on mistaken principles and values, because it may have misapprehended the situation, and because its connection of items may be faulty, its conclusion in any particular case may be in error even though it is binding upon us.

In order to claim for the deliverances of conscience not only binding moral authority but also a greater reliability than is attributable to the conclusions of our reasoning, another, widely accepted, understanding of its nature is put forward. On examination, however, it turns out to characterize conscience in a way which, contrary to intention, renders it less rather than more trustworthy than the view which sees it as expressing the conclusions of some unconscious reasoning process. According to this view conscience is to be regarded as a form of experience, a direct means of perceiving the will of God, a kind of personal revelation. It seems to be this view of conscience which Newman has in mind in the *Letter to the Duke of Norfolk* when he says that it is 'the voice of God in the nature and heart of man',[23] and in *The Grammar of Assent* when he places it 'among our mental acts'[24] as the faculty by which we are able 'to perceive the voice, or the echoes of the voice, of a Master, living, personal, and sovereign'.[25] It supplies 'the dictate of an authoritative monitor bearing upon the details of conduct as they come before us'.[26] When C. C. J. Webb discusses such matters he is careful to make it clear that he does not regard such experiences as providing an infallible insight into truth. Nevertheless he does hold that 'when we "judge of ourselves what is right" . . . we have the living God present with us, speaking to the conscience, supplying grace, enlightening the mind, impelling to charity'.[27]

How far are such claims about the nature and authority of conscience justified? In effect they treat it as a form of religious experience. Hence it will be appropriate to discuss the significance of such claims in terms of a more general discussion of the significance of religious experience as a way of discovering the nature and will of God.

The significance of claims to religious experience

To those who have them practically all forms of experience seem to be a direct, self-validating awareness of what is there. I hear a telephone ringing; I see a cherry tree in blossom; I smell fried onions. Such experiences seem so immediate that generally we do not consider that there can be any reasonable doubt that a telephone is ringing, a cherry tree is in blossom, onions are being fried. If you doubt it, I will say 'listen' or 'look' or 'sniff'. Some forms of experience, however, are not so easily and straight-forwardly confirmed. If I say that I feel a pain in my wrist or that I feel dismal and lonely, you will have to take my word for it, although you may look for confirming modes of behaviour in my conduct. Provided, though, that you accept that I am not trying to deceive you, there would be no reason to doubt that if I claim to feel 'a pain' or to feel 'dismal and lonely' that I am in those states. There are, though, other forms of experience which are more controversial. People, for example, may report feeling utter joy which they maintain is an experience of the reality of God, or feeling drawn towards certain relationships which they maintain is an experience of God 'nudging' or calling them to certain acts of love, or feeling that certain patterns of conduct are morally wrong which they maintain is an experience of the judgment of God. In what they maintain about these experiences they are not using the reference to God as a way of expressing the importance of these feelings for them (though it does imply this); they consider that these feelings have a cognitive significance in that they provide them with a way of apprehending the reality, will and judgment of God. Can, though, these assertions about what is thus experienced be justified?

The first thing that needs to be appreciated about such claims is that there is no reason to doubt the reality of the basic feelings. When people report feeling deep joy or being drawn or a sense of moral outrage, they may generally be presumed to be having such experiences. Secondly, it seems equally clear that for many people the way these feelings are apprehended as experiences of God is something which to them is overwhelmingly convincing. As a result they may say that they 'know' the presence of God in their lives, or they 'know' that God wants them to do this, or they 'know' that God condemns such conduct. When asked how they 'know' such things, they may reply that their experiences are such they would be false to themselves if they said that they did not know it. These things are as clear to them because of their experiences as it is clear to me when I look up that there is a deep red rose surrounded by mock orange in a glass vase opposite to me.

Thirdly, though, sceptics of such claims may hold that what such people claim to 'know' through their experiences are in fact expressing interpretations of their feelings and that these interpretations may be unjustified. Those who offer such criticisms are likely to go on to suggest that there is a fundamental difference between the way I know that there is a red rose there and the way that I claim to know the reality of God in or through a feeling of deep joy. The former is a direct perception; the latter is an inference which needs to be warranted. While, though, this criticism makes an important point, it is important not to exaggerate the differences. As was suggested in chapter 3 on 'Faith, Culture and Doctrine', all our experiences, so far as they are conceptually apprehended by us (and unless they are so apprehended, they must remain as a totally vague awareness of having feelings of 'I know not what'), are inescapably matters of interpretation. Consider, for example, my experience of seeing a red rose. Leaving aside all the complex issues of the physical processes involved – light waves, surfaces that absorb and reflect light, refraction, optic nerves, brain states and so on – in perceiving what is there, I could only 'see' it as 'a red rose' because unity, redness and rose are among the concepts which I have available for apprehending what I am aware of. In this respect, therefore, sceptics of claims to religious knowledge through experience should not exaggerate the distinction between different forms of such knowledge. As Kant pointed out, in every case percepts without concepts are blind: we do not know what we are experiencing until and unless we find concepts by which to apprehend it.

All experiences, therefore, so far as they are apprehended, involve interpretation. The interpretative structures which are adopted, furthermore, may in some cases significantly mould what is taken to be an experience and what it is taken to be an experience of. This does not only happen at the conceptual level, though it does happen here: distinctions are made in different ways and to different degrees of refinement according to the different conceptual divisions that are employed. Interpretative structures may also carry with them ontological commitments and in these cases their application may have considerable influence on what is held to be experienced. The experience of the holy or the experience of deep joy, for example, may be apprehended according to an interpretative structure which sees it as a kind of aesthetic or emotional experience which does not refer to anything or anyone that exists – apart, that is, from the person having that experience. It may, however, be apprehended according to an interpretative structure which sees it as a mode of cognition whereby we grasp that reality which is 'holy' or which evokes deep joy in us. In such cases the choice of the interpretative structure to use is crucial – and the appropriateness of the choice cannot be judged simply by reference to the experience for this would beg the question since it is how the experience is appropriately to be grasped that is at issue. It is also possible that sometimes our experiences are generated by our wishes and expectations rather than by our encounter with reality that is independent of us. Our supposed experiences of the characters of others may thus turn out to be the projection of our own feelings concerning them on to them. In this respect we are all liable to the error of children who blame stones that they trip over for having ill-will towards them!

Since, therefore, all experiences involve interpretation and since religious experience may involve it to a controversial extent, it is not justifiable to refer to religious experience as if it provided self-evidently valid information about the reality, will and judgment of God. This is not to imply that such experiences may not provide such insights. It may be that our feelings in this respect are authentic perceptions of the divine. What it does imply is that any such claims will need to be justified by arguments which show that it is reasonable to interpret the experiences in this way – and more reasonable than to interpret them in another way. When, therefore, people assert that their conscience declares a course of action to be morally wrong, we may properly accept that for them to act in this way would be wrong. If, though, they go on to assert that in this way they are aware of the will of God in this matter, we may legitimately ask how they know this. How do they know that it is God's will that they perceive rather than the moral wishes of their friends, the moral inheritance of their education, or the moral principles of their society? It may be, of course, that they do apprehend the will of God – either directly or through these other agencies – but the case needs to be established.

Where, then, can we turn for moral direction? The answer is nowhere. That is the price and the privilege of our responsibilty as human beings. There are various places where we can seek guidance – the authorities of respected writings, wise counsellors, revered authorities, and creditable communities are all available for us to consult – but in the end we have each to make our decisions for ourselves. What we take to be authorities and how we use their guidance is for us to determine individually. Others may help us but finally we stand alone before God. We may make mistakes, sometimes terrible mistakes. God, though, is to be understood as the one who understands, who cherishes what is good, and who accepts us as we are. We cannot avoid the loneliness of decision-making but we are not alone as we decide. At the end of the parable of the grand inquisitor in Dostoyevsky's *The Brothers Karamazov*, we hear of the response of Christ. The inquisitor has defended his actions in imposing the guidance of the church. He has used his freedom in ways that are implicitly to be condemned and, in a way, the inquisitor seems to know it. And yet he has tried to do what was for people's good. Christ utters no judgment: having looked 'gently into his face . . . he suddenly approached the old man and kissed him gently on his bloodless, aged lips. That was all his answer'.[28] In that parable, perhaps, we may see the divine answer to our moral predicament. It does not absolve us from striving to realize the good and it does not take from us our responsibility for what we choose to do. At the same time it assures us that in the loneliness, sometimes the desperate loneliness, of having finally to make our decisions for ourselves and by ourselves we are not alone, for everlastingly we are embraced in the divine.

Chapter 11

Faith and Religious Language

Philosophers have always been concerned with language since it is by means of language that we apprehend as well as express our thoughts. Their discussions about the nature of truth and justice, beauty and goodness can be interpreted as arising from a concern to understand what we mean when we speak about such things. As we have already noted on various occasions, those who engage in metaphysical and theological reflection are confronted with the initial problem of determining how, in principle, it is possible to speak coherently of that which is ultimate or transcendent or perfect – and of determining the proper significance of such terms as 'ultimate', 'transcendent' and 'perfect'.

When, therefore, twentieth-century Anglo-Saxon philosophy is held to be characterized by a dominant concern with language, it is not doing anything foreign to a major interest in all philosophical activity. It is not even distinctive in recognizing that many of our intellectual puzzles arise from misapprehending the language in which we express our understanding. Three hundred years ago, for instance, John Locke wrote *An Essay concerning Human Understanding* to lay the foundations of a re-examination of our words and ideas since he believed that a fresh evaluation of them might lead to a previously undiscovered 'sort of Logick and Critick'.[1] What, though, does distinguish some recent linguistic philosophy is the subtlety and extensiveness of its investigations into the logical structure and content of what we say – as well as the way in which some linguistic philosophers have considered that genuine philosophy should be restricted to such analytical activities.

The initial development of linguistic philosophy was in part a reaction to the puzzling remarks found in the works of some leading contemporary philosophers. F. H. Bradley, for example, maintained that what is 'less than Absolute' is not real but only an appearance: there is only 'one Reality' and that is 'the Absolute as a whole of experience'.[2] J. McT. E. McTaggart argued that upon careful examination the idea of time turns out to be self-contradictory. Hence time cannot be real. It is only an appearance – or, rather, a misperception. Matter, too, is unreal: the only existing realities are spirits.[3]

It is, admittedly, unfair to take such remarks out of their context and apart from the arguments (in McTaggart's case especially complex arguments which stretch most people's comprehension) which are held to justify them and which clarify what they mean. Nevertheless it does seem clear that basic notions like 'being real' are being employed in strange, if not in self-contradictory, ways in such remarks. It is odd, for example, to say that the desk on which I am writing is 'unreal' or that time is unreal when I have been anxiously waiting for a telephone call. G. E. Moore responded to the oddity of such remarks in a paper entitled 'A Defence of Common Sense'. In it he suggests that philosophers have come to such conclusions because they have not recognized that we may understand the meaning of statements and know, with certainty, that what they state is true although we cannot provide absolute and exhaustive analyses of their meaning.[4] Moore suggests, therefore, that we should not be persuaded by the apparent implications of our attempts to achieve such comprehensive analyses into asserting that 'this desk is unreal' or that 'time is unreal'. Instead we should recognize that while we know implicitly what is meant by talk about 'this desk' or about 'waiting for time to pass', we may not be able to tease out correctly in explicit analyses what our common sense thus understands and knows to be true.

Others attempted to determine the necessary boundaries of what can be significantly asserted and the way in which its proper meaning is to be established by establishing rules for meaningful discourse. The most famous of these attempts is that of Logical Positivism. Originating in the so-called 'Vienna Circle' which included Moritz Schlick, Rudolf Carnap and Friedrich Waismann, its apostle to the British was Alfred J. Ayer and its British gospel, Ayer's *Language, Truth and Logic*. The first edition was published in 1936. The preface to the second edition, which appeared a decade later, provides a clear indication of some of the difficulties in making the basic thesis satisfactory.

The title of the first chapter of *Language, Truth and Logic*, 'The Elimination of Metaphysics,' proclaims one fundamental aim of Logical Positivism. The means by which this philosophical final solution is to be accomplished is through the adoption of the 'verification principle'. According to the formulation given in this first chapter

> a sentence is factually significant to any given person, if, and only if, he knows how to verify the proposition which it purports to express – that is, if he knows what observations would lead him, under certain conditions, to accept the proposition as being true, or reject it as being false.[5]

All other purported statements either are analytic statements (i.e. statements like tautologies which give no new factual information since their predicate is implied in their subject – e.g., 'Bachelors are unmarried men') or are 'not literally meaningful'[6] although they may be emotionally significant[7] for those who utter them. For example, to say that 'this solution is radio-active' may be held to be factually significant because if I place a Geiger counter near to the solution, the instrument will give a higher reading than is due to natural background radiation if the statement is true, and the instrument will not increase its reading if the statement is false. If, on the other hand, I say that 'the ultimate entities constituting this solution are psychically structured' (or that 'all ultimate entities have a psychical structure') but neither I nor any one else can specify any empirical test by which this claim can be shown to be either justified or falsified, then according to the verification principle the claim is not providing us with any cognitively significant information. In other words it is not telling us anything about what is the case – although it may express our emotional attitude to things.

The problem posed by verification and falsification principles

It is important to bear in mind that the logical positivists were attempting to eliminate many traditional philosophical disputes and other beliefs by showing that the claims at issue were meaningless. The verification principle, that is, was put forward as a way to distinguish what is 'literally meaningful' from what is not: it was not used as a way of showing that certain claims are false. If a statement is meaningless, questions of its truth or falsity cannot coherently arise. The application of the principle, however, created various problems. In days before space rockets, it was not possible in practice to verify statements about the conditions on the far side of the moon, but it was odd to have to conclude that any such statement is therefore meaningless. Presumably it never will be possible to check claims about what happened in the past by observing again what happened. It does not seem to be satisfactory, though, to hold that the significant content of statements about historical events report only what can be observed in extant records (e.g. 'King Harold was killed by an arrow in the eye' reports what can be seen *now* in the Bayeaux tapestry and what can be read *now* in documents: it does not tell us about an event that happened *then*). Such strange conclusions from applying the verification principle led rapidly to modifications in its formulation. It was held, for example, that the verificatory procedure need not be possible in practice: what needed to be specified is one which is conceivable in principle. Such modifications, however, still generally succeed in leaving ethical and aesthetic as well as metaphysical and theological claims in the rubbish dump of meaninglessness – even though it was allowed that this wasteland might contain some 'interesting non-sense' in that some of these scrapped claims reflect people's emotional feelings and attitudes.

A fundamental problem, however, arises from considering the status of the verification principle itself. It could not plausibly be held to be analytically true – for if it only provided a particular definition of literal meaningfulness, those who advanced it could not deny the right of others to prefer a different, more comprehensive, definition. On the other hand the principle could not claim to be empirically verifiable for its very postulation was a response to the empirical fact that people treat many statements as meaningful which the principle is intended to discriminate between. But if the principle is not analytic and it is not empirically verifiable, it must be nonsensical. It was an embarrassing conclusion! If an exception were made for the meaningfulness of the principle itself, why not for other things which people desire to affirm?

By means of the verification principle the logical positivists were attempting to lay down *a priori* the conditions for meaningful discourse. After initially sharing this type of approach, Ludwig Wittgenstein concluded that it is fundamentally erroneous because it fails to appreciate the variety and subtlety of language as it is actually used. In *Philosophical Investigations* he comments thus on the things we say:

> Think of the tools in a tool-box: there is a hammer, pliers, a saw, a screw-driver, a rule, a glue-pot, glue, nails and screws. – The functions of words are as diverse as the functions of these objects. (And in both cases there are similarities.)

Of course, what confuses us is the uniform appearance of words when we hear them spoken or meet them in script and print. For their *application* is not presented to us so clearly. Especially when we are doing philosophy![8]

A little later he adds that 'there are *countless* . . . different kinds of use of what we call "symbols", "words", "sentences"'.[9] New ways of using language come into being and old ones fall into disuse. If then, we wish to understand what is being said, Wittgenstein maintains that we must not try to force it into a predetermined categorical scheme. We should instead follow the principle of 'Don't ask for the meaning, ask for the use'. In other words, faced with a remark which puzzles us, we should attempt to discover what it expresses by considering the context in which the remark was made, the way in which it is connected to other remarks, the purpose for which it was made, the response which the person who made it expected to find in those who heard it, the reasons which might be offered to justify making it, and so on. Furthermore, we should not just concentrate on individual remarks but consider the characteristics of the different ways in which we use language – in the language of physics, the language of poetry, the language of law, the language of history, the language of love, and so on. By thus examining what happens in practice we seek to discern the actual content and logical structure of what is said and so, it is to be hoped, avoid misunderstanding it by imposing upon it inappropriate (and independently determined) rules of significant discourse.

Both through his teaching and, after his death, through the publication of his manuscripts and notes, Wittgenstein greatly influenced the development of the varied movement sometimes labelled 'Linguistic Analysis' as the prevailing form of language philosophy. Other leading exponents were Gilbert Ryle, John Wisdom, and John L. Austin. So far as the language used in religion and theology is concerned, the application to it of the techniques and concerns of linguistic analysis has been illuminating. Although some of those who have presented analyses of religious language have been hostile to the claims of faith, their analyses as well as those of others more sympathetic have indicated the complexity of this form of language. In the remainder of this chapter, therefore, we shall note some of the various aspects of religious language that have been identified. Some of the topics have already been mentioned in earlier chapters in other contexts.

Here we will consider how they are components of the rich and complex phenomenon that is the language of religion.

Theism is based upon claims about the reality of God. As such it involves making claims about what is – or what is held to be – the case: God exists, God loves all people, 'God created the heavens and the earth', and so on. Once these claims are examined, however, they are quickly perceived to be importantly unlike other claims which we make. Logical positivists such as Ayer pointed out that theistic assertions about what is the case cannot be verified by empirical tests. We no longer consider it appropriate to decide claims about God by seeing what happens to a fleece left outside[10] or whether a sacrifice is consumed by heaven-sent fire.[11] Both because believers hold such tests to be inappropriate for justifying claims about the reality of God (for God is not to be treated as another object which may or may not be present at a particular time and place) and because they cannot now produce convincing empirical tests in any case, Ayer concluded on the basis of the verification principle that 'all utterances about the nature of God are nonsensical'.[12] Neither theism nor atheism can be meaningfully asserted since 'the notion of a person whose essential attributes are non-empirical is not an intelligible notion at all'.[13]

A different but more disturbing challenge to theistic claims about God was made by Antony Flew on the basis of the 'falsification principle'. This principle maintains that a statement can only be held to be factually significant if we can specify some possible state or event which would, if it occurred, falsify it. For example, I may find it hard to prove that a particular person loves me (since a sceptic may cast doubt on the significance of the evidence which I offer, holding that it may only show that the person wants to humour me, or pities me, or enjoys teasing me, or finds satisfaction in deluding me,) but it is easier to specify what would falsify the claim that that person loves me (e.g. in normal circumstances it would generally be regarded as falsified if it were found that that person persistently let me down, deliberately ignored me, intentionally tantalized me,or attacked me with an axe!). Because, therefore, I can specify what would, if it occurred, falsify the claim, the claim (whether it be true or false) that that person loves me is factually significant. Flew maintains, however, that theistic believers who assert that 'God loves us as a father loves his children' will allow 'no conceivable event or series of events' to be a reason for conceding that the claim is false.[14] Instead, they assert the claim whatever happens to be the case – whether we are rejoicing over a happy relationship or agonizing over someone being painfully destroyed by a cancer – and intend to continue to assert it whatever happens. Consequently, Flew suggests, such claims about God do not actually assert anything about what is the case.

Various responses have been made to these applications of the verification and falsification principles to religious assertions about God. Basil Mitchell, for example, took up Flew's challenge by arguing that believers' claims about God are not to be seen as assertions which believers must give up as soon as experience tells against them. Although believers consider that they have properly convincing grounds for holding them, the claims do not assert provisional hypotheses subject to empirical falsification. They express articles of faith to which the believers are committed, against which they will not allow anything to count decisively, and in terms of which they interpret their experience.[15] E. L. Mascall's response to the verificationist challenge was partly to hold that there is appropriate experiential evidence to verify and thus to show the meaningfulness of theistic claims. In *Words and Images* he argues that 'there is nothing logically impossible in an experience which is not an experience of sense impressions upon the physical organs of the body'[16] and that mystical experience may therefore be held to provide a kind of empirical awareness which meets the requirements of the verification principle. If verificationists object that mystical experience requires a technique and long training, devotion and single-mindedness, and is only attainable by a few people,[17] it can be pointed out in reply that the same is true of the awareness and interpretation of data which allows sub-atomic physicists to make claims about quarks. If verificationists do not seem to be troubled about the meaningfulness of physicists' claims, they should be prepared to accept those of theistic believers. Even less presently attainable, though, is the form of experience which John Hick suggested could be specified to meet the criterion of factual significance laid down by the verification principle. This was the experience of 'continued conscious existence after bodily death'.[18] According to his notion of 'eschatological verification', theistic believers and non-believers do not differ over what they expect to happen in this life but they do differ over their expectations about the time 'when history is completed'. Theists expect to discover that history has 'fulfilled a specific purpose, namely that of creating "children of God"', whereas atheists expect no such experiences.[19] Since, according to Hick, the notions of post-mortem personal existence and eschatological verification are coherent, it is justifiable to claim that theistic claims are meaningful. On the other hand the criterion of falsification cannot be met in this way since if there is no post-mortem conscious experience, we shall never be aware that there is not.

These kinds of response to the verification and falsification principles high-light some of the logical oddity of assertions about the reality of God. Although these assertions make claims about what is the case, they are logically different from claims about the empirical reality in which we find ourselves. They differ in the kind of evidence which is used to justify them, in the kind of expectations by which their truth will be confirmed, and in the degree of commitment which believers give to them. The logical peculiarity of assertions about God is further indicated by what Charles Hartshorne, among others, holds to be the 'necessary' character of claims about the existence of God. According to Hartshorne such claims are 'necessary' in that they refer not only to what is the ground of everything actual but also to the ground of anything that could possibly be actual. Since this is so, it is logically erroneous to seek empirical verification for theism or to attempt to specify situations which, if they came to be, would falsify basic theistic claims. God, as the ontological ground of all, must be compatible with all that is and all that ever could be. What in this case may be held to be shown by the verificationist and falsificationist challenges to theistic claims is that those who present them have not recognized the peculiar status of fundamental assertions about God. These assertions are universal and ultimate in their scope. The question of theism is therefore seriously misunderstood when it is treated as a question of whether God exists as one item among many in the universe (as we may ask if heffalumps exist or if David Pailin has more than one son): the question of theism is the primary metaphysical question of whether reality as a whole is ultimately meaningful or finally absurd, and its logical status must be perceived accordingly. Empirical considerations may contribute to our decision about the truth of such claims about God's reality but they can never decisively verify or falsify them.

The language of encounter and of value

Religious language, however, does not only consist of claims about the reality of God which are universal, fundamental or metaphysical in character. It also contains components whose logical status is most adequately understood in terms of our encounter with other selves. God is not just an idea to be talked about. For believers God is supremely a reality which confronts them. The Jewish theologian, Martin Buber, in his seminal *I and Thou* (first published in 1923) maintained that God is a 'Thou' which is never properly understood when described in third-person terms and even less in the impersonal language of 'it'. He writes that 'God is the Being that is directly, most nearly, and lastingly, over against us, that may properly only be addressed, not expressed'.[20] God is not to be spoken about so much as spoken to.[21] Talk about God as 'He or It' is always allegorical;[22] the reality of God is the reality of 'the Eternal Thou' which 'can by its nature not become It'.[23] In a not unsimilar way around the same time Karl Barth was stressing that God is unique and the gospel discontinuous with all human reasoning processes.[24] God is known only through the sovereignly free 'Word' of God's self-communication with humanity. The proper role for theology is to be nothing more or less than the service of this divine 'word' (a 'ministerium verbi divini').[25]

Knowledge of another personal being through encounter involves the self who comes to that knowledge as well as the self who is thereby come to be known. For Buber such 'knowing' is a matter of a direct relationship between the parties involved.[26] In *Subject and Object in Modern Theology* James Brown points out that so far as a knowledge of God is a matter of such meeting, it is a knowledge which we can attain only so far as we are prepared to open ourselves up to the divine and actively participate in the divine being. The knowledge that is appropriate to theistic faith is not an objective, disinterested decision about the truth but 'the supreme exercise of subjectivity' in which the Object of faith 'is appropriated as truth in a form of living'.[27] William Hordern, in *Speaking of God*, also draws attention to the personal characteristics of authentic talk about God and suggests that as a result the verification of claims about the divine is to be compared to the way in which we verify claims about another person – namely, through engaging in 'the give-and-take' of a personal relationship with that person.[28]

Although some of the ways in which this 'personal encounter' element in religious language is understood may be disputed, it does seem to indicate an important characteristic of most expressions of theistic faith. In talking about God, theistic believers are talking about the divine reality which they consider that they encounter and whose being supremely exemplifies the mysteriousness of other persons. Interpretations of the logic and content of statements about God which do not recognize the personal character of what is known and the personal involvement in the knowing of that other, fail to understand an important part of the nature of the language of theistic faith – although such interpretations may be appropriate to the discussions of the notion of God in disinterested metaphysical speculations.

On numerous occasions, and especially in the previous chapter on faith and morality, it has been pointed out that descriptions of God do not only refer to that which is ultimate in being. By definition God is the proper and adequate object of worship and, as such, is to be conceived as 'that than which a greater cannot be conceived' in value. God and goodness ultimately coincide. This indicates another important characteristic to be included in any comprehensive analysis of religious language. As noted earlier, Richard Braithwaite interpreted 'God is love' as the expression of the moral intention to live lovingly. Although such an attempt to restrict claims about God to the assertion of behaviour-policies and supporting stories is not likely to satisfy theistic believers, it is a reminder that a proper appreciation of theistic claims will perceive that they include value-components. When believers assert that 'God is love', they are not simply describing some-one's character. They are both affirming the character of the ultimate reality and recognizing that character as an expression of the good which they are to seek to actualize in their own lives.

A similar insight, made in relation to the notion of God as creator, is suggested by a comment in Wisdom's fascinating paper 'Gods'. Telling a story of two people who return to 'their long neglected garden' and who disagree about whether a gardener still tends some of the old plants, Wisdom points out that the two not only differ over how they interpret the evidence of the plot, they also differ 'in how they feel towards the garden'.[29] In part that 'feeling' is likely to express itself in moral concerns. The person who considers that the plot is tended by someone will probably consider that a certain respect for the plot is appropriate while the person who holds that no one now tends the plot will not feel any such inhibitions. Similarly persons who believe that 'God created the heavens and the earth' will be likely to understand that belief as involving a concern for the fulfilment of the divine purposes in creation. Because, that is, they believe in the reality of God as creator, they will tend to assert such things as that 'the world is given to us to use according to the will of God, not to do what we like with' or 'we are to be co-creators with God, not destroyers of what God gives us'. The relationship between the beliefs about God and what are considered to be the actual forms of appropriate practice is, however, a complex and controversial one. Believers may – and frequently do – disagree about what their faith requires of them as current debates about divorce, abortion, ecology, nuclear weapons and social legislation illustrate. What seems to be non-controversial is that expressions of theistic faith essentially, and not merely accidentally, involve values and commitment to their realization. Analyses of their meaning which overlook this element in them and treat statements of belief about God as if they are like, say, descriptions of the molecular structure of vitamin D_3, are seriously deficient.

The language of commitment

In the earlier discussion of Flew's falsification challenge to the meaningfulness of theistic claims mention was made of Basil Mitchell's response which includes the point that such claims express articles of faith. They are, that is, claims which not only express what is held to be the case but also what those who hold them are personally committed to. This is reflected in the way that believers speak of believing *in* the reality of God and not merely of believing that such-and-such is the case concerning God. Such 'belief in' presupposes 'belief that' (it is not credible to believe in something or someone which is not there to be believed in) but it goes beyond bare intellectual assent. It is a characteristic of authentic theistic understanding which Søren Kierkegaard frequently stressed. The truth of Christianity only exists, in his view, in 'subjectivity'[30] – 'in an appropriation-process of the most passionate inwardness':[31] an 'objective acceptance of Christianity (*sit venia verbo*)' which entertains it only as a set of correct views is condemned as 'paganism or thoughtlessness'.[32]

William Zuurdeeg and William Hordern similarly point to the way that religious language is 'convictional language': 'the man who speaks of his God, of right and wrong, or of something beautiful, is not describing how he feels, he is pointing to that which has "convicted" him.' Such convictions are not 'a matter of personal taste' but an irresistible result of what is apprehended to be the inherent quality of the convictor. They result in more than intellectual persuasion for they produce a certitude which moves 'the whole life' of the convicted.[33] Religious language is thus to be recognized as dealing 'with the ultimate convictions of a man's life . . . by which he lives and dies' and which determine for a person 'what in life is supremely worthwhile' and dependable.[34] It expresses the fundamental convictions which are presupposed in a person's understanding of everything else. In *Religious Language* Ian T. Ramsey argues that theological phrases are not meant to give labels to 'a group of hard, objective "facts" glanced at by passive observers' but are used to evoke a 'disclosure' of that which lies beyond what is immediately observed.[35] We shall return to this characteristic of religious language later but here it should be noted that he sees such a disclosure as resulting in 'a *total* commitment to the *whole* universe'.[36] What we thus discern, in other words, elicits a response which 'involves our whole personality'.[37] Donald D. Evans puts it that religious language is essentially 'self-involving'.[38] Although the precise nature of this characteristic of religious language may be debated, no adequate analysis of the language of faith can claim to be adequately comprehensive if it omits all recognition of it. Luther's 'Here I stand. I can do no other' reminds us that statements of religious belief do not merely express intellectual judgments. They are also confessions of the faith by which people live and for whose truth they may even die.

Ways of seeing

As well as expressing believers' convictions, religious language also expresses the basic standpoints, perspectives and attitudes which direct their understanding and orientate their lives. Here again the basic point has been identified in somewhat different ways by different analysts. In a response to Flew's falsification challenge to the meaningfulness of statements about God, R M Hare suggests that such assertions are not to be understood as statements of what is the case which offer 'some sort of explanation' for why things are as they are.[39] Talk about God is a disguised way of expressing the principles of interpretation on the basis of which theists understand the world. No event or series of events can compel us to give up such principles because it is in terms of them that we 'decide what is and what is not an explanation' of every event. They describe how we basically see things and make sense of them. A more complex analysis of this aspect of religious language is provided by H. A. Hodges in *Languages, Standpoints and Attitudes*. Initially he distinguishes between languages and standpoints. 'Standpoints' refer to our basic assumptions or absolute presuppositions about the structure of reality and to 'the way of seeing things to which these in turn give rise'.[40] They may include valuative and volitional as well as cognitive elements. A 'language' is understood by Hodges as the expression of a particular standpoint. To use a language is consequently to adopt its standpoint, whether we are wholly conscious of what we are doing or not. Standpoints, however, are not ultimate. According to Hodges' analysis of our intellectual and existential situation, our standpoints are the product of our basic 'attitude' to life as a whole. It is this attitude which constitutes 'the basis' on which the structure of our life rests and which determines 'the direction' of our 'interests' and 'the experiences and activities' which we regard as good.[41] A faith such as theism generally or more specifically Christianity (or a form of Christianity) is a system of belief reflecting an attitude which is worked out in various standpoints, expressed in a particular language, and gives rise to a pattern of life and thought.[42] If, therefore, we wish to appreciate the content of religious language we must recognize that in part at least it describes a person's standpoint and the attitudes underlying it' which together determine what that person takes reality to be and how that person accordingly interprets all experiences.[43]

This characteristic of religious language has been regarded by some as the clue to identifying the proper logical status of references to historical events in statements of the Christian faith. Paul van Buren, for example, in *The Secular Meaning of the Gospel*, maintains that statements of the gospel both describe an empirical event which happened and call for an existential response to that event.[44] These two functions of those statements are seen to be reconcilable when it is realized that statements of faith are statements expressing 'a particular way of seeing the world, other men, and oneself, and the way of life appropriate to such a perspective'[45] and that for the Christian faith the norm of its perspective is given in the historical events of the story of Jesus of Nazareth. So far, then, as the Christian gospel is expressed in terms of reports about Jesus, the basic point of those reports is not grasped unless they are seen to be expressing the perspective on life which constitutes that faith. From an existentialist approach Carl Michalson makes a somewhat similar point in *The Rationality of Faith* when he states that 'the Christian faith is an attitude toward the world which the presence of Jesus of Nazareth in history has made possible'. While for Michalson this attitude comes about 'through the mediation of particular historical events' and so is 'tied to history',[46] it is important to recognize that the function of 'historical language in matters of faith is not to point to past events as such but 'to change situations' now. The language of theistic faith is primarily the language of a challenge 'to receive the world from beyond oneself' – to live in the openness of faith – and the language of Christian faith sees that challenge as presented and the authentic response to it illuminated by the event of Jesus of Nazareth.[47] In such ways, then, van Buren and Michalson suggest another aspect of religious language which needs to be taken account of in any comprehensive analysis of such language.

So far in this rapid survey of some of the analyses of the language of faith we have concentrated on the content of such language. It emerges that statements of theistic faith are intrinsically complex. They make claims about what is the case ultimately and universally; they describe what is of supreme value; they point to what is encountered; they express what has convicting power and has elicited total commitment; they report basic principles of understanding, perspectives and standpoints. And they do all this in the guise of innocuous statements about God which appear, as printed or said, to be comparable to the descriptions which we may give of a friend or of a person whom we have studied. A full analysis of religious language, however, not only reveals this, perhaps unexpected, intrinsic complexity in its content. It also draws attention to the way in which religious language often uses various forms of indirect expression in order to convey that content.

Qualifiers and models

Earlier in this chapter we mentioned how Ian T Ramsey suggests that theological statements do not provide literally applicable descriptions but use language in order to evoke a disclosure of what lies 'beyond' the immediately observable and directly apprehensible. Ramsey's own works particularly draw attention to two ways by which such discernment may be achieved – by the use of 'qualifiers' and by the use of 'models'. In the former case he points to the way in which, when speaking of God, we use some terms that have a relatively straightforward sense in ordinary discourse – words like 'wise', 'cause', 'good' and so on – but then qualify them by adverbs such as 'infinitely', 'first' and 'absolutely'.[48] We thus talk of God not as being wise but as 'infinitely wise', not as a cause of something but as 'the first cause of everything', not as good but as 'absolutely good'. The function of these 'qualifiers', as Ramsey describes these adverbs, is not just to point out that God is wiser than we are, prior to our derivative causal acts, better than we manage to be. It goes further, for it seeks to point us along the intellectual path of considering ever increasingly superior states of wisdom, causality and goodness until it dawns upon us that when we talk of God we talk of that whose qualities are intrinsically and logically different from those of all other beings. In the case of God we are not talking of that which is comparatively superior: we are talking of that which evokes 'adoration, wonder, worship, commitment'.[49]

Ramsey's exploration of the nature and logic of 'models' in religious language is valuably illuminated by his knowledge of the use of models in the thought of the natural sciences. Basically he suggests that theology thrives on the employment of a diversity of models[50] which both separately and in conjunction seek to evoke revealing insights into the nature of that which we cannot grasp directly, namely, the nature and will of God and the relationship between the divine and the human. In this respect it is important to appreciate that the most fruitful models are not those which aim to 'picture' what they disclose by providing a scaled-down reproduction of it but are those which act as 'analogue' models. The latter generate insights through their 'similarity-with-a-difference' in relation to what they seek to disclose.[51] Although such analogue models allow us to talk coherently of what we cannot grasp directly, they are always liable to be misunderstood (and frequently have been misunderstood in the history of religious thought as the case of the models used in relation to atonement theology illustrates) as providing literally applicable descriptions. Ramsey properly insists that where models are used in religious language they must be recognized as such and interpreted accordingly.

Indirect language

As was mentioned in the chapter on the attributes of God, theologians such as Edwyn Bevan and Paul Tillich have explored how religious language uses symbolic means of expression to talk about the divine. According to the former theology aims to arrive at precise concepts but can never satisfy that aim because God always lies beyond what we can apprehend. It has, therefore, to recognize that its descriptions of God need to use symbols – that is, to use something which is 'presented to the senses or the imagination' to stand for something which it cannot grasp except by some such indirect means.[52] Bevan is concerned to affirm, however, that such symbolic descriptions do convey information about God:

to say that a conception has symbolical *truth* . . . implies a belief

that God, although unimaginable, is really such that a response of
that kind [i.e. as indicated by the symbol] is the appropriate
response to Him. It means that the symbolic expression is the best
possible way the truth could be expressed in terms of human
ideas.[53]

Tillich, in emphasizing the symbolic nature of God-talk, carefully
distinguishes between 'signs', which are arbitrary and can be
changed at will, and 'symbols', which have an ontological relationship (he speaks of it as one of 'participation in') with that to which
they point.[54] Symbols are not producible to order; they emerge as
they manifest themselves in a culture as effective ways of achieving
awareness of that which concerns us ultimately. Studies such as
these both draw attention to another of the indirect methods by
which religious language communicates understanding of the divine
and remind us that attempts to treat its statements literally are
highly likely to result in serious misunderstandings of their content.

Other attempts to identify indirect methods of communication
found in religious language have emphasized that analogical and
metaphorical usages are to be found. Theologians have long been
interested in the different kinds of analogical description and in
discovering their applicability to our perceptions of the divine. They
have explored the notion of analogy as a way of saying something
specific and precise about God without at the same time saying too
much and so producing an unwarrantably anthropomorphic image
of the divine. The problem that remains for any analogical
description of God is how to determine what may legitimately be
inferred from it (because what it conveys does have that content)
and what may not be thus inferred (because this is to treat the
analogical predication too literally). To put the issue in concrete
terms: if it is held that it is correct to speak of God analogically as
'parent', what is to be understood both about God and about God's
relationships and activities in respect of you and me and everyone
else as a result of that divine parenthood? The more that is held to
be implied, the more the criticism is likely to be raised that we are
fashioning God in a human image; the less that is held to be implied
in order to respect the otherness and mystery of God, the emptier
do these analogical descriptions turn out to be. In the case of
metaphors the problem becomes even more acute as metaphorical
usage is generally held to be even more allusive and imprecise. As
Sallie McFague suggests in her interesting study, *Metaphorical
Theology*, metaphorical statements 'always contain the whisper, "it

is *and it is not*"'. To see theological descriptions as metaphorical is to stress the 'dissimilarity, distinction, tension' between 'the transcendence of God and the finitude of creation'.[55] While such metaphorical theology does affirm that there are 'connections' between the divine and the human, it sees these connections as being 'of a tensive, discontinuous, and surprising nature'.[56] On the other hand metaphorical thinking, which is 'seeing one thing *as* something else', is arguably 'the basis of human thought and language'.[57] If so it is unavoidable in religion as elsewhere. Once again, however, we are reminded of the dangers of treating remarks about God too literally – and of the need to choose appropriate metaphors for the divine qualities. Sallie McFague justifiably protests against the way in which traditional metaphors for God have been predominantly masculine.

The most common communication of religious insights, however, is not usually through the statement of individual, abstract, doctrinal propositions. It is through the telling of stories, myths, tales, and parables. These too are properly to be understood as an indirect means of communication either because they are identifiable as imaginative fictions anyway (the stories of creation, of Adam and Eve, of Job, of Jonah, of the birth of Jesus, of the good Samaritan, and of the prodigal son come readily to mind) or because they use reports of historical events to point to insights into the nature of that which lies beyond those events as historical phenomena (the history of Israel and the story of Jesus are good examples). The value of the story-form in relation to other forms of indirect communication is considerable. For one thing we basically understand things and persons by grasping their story: who I am is discovered (by me and by others) by telling the story of my life. A story, furthermore, embodies in its structure a recognition of the basic temporal ordering of reality and of the interconnectedness of things. No one and no thing is a discrete individual: everyone and everything is fashioned by relationships with others. Stories bring this out. A story is also open to imaginative development by those who relate it and those who hear it. It need not be regarded as a final statement of what is the case but as containing an invitation to discern through it new interpretative insights. A story, finally, may be regarded as providing an essentially indirect grasp of truths which we are unable to grasp directly. In these respects when believers sing 'Tell me the old, old story' they may be nearer to a recognition of how we grasp the fundamental truths of reality – the nature of the divine mystery and of the purpose and destiny of human being – than they realize. Story forms, however we name them, may well not be merely attractive ways of illustrating an insight into God: they may be the most adequate way of grasping and communicating that insight. This, too, is a perception which is emerging from current studies of religious language.

Religious faith seeks to provide an understanding of reality which offers, as F. W. Dillistone puts it, the hope of 'a total integration and a final reconciliation' of all the various components of our experiences of it.[58] In order to express claims to such an understanding (or, perhaps better, faith's inklings of what such an understanding will be like), it is not surprising that religious language turns out to have a complex structure and to use indirect methods of communication. The great advantage for faith of twentieth-century developments in linguistic philosophy is that they have enhanced our awareness of the complex character and inherent elusiveness of the content of statements about God. The danger of the application of these philosophical techniques to religious language has been (and still, to some extent, is) that an analyst, having identified one component in such language, then falls into the error of holding that that is all that is present in the language. It is the error of the chemical analyst who identifies carbon as present in a substance and then says that the substance is carbon. Further investigation might show that oxygen and hydrogen are also present and in determinate relationships which show that the substance is sugar. It is an elementary mistake but one into which some recent analyses of religious language have fallen. The remedy is not to deny the results of the various individual analyses but to see that many of them at least give insight into the structure of a complex whole.

Finally, the complex and elusive nature of religious language should perhaps make those addicted to the clear concepts and precise expressions of ideal philosophy of religion recognize that it may be otherwise that the divine is to be grasped. Charles Hartshorne, who can never be accused of not seeking clarity and precision in thought about God, once told me that Wordsworth's 'The Simplon Pass' had special interest and value for him. The poem ends:

> Tumult and peace, the darkness and the light –
> Were all like workings of one mind, the features
> Of the same face, blossoms upon one tree,
> Characters of the great Apocalypse,
> The types and symbols of Eternity,
> Of first, and last, and midst, and without end.

Perhaps the study of religious language should make believers and theologians more sensitive to the need for poetry and stories as they consider the mysteries of the divine that is unbounded, undemanding Love.

Conclusion

Finishing a book such as this, both for the author and for the reader, is rather like the deflating experience of being awarded a degree. Those who have really benefited from the course will be more aware of problems than of solutions. This is as it should be. An introductory study such as this 'Groundwork' is intended to indicate the start of various routes for exciting intellectual adventures rather than to commemorate the successful attainment of a summit. In the case of theistic faith, furthermore, no one has yet finally attained those summits and no one ever will. God always lies beyond our grasp. Theological understanding thus offers the fascinating but tantalizing goal of an unending quest. The believer is one who seeks understanding rather than one who complacently considers that it has been achieved. In this respect the criticisms of unbelievers and the doubts of sceptics are to be gladly received for they push faith towards finding deeper, clearer and more comprehensive understanding.

Those, therefore, that find some of the ideas presented in this book disturbing should see them as a challenge to be faced rather than as an infection to be avoided. For far too long in the modern world theistic faith generally and Christian theistic faith in particular has suffered a credibility gap because those who confess it have seemed either unwilling or unable to meet fundamental criticisms of their belief. The need is for believers and, even more, for those who present to others the claims of faith to be aware of what the problems are. It is not a failure to find solutions but a refusal to admit that problems exist which destroys the possibility of authentic faith. In terms of personal growth, furthermore, the problems raised by philosophical considerations of the contents of faith point the paths to mature self-understanding. By being exposed to the light of critical rationality our awareness of what we believe and why – and our discovery of what we ought to believe and why – will be enhanced. As was said at the start of this study: to believe that

God is the truth implies that the search for truth can never be alien to a fundamental faith in God.

At the close of the previous chapter it was hinted that sometimes poetry may provide a more satisfactory means of perceiving and communicating religious insights than doctrinal propositions. This, however, is not to be taken as an excuse for revelling in obscurantism. Rather, as Whitehead once suggested, we are always to seek clarity – and then to distrust it! In this quest for understanding, we should not be afraid to use our imagination. It is through this faculty for achieving novel ways of perceiving things and their relationships that we are likely to find the solution to our intellectual problems. It is even arguable that it is through our imagination that God speaks to us. Theological and philosophical training which so moulds people's thinking that the capacity for imaginative novelty is stifled under a heap of dead learning is to be abhorred. The point of knowing what others have said is not so that we can repeat their ideas after them – the intellectual burping that so often is confused with ability – but to add to the stock of resources on which we can use our imagination and develop our insights. Those, therefore, who take this book seriously will not stay with it. They will argue with its ideas, read other works on the subject, and come out with their own thoughts – which they too will submit to the criticism of others.

What, finally, is the aim of understanding faith? It is to find the story of reality which renders it meaningful and our lives in it significant. As Newman indicates in his *Grammar of Assent*, we can only believe that whose content we apprehend and of whose rational probability we are persuaded. By considering the issues which have been raised in this book and many other issues which there has been no space to discuss, we seek to apprehend the story of God, humanity and the world in a form that is rationally warranted and personally captivating. At the end of the chapter on 'Adventure' in his *Adventures of Ideas*, Alfred North Whitehead wrote that 'truth of belief is important, both in itself and in its consequences'. Falsehood 'lacks the magic by which a beauty beyond the power of speech to express can be called into being, as if by the wand of an enchanter. It is for these reasons that the civilization of a society requires the virtues of Truth, Beauty, Adventure and Art.'[1] It is for the same reasons that the philosopher of religion examines faith. Error is to be exposed and understanding developed so that truth may flourish, life may be creative, and God may be all in all.

Notes

Preface

1. John Oman, *Honest Religion*, Cambridge University Press 1941, p. 19.

Chapter 1 Faith, Religion and Philosophy

1. Anselm, *Proslogion*, ch. 1.
2. Paul Tillich, *Dynamics of Faith*, New York, Harper Torchbooks 1957, p. 1.
3. Paul Wiebe, *The Architecture of Religion*, San Antonio, Texas, Trinity University Press 1984, p. 32.
4. Ibid., p. 27.
5. Melford E. Spiro, 'Religion: Problems of Definition and Explanation', printed in Michael Banton (ed.) *Anthropological Approaches to the Study of Religion* Tavistock 1966, p. 96.
6. Cf. Ninian Smart, *The Phenomenon of Religion*, Macmillan 1973, pp. 42f.
7. Harvey Cox, *The Seduction of the Spirit*, Wildwood House 1974, p.14.
8. William James, *The Varieties of Religious Experience*, Longmans Green 1952, p. 27.
9. Anselm, *Proslogion*, ch. 2.
10. Cf. Charles Hartshorne, *A Natural Theology for Our Time*, La Salle, Illinois, Open Court 1967, pp. 3ff.
11. Cf. Paul Tillich, *Systematic Theology*, Vol. 1, Nisbet 1953, p.14.
12. Ibid., p. 231.
13. Ibid., p. 265.
14. Luke 10.27.
15. Søren Kierkegaard, *Concluding Unscientific Postscript*, trans. D. F. Swenson and W. Lowrie, Princeton University Press 1941, p. 182.
16. Nathan Söderblom, 'Holiness', in *Encyclopaedia of Religion and Ethics*, T. & T. Clark 1908ff.
17. Rudolf Otto, *The Idea of the Holy*, trans. J. W. Harvey, Oxford University Press 1950, pp. 5–7.
18. Cf. II Samuel 6.6ff.; Isaiah 6.5ff.; Job 40.1f. and 42.6.
19. Revelation 4.8ff.
20. Friedrich D. E. Schleiermacher, *On Religion: Speeches to its Cultured Despisers*, trans. J. Oman, New York, Harper Torchbooks 1958, p.14.
21. Ibid., p.36.
22. Friedrich D. E. Schleiermacher, *The Christian Faith*, trans. and ed. H. R. Mackintosh and J. S. Stewart, T. & T. Clark 1928, p.16.

23. John Ellis, *An Enquiry, Whence Cometh Wisdom and Understanding to Man?*, London 1757, pp. 38f. According to the Preface this work gives 'abstracts from larger works' which were 'intended for a continuation to the first volume on divine knowledge' – see next note.

24. John Ellis, *The Knowledge of Divine Things from Revelation, Not from Reason or Nature*, London 1747, p. 438.

25. Karl Barth, *The Epistle to the Romans*, trans. E. C. Hoskyns, Oxford University Press 1933, pp. 37 and x.

26. Karl Barth, *Dogmatics in Outline*, trans. G. T. Thomson, SCM Press 1949, p. 23.

27. Edward, Lord Herbert of Cherbury, *De Veritate*, trans. and introduction M. H. Carré, Bristol University Press 1937, p. 296; cf. pp. 291–303.

28. Immanuel Kant, *Religion Within the Limits of Reason Alone*, trans. T. M. Greene and H. H. Hudson, New York, Harper Torchbooks 1960, p. 79.

29. Matthew Arnold, *Literature and Dogma*, Smith, Elder 1876, p. 21.

30. Ibid., p. 20.

31. Richard B. Braithwaite, 'An Empiricist's View of the Nature of Religious Belief', reprinted in Ian T. Ramsey (ed.), *Christian Ethics and Contemporary Philosophy*, SCM Press 1966, p. 63.

32. I John 4.20.

33. Søren Kierkegaard, *Concluding Unscientific Postscript*, pp. 182, 187.

34. Ibid., p. 447.

35. Søren Kierkegaard *Philosophical Fragments*, trans. D. F. Swenson, Princeton University Press 1936, p. 88.

36. Alfred North Whitehead, *Religion in the Making*, Cambridge University Press 1927, pp. 6f.

37. Alfred North Whitehead, *Process and Reality*, Corrected edition, ed., D. R. Griffin and D. W. Sherburne, New York, The Free Press 1978, pp. 15f.

38. Cf. Paul Tillich, *Systematic Theology*, Vol. 1, pp. 67ff. and *The Courage to Be*, Nisbet 1952, passim.

39. Quoted in William James, *Varieties of Religious Experience*, p. 497.

40. Gerardus van der Leeuw, *Religion in Essence and Manifestation*, trans. J. E. Turner, George Allen & Unwin 1964, pp. 681f.

41. Ludwig Feuerbach, *The Essence of Christianity*, trans. G. Eliot, New York, Harper Torchbooks 1957, p. 12.

42. Sigmund Freud, *The Future of an Illusion*, trans. W. D. Robson-Scott, Hogarth Press 1962, p. 26.

43. Cf. Gordon D. Kaufman, *An Essay on Theological Method*, Missoula, Montana, Scholars Press 1975 and *The Theological Imagination*, Philadelphia, Westminster Press 1981.

44. Ludwig Wittgenstein, *Philosophical Investigation*, trans. G. E. M. Anscombe, Basil Blackwell 1963, I, 66f., pp. 31f.

45. Paul Tillich, *Biblical Religion and the Search for Ultimate Reality*, Nisbet 1955, p. 8.

46. Whitehead, *Process and Reality*, pp. 4 and 3.

47. L. Wittgenstein, *Philosophical Investigations*, I, 123f., p. 49.

48. M. J. Charlesworth, *Philosophy of Religion: The Historic Approaches*, Macmillan 1972.

49. Plato, *The Republic*, trans. H. D. P. Lee, Penguin Books 1955, 508f., p. 273.

50. Ibid., 505, p. 269.

51. Iris Murdoch, *The Sovereignty of Good*, Routledge & Kegan Paul 1970, p. 69.

52. Plotinus, *Select Works*, ed., G. R. S. Mead, G. Bell and Sons 1914, p. 316.

53. Charles Hartshorne, *The Logic of Perfection and Other Essays in Neoclassical Metaphysics*, La Salle, Illinois, Open Court 1962, pp. viiif.

54. Hartshorne, *A Natural Theology for Our Time*, pp. 45f.

55. Thomas Aquinas, *Summa Contra Gentiles*, I. 9, 1; IV, 1, 4.

56. Ibid., IV, 1, 11.

57. Cf. ibid. I, 4.

58. Cf. John Locke, *An Essay Concerning Human Understanding*, Book 4, chs. 16–19.

59. Samuel Clarke, *A Discourse concerning the Being and Attributes of God, the Obligations of Natural Religion, and the Truth and Certainty of the Christian Revelation*, London 1732, p. 126.

60. Ibid., pp. 147, 149.

61. Ibid., pp. 455f.

62. Cf. Immanuel Kant, *Critique of Pure Reason*, trans. N. K. Smith, Macmillan 1958, p. 29: Kant himself actually speaks of finding it 'necessary to deny knowledge, in order to make room for *faith*'.

63. William Ockham, *Predestination, God's Foreknowledge, and Future Contingents*, trans. M. M. Adams and N. Kretzmann, New York, Appleton-Century-Crofts 1969, p. 90.

64. Henry Longueville Mansel, *The Limits of Religious Thought*, Oxford 1858, p. 47.

65. Ibid., pp. 198f.

66. Ibid., pp. 126f.

67. Thomas F. Torrance, *Theological Science*, Oxford University Press 1969, p. 9.

68. Ibid., p. 37.

69. Quoted in Werner Jaeger, *The Theology of the Early Greek Philosophers*, Oxford University Press 1967, p. 47.

70. Dewi Z. Phillips, *The Concept of Prayer*, Routledge and Kegan Paul 1965, p. 10.

71. Ibid., pp. 22f.

72. Ibid., p. 3.

73. Ibid., p. 28.

74. Cf. Edwin Hatch, *The Influence of Greek Ideas and Usages upon the Christian Church*, Williams and Norgate 1890.

75. Cf. Maurice F. Wiles, *The Remaking of Christian Doctrine*, SCM Press 1974; *Working Papers in Doctrine*, SCM Press, 1976; 'Christianity without Incarnation' and 'Myth in Theology' in John Hick (ed.), *The Myth of God Incarnate*, SCM Press 1977.

76. Cf. John Hick, 'Jesus and the World Religions' in *The Myth of God Incarnate*; *God and the Universe of Faiths*, Macmillan 1973.

Chapter 2   Faith, Theology and Reason

1. Jean-Paul Sartre, *Existentialism and Humanism*, trans. P. Mairet, Methuen 1948, p. 48.
2. Ibid., p. 54.
3. Schubert M. Ogden, 'The Strange Witness of Unbelief' in *The Reality of God*, SCM Press 1967, pp. 134, 136.
4. Ibid., p. 140.
5. Ibid., p. 141.
6. Ibid., p. 139.
7. John Macquarrie, *Principles of Christian Theology*, SCM Press 1966, pp. 1f.
8. Schubert M. Ogden, *The Point of Christology*, SCM Press 1982, p. 4.
9. John Baillie, *Invitation to Pilgrimage*, Penguin Books 1960, pp. 41f.
10. John Locke, *Essay concerning Human Understanding*, Book 4, ch. 17, para. 24.
11. Cf. David Hume, *A Treatise of Human Nature*, ed., L. A. Selby-Bigge, Clarendon Press 1888, pp. xxf.
12. Ibid., p. 264.
13. Ibid., p. 266.
14. Sir William Hamilton, *Lectures on Metaphysics*, ed., H. L. Mansel and J. Veitch, Edinburgh and London: Blackwood 1877, Vol. I, p. 153.
15. Sir William Hamilton, *Discussions on Philosophy and Literature, Education and University Reform*, Longman, Brown, Green and Longmans 1852, p. 601.
16. John Stuart Mill, *An Examination of Sir William Hamilton's Philosophy*, Longmans, Green 1865, p. 5.
17. S. Kierkegaard, *Concluding Unscientific Postscript*, p. 182.
18. Alfred C. Ewing, 'Reason and Intuition' in *Non-Linguistic Philosophy*, George Allen and Unwin 1968, p. 36.
19. Ibid., p. 37.
20. Whitehead, *Process and Reality*, p. 39.
21. (Dr Hildrop), *Reflections upon Reason*, London 1729, pp. 1f.
22. G. J. Warnock, 'Reason' in *The Encyclopaedia of Philosophy*, ed. Paul Edwards, New York, Macmillan.
23. J. Baillie, *Invitation to Pilgrimage*, p. 42.
24. J. Locke, *Essay concerning Human Understanding*, Book 4, ch. 17, para. 4.
25. John Henry Newman, *The Grammar of Assent*, ed. I. T. Ker, Clarendon Press 1985, pp. 227f. (p. 353 in 1889 edition).
26. Stephen Toulmin, *The Uses of Argument*, Cambridge University Press 1958, pp. 7f.
27. Stephen Toulmin, *Human Understanding*, Vol. 1, Clarendon Press 1972, pp. viif.
28. Cf. A. C. Ewing, 'Reason and Intuition' in *Non-Linguistic Philosophy*, p. 55.
29. Ibid., p. 41.
30. Ibid.
31. Cf. ibid., p. 53.

32. Ibid.
33. Cf. ibid., pp. 43f.
34. Cf. ibid., pp. 53–60.
35. Psalm 91. 8ff.

Chapter 3   Faith, Culture and Doctrine

1 H. Richard Niebuhr, *Christ and Culture*, Faber and Faber 1952, p. 46.
2. Matthew 5.42.
3. Niebuhr, *Christ and Culture*, p. 56.
4. Cf. John Hick, 'Jesus and the World Religions' in *The Myth of God Incarnate*, p. 176; 'The Essence of Christianity' in *God and the Universe of Faiths*, p. 117.
5. Cf. Matthew 10.29.
6. Anselm, *Proslogion*, ch. 8.
7. Thomas Aquinas, *Summa Theologiae*, Part I, Qn. 9, Art. 1; Part I, Qn. 13, Art 7.
8. E. L. Mascall, *Existence and Analogy*, Longmans, Green 1949, pp. 142f.
9. Whitehead, *Process and Reality*, pp. 342f.
10. E. Hatch, *The Influence of Greek Ideas and Usages upon Christianity*, pp. 1ff.
11. Ibid., p 351
12. Adolf Harnack, *The Expansion of Christianity in the First Three Centuries*, trans. J. Moffatt, Williams and Norgate 1904, Vol. I, pp. 391f.
13. Adolf Harnack, *What is Christianity?*, trans. T. B. Saunders, Williams and Norgate 1901, pp. 13f; cf. Adolf Harnack, *The History of Dogma*, trans. N. Buchanan, New York, Dover 1961, Vol. VII, pp. 272f.
14. Rudolf Bultmann, 'New Testament and Mythology', in *New Testament and Mythology and Other Basic Writings*, ed. and trans. S. M. Ogden, SCM Press 1984, p. 14.
15. Cf. Charles M. Wood, *The Formation of Christian Understanding*, Philadelphia, Westminster Press 1981, pp. 17, 58ff.
16. Paul Tillich, *Systematic Theology*, Vol. 1, p. 8, cf. pp. 67ff.
17. Paul M. van Buren, *The Secular Meaning of the Gospel*, SCM Press 1963, pp. 1f.
18. José Míguez Bonino, *Revolutionary Theology Comes of Age*, SPCK 1975, p. 91.
19. Ibid., pp. 89f.
20. Jürgen Moltmann, *The Crucified God*, trans. R. A. Wilson and J. Bowden, SCM Press 1974, p. 338.
21. Cf. ibid., pp. 332–5.
22. Gustavo Gutierrez, *A Theology of Liberation*, trans. C. Inda and J. Eagleson, SCM Press 1974, p. 307.
23. James H. Cone. *Black Theology and Black Power*, New York, Seabury Press 1969, quoted in Alistair Kee (ed.), *A Reader in Political Theology*, SCM Press 1974, p. 118.
24. Cf. ibid., pp. 120f.
25. James H. Cone, *God of the Oppressed*, New York, Seabury Press 1975, p. 136.

26. Rosemary Radford Ruether, *To Change the World: Christology and Cultural Criticism*, SCM Press 1981, p. 56.

27. Harnack, *What is Christianity?*, p. 11.

28. John Henry Newman, *An Essay on the Development of Doctrine*, Longmans, Green 1890, p. 171.

29. Cf. Wiles, *The Remaking of Christian Doctrine*, pp. 17f.

30. These seven points are discussed in David A. Pailin 'Authenticity in the Interpretation of Christianity' in Michael Pye and Robert Morgan (eds), *The Cardinal Meaning*, The Hague, Mouton 1973, pp. 127ff.

Chapter 4   Faith, Hermeneutics and the Bible

1. John Locke, *A Second Vindication of the Reasonableness of Christianity*, in *Works*, Volume III, London 1768, p. 190.

2. Christopher Evans 'Should the New Testament be taught to Children?' in *Is 'Holy Scripture' Christian? and Other Questions*, SCM Press 1971, pp. 37ff.

3. Augustine, *In Epistolam Joannis ad Parthos Tractatus*, 7, 5.

4. Harry A. Williams, 'Theology and Self-Awareness' in A. R. Vidler (ed.), *Soundings*, Cambridge University Press 1962, pp. 82 and 80.

5. Karl Barth, *The Word of God and the Word of Man*, trans. D. Horton, New York, Harper Torchbooks 1957, pp. 60f.

6. Decree of 8 April 1546, translation in J. Waterworth, *Canon and Decrees of the Council of Trent*, C. Dolman 1848, pp. 19f.

7. J. H. Newman, *An Essay on the Development of Christian Doctrine*, pp. 88f.

8. Isaac Watts, *The Improvement of the Mind*, ch. VIII, in *Works*, compiled by G. Burder, London 1810, Vol. V, pp. 228ff.

9. Samuel Davidson, *Sacred Hermeneutics*, Thomas Clark 1843, pp. 1f.; cf. Frederick W. Farrar, *History of Interpretation*, Macmillan 1886, pp. 475 n 7 and 476 n 12.

10. Friedrich D. E. Schleiermacher *Hermeneutics: The Handwritten Manuscripts*, ed., H. Kimmerle, trans. J. Duke and J. Forstman, Missoula, Montana, Scholars Press 1977, p. 184.

11. Ibid., p. 182.

12. Cf. ibid., p. 183.

13. Harnack, *The Expansion of Christianity*, Vol. I, p. 397.

14. Harnack, *What is Christianity?*, pp. 179f.

15. R. Bultmann, 'New Testament and Mythology', p. 12.

16. Ibid., p. 1.

17. Cf. ibid., p. 3.

18. Ibid., p. 9.

19. Ibid.

20. Cf. ibid., p. 23.

21. Ibid., p. 15.

22. Ibid., p. 17.

23. Cf. ibid., p. 42.

24. Hans-Georg Gadamer, *Truth and Method*, Sheed & Ward 1975, p. 260.

25. Ibid., p. 445.

26. W. K. Wimsatt, Jr, *The Verbal Icon*, Methuen 1970, p. 4. This is from the essay 'The Intentional Fallacy' written by W. K. Wimsatt, Jr and Monroe C. Beardsley.

27. Cf. ibid., p. 6.

28. Ibid., p. 10.

29. Sallie TeSelle, *Speaking in Parables*, Philadephia, Fortress Press 1975, pp. 69, 71.

30. Frank Kermode, *The Genesis of Secrecy*, Cambridge, Massachusetts, Harvard University Press 1979, p. 15.

31. Sir William Hamilton, *Lectures on Logic*, ed. H. L. Mansel and J. Veitch, Blackwood 1866, Vol. II, p. 217.

32. William Golding, *The Hot Gates*, Faber & Faber 1970, pp. 98, 100.

33. Samuel Taylor Coleridge, *Confessions of an Inquiring Spirit*, ed. H. St. J. Hart, A. & C. Black 1956, p. 42.

34. Ibid., p. 80.

Chapter 5   Faith, History and Revelation

1. Gotthold E. Lessing, 'On the Proof of the Spirit and of Power', in Henry Chadwick (ed.), *Lessing's Theological Writings*, A. & C. Black 1956, p. 53.

2. Alfred Lord Tennyson, 'In Memoriam', Preface, Stanzas 5 and 6.

3. Ibid., LIV, Stanzas 4 and 5.

4. Rudolf Bultmann, *Faith and Understanding*, trans. L. P. Smith, SCM Press 1969, p. 277.

5. Rudolf Bultmann, *Primitive Christianity in its Contemporary Setting*, New York: Living Age Books 1957, p. 197.

6. Bultmann, *Faith and Understanding*, p. 132.

7. Ibid., p. 137.

8. Ibid., p. 138.

9. Lessing, 'On the Proof of the Spirit and of Power', p. 54.

10. Ibid., p. 55.

11. Cf. S. Kierkegaard *Philosophical Fragments*, pp. 44ff.

12. Cf. ibid., p. 53.

13. Alan Richardson, *History Sacred and Profane*, SCM Press 1964, p. 13.

14. Alan Richardson, *Christian Apologetics*, SCM Press 1947, p. 11.

15. Wolfart Pannenberg, *Jesus-God and Man*, trans. L. L. Wilkins and D. A. Priebe, SCM Press 1968, p. 108.

16. Ibid., p. 135.

17. Bultmann, 'New Testament and Mythology', p. 38.

18. Ibid., p. 37.

19. Ibid., p. 39.

20. Lessing, 'On the Proof of the Spirit and of Power', p. 55.

21. John 1. 14; cf. I John 1.1ff.

22. John 3.17.

23. Ogden, *The Reality of God*, p. 184.

24. Grace M. Jantzen, *God's World, God's Body*, Darton, Longman & Todd 1984.

25. Alfred North Whitehead, *Adventures of Ideas*, Cambridge University Press 1933, p. 209.

26. Exodus 20.1.
27. Isaiah 1.2, 10, 18, 24.
28. Mark 9.7.
29. Hebrews 1.1f.
30. Cf. John 4.6ff.
31. Matthew 10.34; Luke 12.49.
32. Thomas Gray, 'Elegy written in a Country Church-yard', Stanza 14.
33. Cf. J. Hick, *God and the Universe of Faiths*, p. 136.

Chapter 6   Faith, God and the Natural World

1. John Ray, *The Wisdom of God Manifested in the Works of the Creation*, London 1691.
2. William Paley, *Natural Theology* (first published in 1802) in *Works*, ed. D. S. Wayland, London 1837, Vol. IV, p. 355.
3. Jacques Monod, *Chance and Necessity*, trans. A. Wainhouse, Collins 1972.
4. Arthur R. Peacocke, *Creation and the World of Science*, Clarendon Press 1979.
5. Charles Birch and John B. Cobb, Jr, *The Liberation of Life*, Cambridge University Press 1981.
6. David J. Bartholomew, *God of Chance*, SCM Press 1984.
7. Cited in Owen R. Jones 'Philosophical Reflections on Creation', in Ian G. Barbour (ed.), *Science and Religion: New Perspectives on the Dialogue*, SCM Press 1968, pp. 232f.
8. (John Hutchinson) *Moses's Principia*, Part I. London 1724, Part II, London 1727.
9. Cf. A. R. Peacocke, *Creation and the World of Science*, pp. 94f.
10. Bartholomew, *God of Chance*, p. 75.
11. Cf. David A. Pailin, 'God and Creation – A Process View' in *Epworth Review*, January 1982, and 'God as Creator in a Whiteheadian Understanding' in *Whitehead und der Prozessbegriff*, ed. H. Holz and E. Wolf-Gazo, Freiburg and Munich, Verlag Karl Alber 1984.
12. Cf. C. Hartshorne, *Man's Vision of God*, New York, Harper & Row 1941; *The Divine Relativity*, New H   ale University Press 1948; *The Logic of Perfection*, La Salle, Illinois, ` .n Court 1962; and articles cited in the previous note for more on this view of the relationship between God and the world.
13. Kaufman, *Essay on Theological Method*, p. 14.
14. Kaufman, *The Theological Imagination*, p. 50.
15. Cited in John Hick, *Evil and the God of Love*, Collins 1968, p. 5n.
16. Søren Kierkegaard, *Gospel of Sufferings*, trans. A. S. Aldworth and W. S. Ferrie, James Clarke 1955, p. 33.
17. F. R. Tennant, *Philosophical Theology*, Vol. II, Cambridge University Press 1928, p. 198.
18. Ibid., p. 201.
19. J. Hick, *Evil and the God of Love*, pp. 371f.
20. Baruch Spinoza, *Ethics proved in geometrical order*, trans. A. Boyle, Dent 1959, p. 36.

21. Ibid., p. 186.

22. Gottfried Wilhelm Leibniz, *Principles of Nature and of Grace, Founded on Reason* (1714), para. 10, in Leibniz, *The Monadology and Other Philosophical Writings*, trans. and ed. R. Latta, Oxford University Press 1898, p. 417.

23. Ibid., para. 12, p. 418.

24. John Stuart Mill, 'Theism' in *Three Essays on Religion*, Longmans, Green, Reader and Dyer 1874, pp. 186f.

Chapter 7   Faith and the Attributes of God

1. John Robinson, *Observations Divine and Morall for the Furthering of Knowledge, and Vertue*, n.p., 1625, p. 2.

2. Aquinas, *Summa Theologiae*, Part I, Qn. 63, Art. 2 and Part I, Qn. 36, Art 4.

3. Anselm, *Proslogion*, ch. 2.

4. Aquinas, *Summa Theologiae*, Part I, Qn. 13, Art 5.

5. Edwyn Bevan, *Symbolism and Belief*, Boston, Beacon Press 1957, p. 14.

6. Paul Tillich, *Dynamics of Faith*, p. 44.

7. Ibid., p. 42.

8. Cf. ibid., p. 41.

9. Ibid., p.45.

10. Sallie McFague, *Metaphorical Theology. Models of God in Religious Language*, Philadelphia, Fortress Press 1982, p. 17.

11. Ibid., p. 40.

12. Cf. Charles Hartshorne, *Man's Vision of God*; *The Divine Relativity*; *The Logic of Perfection*; *A Natural Theology for Our Time*; *Creative Synthesis and Philosophic Method*, SCM Press 1970; *Omnipotence and Other Theological Mistakes*, Albany, State University of New York 1984.

13. Anselm, *Proslogion*, ch. 8.

14. Aquinas, *Summa Theologiae*, Part I, Qn. 9, Art. 1.

15. Ibid., Part I, Qn. 6, Art. 2, Resp. 1.

16. I John 1.9; cf. I John 4.12.

17. Anselm, *Proslogion*, ch. 5.

18. Cf. Hartshorne, *Creative Synthesis and Philosophic Method*, ch. XI.

Chapter 8   Faith and the Existence of God

1. J-P. Sartre, *Existentialism and Humanism*, pp. 33f.

2. J. Monod, *Chance and Necessity*, pp. 160, 167.

3. Cf. Thomas H. Huxley, *Science and Christian Tradition*, Macmillan 1894, p. 310.

4. J. J. C. Smart, 'The Existence of God' in Antony Flew and Alasdair MacIntyre, *New Essays in Philosophical Theology*, SCM Press 1955, p. 41.

5. Alasdair MacIntyre, 'The Logical Status of Religious Belief' in Stephen Toulmin, Ronald W. Hepburn, Alasdair MacIntyre, *Metaphysical Beliefs*, SCM Press 1957, p. 202.

6. Cf. Martin Buber, *I and Thou*, trans. R. G. Smith, T. & T. Clark 1937, pp.80f.

7. Dorothy M. Emmet, *The Nature of Metaphysical Thinking*, Macmillan 1945, p. 4.

8. P. Tillich, *Systematic Theology*, Vol. 1, p. 227.

9. Cf. C. Hartshorne, *A Natural Theology of Our Time*, chs. 2 and 3.

10. Plato, *Laws*, Book X, 894ff., trans. in B. Jowett, *The Dialogues of Plato*, Clarendon Press 1953, Vol. IV, pp. 464f.

11. Aristotle, *Metaphysics*, Book Lambda, 1071f., trans. R. Hope, Ann Arbor, University of Michigan Press 1960, pp. 256f.

12. Cf. J. Ray, *The Wisdom of God Manifested in the Works of the Creation*, p. 133.

13. William Derham, *Astro-Theology: Or, A Demonstration of the Being and Attributes of God from a Survey of the Heavens*, seventh edition, London 1738, p. 161.

14. William Derham, *Physico-Theology: Or, A Demonstration of the Being and Attributes of God from his Works of Creation*, sixth edition, London 1723, pp. 197f.

15. Cf. W. Paley, *Natural Theology* in *Works*, Vol. IV, pp. 94, 115, 131f., 248, 227.

16. Ibid., p. 290.

17. F. R. Tennant, *Philosophical Theology*, Vol. II, p. 79; cf. p. 80.

18. Cf. ibid., p. 117.

19. Ibid., p. 81.

20. Ibid., pp. 84f.

21. Ibid., p. 87.

22. Ibid., p. 89.

23. Ibid., p. 93.

24. Ibid., p. 103.

25. Ibid., p. 104.

26. Ibid., p. 116.

27. Cf. Immanuel Kant, *Critique of Practical Reason*, trans. T. K. Abbott, Longmans 1909, p. 206.

28. Ibid., p. 221.

29. A. E. Taylor, *Does God Exist?*, Collins 1961, p. 133.

30. Ibid., p. 135.

31. A. C. Ewing, *Value and Reality: The Philosophical Case for Theism*, Allen & Unwin 1973, p. 198.

32. Ibid., p. 204.

33. Hastings Rashdall, *The Theory of Good and Evil*, Oxford University Press 1924, Vol. II, pp. 211f.

34. Herbert H. Farmer, *Towards Belief in God*, SCM Press 1942, p. 50.

35. Ibid., p. 40.

36. Buber, *I and Thou*, pp.80f.

37. Cf. ibid., p. 112.

38. John Baillie, *The Sense of the Presence of God*, Oxford University Press 1962, p. 73.

39. Ibid., pp 88f.

40. Cf. Ogden, *The Reality of God*, p. 31.

41. Ibid., p. 44.

42. Ibid., p. 37.

43. Ibid., p. 34.

44. Ibid., p. 31.

45. Ibid., p. 34.

46. Ibid., p. 37.

47. Ibid.

48. Ibid., p. 42.

49. Ibid., p. 21.

50. Hans Küng, *On Being a Christian*, trans. E. Quinn, Collins 1977, p. 77.

51. Ibid., p. 70.

52. Hans Küng, *Does God Exist?*, trans. E. Quinn, Collins 1980, pp. 575f.

53. Küng, *On Being a Christian*, p. 77.

54. Cf. Küng, *Does God Exist?*, pp. 548f.

55. Charles Hartshorne, *Anselm's Discovery*, La Salle, Illinois, Open Court 1965.

56. Anselm, *Proslogion*, ch. 2.

57. René Descartes, *Meditations on First Philosophy*, Meditation V, in *The Philosophical Works of Descartes*, trans. E. S. Haldane and G. R. T. Ross, Cambridge University Press 1931, p. 180; cf. also G. W. Leibniz, *Monadology*, paras. 40ff., and *Discourse on Metaphysics*, para. 23 for other versions of the argument.

58. Ian T. Ramsey, 'Contemporary Philosophy and the Christian Faith' in *Religious Studies*, Vol. 1, no. 1, October 1965, p. 55.

Chapter 9   Faith, Death and Immortality

1. S. G. F. Brandon, *History, Time and Deity*, Manchester University Press 1965, pp. 10f.

2. Ibid., p. 2.

3. I Corinthians 15.12, 14, 19.

4. Cf. A. G. N. Flew, 'Can a Man Witness his Own Funeral' in *Hibbert Journal*, London 1956.

5. John McTaggart Ellis McTaggart, *Human Immortality and Pre-Existence*, Edward Arnold 1916, pp. 74, 77; this work reprints chs. III and IV of McTaggart's *Some Dogmas of Religion*, Edward Arnold 1906 – the quotations are on pp. 113f., 115.

6. Plato, *Phaedo*, 76, contained in N. Smart, *Historical Selections in the Philosophy of Religion*, SCM Press 1962, p. 26. (Another translation is in Plato, *The Last Day of Socrates*, trans. H. Tredennick, Penguin Books 1954, p. 101.)

7. Ibid., pp. 29f. (105ff. in Tredennick).

8. Reinhold Niebuhr, *An Interpretation of Christian Ethics*, SCM Press 1936, p. 116.

9. C. Hartshorne, *A Natural Theology for Our Time*, p. 108.

10. John 14.19.

11. I Corinthians 15.20.

12. II Corinthians 4.14.

13. Genesis 3.5.

14. Matthew 15.18.
15. Whitehead, *Process and Reality*, p. 346.

Chapter 10   Faith, Morality and Experience

1. James 2.17.
2. I John 3.18f.
3. Friedrich Nietzsche, *Twilight of the Idols and The Anti-Christ*, trans. R. J. Hollingdale, Penguin Books 1968, p. 69.
4. Ibid., p. 70.
5. R. B. Braithwaite, 'An Empiricist's View of the Nature of Religious Belief' in I. T. Ramsey (ed.), *Christian Ethics and Contemporary Philosophy*, p. 59.
6. Ibid., p. 63.
7. Ian T. Ramsey, response to Braithwaite's paper first published in the *Cambridge Review* on 3 March 1956 and reprinted in I. T. Ramsey (ed.) *Christian Ethics and Contemporary Philosophy*, p. 86.
8. John Keats, 'Endymion', ll. 1–5.
9. Alfred North Whitehead, *The Function of Reason*, Boston, Beacon Press 1958, p. 4.
10. Ibid., p. 8.
11. Whitehead, *Process and Reality*, p. 343.
12. Antony Flew, 'Divine Omnipotence and Human Freedom' in A. Flew and A. MacIntyre (eds), *New Essays in Philosophical Theology*, pp. 154f.
13. Ibid., p. 168.
14. J. L. Mackie, 'Evil and Omnipotence', in Basil Mitchell (ed.), *The Philosophy of Religion*, Oxford University Press 1971, pp. 100f.
15. John Henry Newman, 'A Letter to the Duke of Norfolk', in *Certain Difficulties Felt by Anglicans in Catholic Teaching*, Longmans, Green 1890, Vol. II, p. 261.
16. Samuel Taylor Coleridge, *Aids to Reflection*, G. Routledge, n.d., Aphorism lxxxi, p. 83.
17. Newman, *An Essay in Aid of a Grammar of Assent*, p. 169 (p. 260 in 1889 edition).
18. Ibid., p. 214 (p. 331).
19. Ibid., p. 187 (p. 288); cf. p. 196 (pp. 302f).
20. Ibid., p. 233 (p. 362).
21. Ibid., p. 245 (p. 381).
22. Ibid., p. 196 (p. 302).
23. Newman, *Certain Difficulties Felt by Anglicans in Catholic Teaching*, Vol. II, p. 248.
24. Newman, *An Essay in Aid of a Grammar of Assent*, p. 73 (p. 105).
25. Ibid., p. 77 (p. 112).
26. Ibid., p. 74 (p. 106).
27. C. C. J. Webb, *Religious Experience*, Oxford University Press 1945, p. 44.
28. Fyodor Dostoyevsky, *The Brothers Karamazov*, trans. D. Magarshack, Penguin Books 1982, p. 308.

Chapter 11   Faith and Religious Language

1. J. Locke, *Essay concerning Human Understanding*, Bk. 4, ch. 21, para. 4.

2. F. H. Bradley, *Appearance and Reality*, Oxford University Press 1969, pp. 403, 405.

3. Cf. John McTaggart Ellis MacTaggart, *The Nature of Existence*, Cambridge University Press 1927, Vol. II, chs. 23ff.

4. Cf. G. E. Moore, 'A Defence of Common Sense' in J. H. Muirhead (ed.), *Contemporary British Philosophy: Personal Statements*, Second Series, Allen & Unwin 1925, pp. 198, 194.

5. Alfred J. Ayer, *Language, Truth and Logic*, New York, Dover Publications, n.d., p. 35.

6. Cf. ibid., p. 5.

7. Cf. ibid., pp. 44, 108.

8. L. Wittgenstein, *Philosophical Investigations*, I, 11, p. 6.

9. Ibid., I, 23, p. 11.

10. Cf. Judges 6.36ff.

11. Cf. I Kings 18.38.

12. A. J. Ayer, *Language, Truth and Logic*, p. 115.

13. Ibid., p. 116.

14. Antony Flew, 'Theology and Falsification' in A. Flew and A. MacIntyre, *New Essays in Philosophical Theology*, pp. 97f.

15. Cf. Basil Mitchell, 'Theology and Falsification', in ibid., pp. 103ff.

16. E. L. Mascall, *Words and Images*, Longmans, Green 1957, p. 10.

17. Cf. ibid., p. 12.

18. John Hick, 'Theology and Verification', printed in John Hick (ed.), *The Existence of God*, New York, Macmillan 1964, p. 258.

19. Ibid. p. 261.

20. Buber, *I and Thou*, pp. 80f.

21. Cf. ibid., p. 75.

22. Ibid., p. 99.

23. Ibid., p. 112.

24. Cf. Karl Barth, *The Epistle to the Romans*, p. 35.

25. Ibid., p.x.

26. Cf. Buber, *I and Thou*, p. 11.

27. James Brown, *Subject and Object in Modern Theology*, SCM Press 1955, p. 192.

28. Cf. William Hordern, *Speaking of God*, Epworth Press 1964, pp. 175f.

29. John Wisdom, 'Gods', in Antony Flew (ed.), *Logic and Language*, First Series, Oxford: Basil Blackwell 1955, p. 193.

30. Kierkegaard, *Concluding Unscientific Postscript*, p. 116.

31. Ibid., p. 182.

32. Ibid., p. 116.

33. W. Hordern, *Speaking of God*, p. 68.

34. Ibid., pp. 104f.

35. Ian T. Ramsey, *Religious Language*, SCM Press 1957, p. 26.

36. Ibid., p. 37.

37. Ibid., p. 29.
38. Cf. Donald D. Evans, *The Logic of Self-Involvement*, SCM Press 1963.
39. R. M. Hare, 'Theology and Falsification' in A. Flew and A. MacIntyre, *New Essays in Philosophical Theology*, p. 101.
40. H. A. Hodges, *Languages, Standpoints and Attitudes*, Oxford University Press 1953, p. 15.
41. Ibid., pp. 50f.
42. Cf. ibid., pp. 53–60.
43. Cf. ibid., p. 65.
44. Cf. P. M. van Buren, *The Secular Meaning of the Gospel*, p. 71.
45. Ibid., p. 156.
46. Carl Michalson, *The Rationality of Faith*, SCM Press 1964, p. 14.
47. Ibid., pp. 145f.
48. Cf. I. T. Ramsey, *Religious Language*, ch.2.
49. Ibid., p. 68.
50. Cf. I. T. Ramsey, *Models and Mystery*, Oxford University Press 1964, p. 60.
51. Ibid., p. 10.
52. E. Bevan, *Symbolism and Belief*, p. 11.
53. Ibid., p. 340.
54. Cf. P. Tillich *Dynamics of Faith*, ch.3; *Systematic Theology*, Vol. I, pp. 264ff.
55. S. McFague, *Metaphorical Theology*, p. 13.
56. Ibid., p. 14.
57. Ibid., p. 15; further insight into metaphorical usage can be found in Janet Martin Soskice, *Metaphor and Religious Language*, Clarendon Press 1985 (I did not have access to this work before I finished this study).
58. F. W. Dillistone, 'The Function of Symbols in Religious Experience' in F. W. Dillistone (ed.), *Myth and Symbol*, SPCK 1966, p. 14.

Conclusion

1. Whitehead, *Adventures of Ideas*, pp. 364f.

Index